BLACK AMERICANS IN HIGHER EDUCATION

Narrating the realities of teacher burnout, the reception of a Black intelligentsia, and HIV awareness in local communities, *Black Americans in Higher Education*, the eighth volume of *Africana Studies*, explores higher education across the United States as inextricably related to contemporary issues facing African Americans.

Featuring the work of Terrell M. Thomas, Gwendolyn D. Alfred, Kevin B. Thompson, Jasmine Williams, TaNeisha R. Page, Drew D. Brown, Grace A. Loudd, Derek Wilson, DaVonte Lyons, Jacqueline Gerard, Tanisha Stanford, Lanetta Dickens, Brittany C. Slatton, and James L. Conyers, Jr., this collection presents a deeper, cross-cultural understanding of higher education that conveys the many ways its intersections can promote the agency of African Americans.

James L. Conyers, Jr., PhD, is university professor of African American Studies and director of the African American Studies Program at the University of Houston. Additionally, he is the editor of the series *Africana Studies: A Review of Social Science and Research* at Taylor & Francis Group. His most recent publication is *Africology: Interdisciplinary Thought and Praxis*.

BLACK AMERICANS IN HIGHER EDUCATION

A Review of Social Science Research, Volume 8

Edited by James L. Conyers, Jr.

Routledge
Taylor & Francis Group

NEW YORK AND LONDON

First published 2020
by Routledge
52 Vanderbilt Avenue, New York, NY 10017

and by Routledge
2 Park Square, Milton Park, Abingdon, Oxon, OX14 4RN

Routledge is an imprint of the Taylor & Francis Group, an informa business

Library of Congress Cataloging-in-Publication Data
Names: Conyers, James L., Jr., editor.
Title: Black Americans in higher education : a review of social science
research / Edited by James L. Conyers, Jr.
Description: New York, NY : Routledge, 2020. | Series: Africana studies ;
Volume 8 | Includes bibliographical references.
Identifiers: LCCN 2019034542 (print) | LCCN 2019034543 (ebook) | ISBN
9780367218638 (hardback) | ISBN 9780367218652 (paperback) | ISBN
9780429266560 (ebook)
Subjects: LCSH: African Americans--Education (Higher)--Social aspects. |
Educational sociology--United States. | Teacher morale--United States.
Classification: LCC LC2781 .B416 2020 (print) | LCC LC2781 (ebook) | DDC
378.1/982996073--dc23
LC record available at https://lccn.loc.gov/2019034542
LC ebook record available at https://lccn.loc.gov/2019034543

ISBN: 978-0-367-21863-8 (hbk)
ISBN: 978-0-367-21865-2 (pbk)
ISBN: 978-0-429-26656-0 (ebk)

Typeset in Bembo
by Lumina Datamatics Limited

This publication is dedicated to the memory of the late Dr. John Henrik Clarke.

CONTENTS

FIGURES

TABLES

CONTRIBUTORS

Gwendolyn D. Alfred, DMA, is an assistant professor of music at Texas Southern University.

Aisha Asby, PhD, is a Certified Financial Educator.

Drew D. Brown, PhD, is an assistant professor of Africana studies at the University of Delaware. His most recent publication is Brown, Drew D. (2017). "'Girls Don't Play No Ball': The Invisibility of Black Women Athletes in Film" in *Africana Social Stratification: An Interdisciplinary Study of Economics, Policy, and Labor*, ed. J. L. Conyers.

Courtney Bryant is an independent researcher.

James L. Conyers, Jr., PhD, is a university professor of African American studies and director of the African American Studies Program at the University of Houston. Additionally, he is the editor of the series *Africana Studies: A Review of Social Science and Research* at Taylor & Francis Group. His most recent publication is *Africology: Interdisciplinary Thought and Praxis*.

Michara DeLaney, PhD, is an assistant dean for equity, diversity, and inclusion at Stephen F. Austin State University.

Lanetta Dickens, MA, is a doctoral student in literacy leadership at San Houston State University. Her most recent publication is Dickens, L. (2012). Guest Post: African American Studies Intern Lanetta Dickens Reviews Hip Hop Conference. Special Collections Blogs. University of Houston Libraries.

Terence Finley, MBA, PhD, is an executive staff member in the Office of Business Affairs and is a Leadership Development and Organizational Excellence Officer at Prairie View A & M University, Prairie View, Texas.

Pamela R. Finley, PhD, is an independent researcher.

Jacqueline Gerard, MA, is currently an independent writer and researcher in Houston.

Danielle Hairston-Green is currently the director for Human Development and Relationships Institute at the University of Wisconsin Division of Extension. Danielle's most current research examines the frequency and level of distress associated with microagression among students at a historically black university (HBCU) and the impact of food insecurity and homelessness among college students at an HBCU. Her most recent research examines the perceptions of mentors and mentoring relationships among doctoral students and postdoctoral researchers. Danielle is also the president and founder of Embracing ARMS, Inc., a non-profit youth and parent empowerment program and the former VP and member of the board of control for the Harrisburg City School district. She holds a PhD in educational leadership (Higher Education Administration) from Prairie View A&M University, a master's degree in community psychology and social change, and a bachelor's degree in criminal justice from Penn State University and a National Certification in human development and family studies.

Grace A. Loudd, PhD, is an assistant professor of social work at Texas Southern University, Department of Social Work. Her most recent publication is Buzi, R. S., Weinman, M.L., Smith, P. B., Loudd, G., & Madanay, F. (2018). HIV stigma perceptions and sexual risk behaviors among black young women. *Journal of HIV/AIDS & Social Services*, 17(1), 69–85. doi:10.1080/15381501.2017. 1407726.

DaVonte Lyons, MA, is currently a doctoral student in African Studies at Howard University.

TaNeisha R. Page, PhD, research focuses on stratification and social classes. Additionally, she has drawn interest in African Americans in the workplace and in education.

Richard F. Price, is a doctoral student within the Educational Leadership Program at Prairie View A&M University. As a school administrator employed within an urban K-12 district, his research centers on the implementation and impact of socially justified educational methodologies for students of color.

Brittany C. Slatton, PhD, is currently professor of sociology at Texas Southern University. Her most recent publication is Slatton, Brittany C. Slatton & Carla D. Brailey (Eds.). 2019. *Women and Inequality in the 21st Century*. New York: Routledge.

Tanisha Stanford, MA, research focuses on the socio-psychological experiences of the African American family.

Terrell M. Thomas, EdD, is currently an administrator in the Houston Independent School District.

Kevin B. Thompson, PhD, is the program manager in African American studies and adjunct instructor of African American Studies (AAS) at the University of Houston. His most recent publication is Thompson, K. B. (2016). The Negative Imagery of Hip Hop: A Brief Analysis. In James L. Conyers, Jr. (Ed.), *Qualitative Methods in Africana Studies* (pp. 329–339).

Jasmine Williams, PhD, is an assistant professor of education at Fayetteville State University. Her most recent publication is Williams, J. (2018). Reflections on Leadership from the Perspective of an Educational Leadership Doctoral Student, In T. Hicks & L. Watson (Eds.), *Black Administrators in Higher Education: Autoethnographic Explorations and Personal Narratives*.

Derek Wilson, PhD, is an associate professor of psychology at Prairie View A&M University. Her most recent publication is Metofe, P., Wilson, D., & Graves, K. (2018). The Relationship among Black Consciousness, Self-esteem, Self-efficacy and Academic Achievement in African American Students. In James L. Conyers (Ed.), *Africana Methodology: A Social Study of Research, Triangulation and Meta-theory*.

Lucian Yates, III, PhD, is professor, provost, and VP for academic and student affairs at Kentucky State University. His most recent publication is Wright, B. L., Bryan, N., Sewel, C. J. P., Yates, L., Robinson, M., & Thomas, K. (2019). *GUMBO for the Soul: Males of Color Share Their Stories, Meditations, Affirmations, and Inspirations*.

ACKNOWLEDGMENTS

Each publication provides an outlook and reflection of the journey, process, and grind of the assignment. Continually celebrated, my family, both genetic and extended, is the base and support foundation of my continued learning. Transitioned, but vibrant, is the spirit of my father James L. Conyers, Sr. and mother Agnes Conyers. Of course, the friendship, partnership, and marriage to my transitioned spouse of over 25 years, Jacqueline I. Pierce-Conyers, is always relative. Indeed, my lions Chad A. Hawkins, Sekou Conyers, and Kamau Conyers are my muse to retain common sense, patience, and tenacity. Indeed, my girlfriend Kimberly M. Gay is outstanding companion and free librarian. The workspace of the AAS Team in the College of Liberal Arts and Social Sciences offers support and has access to me on the daily: Jasmine Grant, Dr. Kevin Thompson, Dr. Crystal Edwards, Mason Carter, Van Rountree, and Angela Williams Phillips are comrades. This circle of professionals assists in outlining the parameters of trajectory for the development and establishment of the bachelor of arts degree in African American studies at the University of Houston. Faculty team members and colleagues at University of Houston (U of H) have been inspiring and supportive: Drs. Shayne Lee, Donna Stokes, Cedric Tolliver, Demetrius Pearson, Billy Hawkins, Nicholas Kanellos, Gerald Horne, Linda Reed, Phil Howard, George Gamble, Dean Antonio Tills, Elywn Lee, and Rheeda Walker. Friends in the way of Anthony Robinson, Zane Corbin, Joe Taylor, and James Bullock provide valuable sounding boards and companionship. Mentors in the way of Drs. Molefi Kete Asante, James B. Stewart, Delores Aldridge, and Pastor William A. Lawson have continued to be encouraging and play a part in my growth and development as a human.

INTRODUCTION

James L. Conyers, Jr.

Terrell M. Thomas' article titled *The Thrill Is Gone* is a narrative of the realities of teacher burn out. Signaled are the concepts of principal leadership and possible prevention methods and of implementation for effective teaching and supervision. The author outlines the boundaries of investigative realities of teachers' expectations and professional development. Stationed in the experiences of educational institutions, the fusion of this paper addresses the functional outcome assessment of the elementary and secondary teaching profession.

Gwendolyn Alfred offers a humanistic analysis of Africana musicology within a literary cannon to assess William Grant Still's score, *Troubled Island*. Using research tools of ethnomusicology, Alfred locates the study within the context of Americana historiography, in the period of 1949 in New York City. Here, in this place and time, African Americans were transitioning from the period of the Nadir to sectionalism of the progressive Republican era. Nonetheless, the opera performance of *"Troubled Island"* takes a global pan Africanist perspective of Haiti and one of its early leadership figures J. Dessalines. Finally, Alfred has placed the idea of reclamation, in probing this topic from an Afrocentric perspective, within a cultural aesthetic cognitive emphasis.

Kevin B. Thompson's article *The Black Male Teacher* approaches insight on the recruitment, retention, and reference of African American male teachers. Historically, the teaching profession has been flexible to the reception and placement of the approaches of the African American middle-class strata. Referenced in this profession is the development of a social consciousness and Black intelligentsia. Comparative to this phenomenon is the Black community, regarding the culture of African American politics, economics, and a collective consciousness. Linked to this is an ethos and motif of the African American male practitioner in the classroom, despite the fact that the thought, thinking, and theory address how gender plays a role in the intellectual breakdown and breakthroughs of acumen. Additionally, the persona of the African American teacher recommends support and a substantial role model for African American males in the elementary and secondary grade levels. Overall, Thompson challenges our intellect regarding agency to stretch practitioner's assessment of African American students in processing issues and schemes within educational institutions.

Jasmine Williams in the article titled *Cultured Pearls* places emphasis on research tools used by white practitioner's pedagogy in urban schools. Designated as a structural paradigm, test scores and student achievement are emphasized. The use of the terminology of *cultural dissonance* regulates the bridge that exists in academic pluralism. Gender is relative, concerning the gap and interpretive analysis of the learning styles differences of right and left brain curricula. Overall, the authors posit the idea that cultural competency is a priority and relative to the learning module of urban district students.

TaNeisha R. Page's article titled *African Americans in Higher Education* draws accent on developing an understanding of culture and identity. Education has been historically a rubric for measuring the Black middle class in America. Even more important, the acquisition of retaining a degree of higher education, has been one of the few vehicles, which has allowed African Americans to prosper a quality of life in careerism and become homeowners. On the other hand, culture has been segmented in two categories: (1) tradition and (2) popular. Agreeably, the author notes that higher education is a mode of progression for upward mobility of African Americans, and the outcome assessments are positing alternate descriptors. In closing Page's use of historical overview, serve as a research tool and instrument of evaluation to illustrate predictors for African Americans proposition for advancement.

Drew D. Brown's article *Kemet-kA: The African Spirit in Sport* offers a sport and race analysis of African Americans. Brown makes the contention of Africana culture, which is vibrant through retention or creation in Americana sport. He signals the historical foundation of this discussion in classical African civilization in ancient Egypt. Stretched in analogy, the author cites how sport does have impact on our society, with regard to motifs in the form of heroes and role models.

Grace A. Loudd in her article titled *Feminist Standpoint Theory and Women's Sexuality* performs a quantitative assessment of examining the issue of implications of HIV prevention methods for women. Loudd initiates this conversation with statistical data from the World Health Organization (WHO), challenging their ideas and definition of sexuality. Pointing toward the ideas of prevention, the data reveals 51% of the American population are women, but in turn, women make up a disproportionate percentage of individuals who are HIV positive. Loudd points out that in women who have contracted the disease in higher percentages, the disease comes from sexual contact through semen and vaginal penetration. Overall, Loudd notes, the public health community is providing more education, information, and knowledge to produce prevention plans for HIV awareness.

Derek Wilson, Courtney Bryant, and Aisha Asby's article *Evaluation of the Relationship Among Moral Foundations, C.J. and Perception of Terrorism in College Students Attending HBCU's* is informative and outlines the parameters of Black college student's cultural psychology. Situated as a quantitative study, the authors measure (how) the impact of terrorism on the psyche of African American students. Experiencing a history of occupation, lynching, and institutional racism, Black people have endured, engaged, and interacted to resolve in adaptive reality. Enabled within the institutional framework of segregation, mainstream America terrorized the Black community for arbitrary and cupreous justification reasoning. The author's analysis draws on the use of alternate tools of analysis in describing and evaluating African American students' psychology.

DaVonte Lyon's essay on *Africana Philosophy* is a fresh analysis of African existence, meaning, and essentiality. Lyons offers an Afrocentric perspective in his rationale, purpose, and reasoning to examine Africana phenomena. Based on the regulation of time and space, Africana thought centers on the science of humanism and thinking. Using ancient Kemetic culture as a reference and resource, the concepts of spirit and soul extend to examine the aspects of questions, ideas, and boundaries that we engage in, to measure our lives. Lyons has opened the conversation for Africana Studies scholars to embark on the assessment of defining the relative constituents of Black culture.

Jacqueline Gerard, in her essay *Black Identity and White Culture*, discusses the structural aspects of Black popular culture. Using the *Lemonade* score—cannon established by the artist *Beyoncé*—Gerard examines the aesthetics of Black feminism, social identity, and definition of beauty. Retaining the thought of Black feminism is the crux of this article. In this way, we have a foundation to examine the Black aesthetic from an Afrocentric perspective.

Tanisha Stanford's *Critical Analysis of Reclaiming the Psyche Through Research Methods* is an exploratory examination of social science within the discipline of Africana Studies. The concept of thought and praxis is the exploratory lab for examining the process and journey of thinking related to Africana ethos and motif. The author use of the Afrocentric paradigm pivots an alternative analysis of describing and evaluating the Black experience.

Lanetta Dicken's article titled *Taking Action in Hope* is an educational analysis of the public school system in New Orleans. Focused on the transition, transformation, and transcendence of public education after Hurricane Katrina, Dickens signals the points of retention and attrition of public school students in New Orleans. Unfortunately, during this aftermath of Katrina, the public school system in New Orleans has not pivoted toward stabilization. Whereas, currently, the elementary and secondary school systems are designed based on public charter schools organized out of individual parishes.

Brittany C. Slatton's article titled *Race Talk at the Intersection of Gender and Class* examines the phenomena of white male privilege. Using the parameters of intersectionality talk, the rubric of hegemony of race and gender limits the concept and possibilities of diversity. Slatton outlines how this concept of race and talk is the conceptual framework in which white males used to provide a narrative or conceptual base in describing and evaluating the humanistic experience. Equally important, she reports with precision the cannon of rhetorical strategies employed in these race talk engagements: justify, persuade, blame, defend racial positions to themselves, and defend racial positions to others.

James L. Conyers, Jr., in the essay *The Thirteenth Amendment* sequesters issues related to Africana agency and sovereignty. It is this amendment, recorded in Americana history and culture, that pivots African Americans as humans in the space of Americana historiography.

Conclusion

What becomes the measure and value of education? Context for this engagement for involuntary migrants measures up to a tool of liberation. Volume 8 has focused on African Americans in higher education. As a phenomenon of modern-day issues related to Black Americans, perhaps education is one of the tools that African Americans can use for attaining agency in contemporary America. Phrased differently, the use of an alternative resolve to retain the quality of life might be a variable for consideration. Security, financial wealth, and occupational stability are uncommon to mention in both the private and public sectors. In turn, whatever base of employment we engage, the context of culture provides a prism for Black people to define, defend, and develop their interpretation and sense of realty. Nonetheless, we are engaged to sustainability for the advancement of the African American community as a disclosed priority. Continuing onward, this collection of essays seeks to examine education from an interdepartmental lens, which captures theory, practicum, and resolution of critical thinking of Black people. Finally, the concept of education without worldview and interpretative analysis is limited in its functional capability to pivot or advance people. Regarding the Africana community, the concept of education administers an alternative role in offering consciousness, to be used as a strategy in anchoring cultural liberation.

The Afrocentric mode of education seeks to provide tools of liberation for people of African descent. In this way, the concept of learning is life long, with an emphasis pivoted toward the retaining and acquisition of mastery of knowledge and information. Volume 8 of the serial Africana Studies attempts to ask and raise alternative query, in the vortex of the contemporary Americana society. What does it mean to be safe, secure, and sustained in one's profession and everyday life? Directed from an Afrocentric perspective the concept of being occupied is relevant for all Americans, which can transcend, race, ethnicity, and gender. Celebrating the golden-year anniversary of Africana studies in the academy, the movement of the Afrocentric idea pushed the development of terminal and doctoral granting degrees in the discipline. Referencing the thought of struggle and worldview has jump started the academy to examine, engage, and extrapolate ideas related to the diversity and discussion of Africana phenomena.

The Afrocentric idea in education has engaged the academy of higher learning for almost 50 years. Using the interdisciplinary matrix of Africana studies, scholars and students have secured space to raise alternative query regarding the cosmology, axiology, ontology, and epistemology of Africana phenomena. In the contemporary period of nostalgia conservatism, the concept of functional literacy and education has been shelved. Instead, we are reduced to news pundits and propaganda. In closing, the context and preparation of this volume attempted to present a fresh perspective and worldview of examining the field and function of higher-education intersection with the progressive advancement of the African American community.

1

THE THRILL IS GONE

A Romance Gone Bad, a Teacher's Story of Burnout, and the Signs Principals Should Look Out For

Terrell M. Thomas

We've all been there. You've just met the most amazing person in the world, and you love spending time with him or her. You're on cloud 9. Everything about them is perfect. However, as time goes on, you learn more about them and notice subtle signs that things aren't perfect. Then, it happens. You realize things aren't as great as they seem, and the relationship begins to sour. This plot may sound like another Hollywood romance script or the newest network sitcom, but this story is actually about something worse.

This storyline is about how a couple of teachers became disenchanted with teaching and how they left their passion and the profession behind. As an educational leader, there are a number of daily duties and situations that you are required to handle. It is easy to miss signs of a frustrated teacher or teachers on the verge of burning out. Once a teacher loses his or her passion, the educational leadership on campus needs to come together and support that teacher in his or her time of need. The teachers cited issues with communication, feeling unappreciated and the displeasure of being in a test-driven environment as some of the reasons for leaving teaching. The following narratives provide administrators some insight on ineffective leadership behaviors and signs of a teacher at risk of leaving.

Communication

One topic that many of the teachers complain about is communication. One teacher explains how little contact she had with her administration and her lack of support. "There was rarely any administrative support/feedback outside of the mandated semi-annual observation which sometimes didn't happen, and often happened in a very rushed manner." She felt a growing disconnect between her and the administration, and there was little time for them to form a relationship. Another teacher explains how her campus mentor had no relationship with her and provided no real support. She explains, "I only saw her mentor once and the support was worthless." Another teacher stated, "In terms of concrete support, there was very little given." Another teacher shared how inappropriate communication was a problem on her campus.

> Administrators, other administrators, assistant principals in meetings would curse about teachers and just complain, and talk about how busy and angry they were. And, I mean, I thought that their focus would have been on, like, what can we do? We are busy, here's the action items, like let's do this, but instead time was taken us with, you know, angry and mean and really, really rude comments about teachers—lewd comments about teachers. And the principal would sit there in silence, cause she seemed, like scared of dealing with that.

How can we expect our students to succeed in the classroom when the teachers do not feel they have an open line of communication with the leadership on campus or when there is unprofessional communication among administrators and teachers? It is important that early career teachers establish healthy and open relationships with their fellow teachers and administration. Growth-fostering connections are characterized by mutuality, empowerment, and the development of courage (Le Cornu, 2013). Although a lack of communication may not seem like a big problem, it can lead to more serious problems in the administration-and-teacher relationship if unsettled.

Feeling Undervalued

Lack of communication in a relationship can lead to uncertainty, and feelings can be hurt. The former teachers also mentioned their feeling unappreciated by their principal and other administrators as another factor in their dissatisfaction with teaching. As an administrative leader, one must be mindful of the needs of teachers and staff on campus. You can never be too busy to neglect those that are looking to you for support and growth. Aoki (1990) states, "The word principal was at one time understood as 'principal teacher'–first or leading teacher." The teachers spoke on feelings of little to no support from their principals and other administrators. Once teacher explained, "In general, there was a lack of support outside of support received from other teachers." One teacher shared his feelings of frustration and disappointment with the way he was supported by his administrative team. He came into his campus thinking that he had the support of the school leadership and fellow teachers but soon found out that it was not the case. He shared,

> There were plenty of times when I felt like I was an expendable tool. Our administrators felt they could ask anything of you because you were new.

The veteran teachers weren't any better. They were very disrespectful and didn't want to listen to anything that I had to share.

Another teacher expressed a similar feeling,

I was like the low man on the totem-pole. It kind of made me want to rethink exactly what I wanted to do and where I wanted to do it at. I mean, when they say "give back to the community and, you know, work with people who really need your help," it's not as easy as it sounds.

The early career teachers expressed the difficulty they had in trying to receive the support they needed to help their children.

Neither my teacher preparation program nor my administrators offered the support I needed when I was in the classroom. I also didn't have the greatest relationship with my fellow teachers. School wasn't exactly the greatest place for me. I didn't feel empowered or valued on the campus. My input wasn't important.

The teachers mentioned how the administrators on their campus lost track of how difficult it is to be a teacher in the classroom. She later went on to state, "I also felt like the institution I worked for generally didn't value the work of teachers, and felt teachers were expendable." One teacher shared,

I didn't have a mentor or any kind of support to help me. The only support I received as a teacher was through verbal acknowledgement and praise for certain actions. In terms of concrete support or feedback outside of the mandated semi-annual observation which sometimes didn't happen, and often happened in a very rushed manner. There were no relevant professional development sessions aimed at supporting teachers to better achieve student goals. In general, there was a lack of support outside of support received from other teachers.

An additional teacher expressed similar sentiments, "I didn't feel valued as a teacher. My input was not well received. It wasn't a positive place to work." One teacher explained,

We had an extremely dysfunctional administrative team. It was a divisive environment. It wasn't a team environment. ...the bigger picture of the school itself being pretty severely dysfunctional at times was harder to deal with. I always tell people when they ask why I left teaching, it wasn't the kids, it was the adults. We had an extremely dysfunctional administrative team that I then strangely tried to join in my last year to try to correct things from the inside, but that's another story. It was kind of an "every man for himself" type of thing. And it wasn't benefiting the students in the way that it should have been.

This type of dissatisfaction not only affects the students in the classroom but also the campus climate. Cress (2008) explains, "Campus climate is the metaphorical temperature gauge by which we measure a welcoming and receptive, versus a cool and alienating learning environment."

The teachers felt that they did not have much of relationship with their administration and felt very unrecognized. Le Cornu (2013) states, "...in order for the new teachers to feel confident and competent they needed to be sustained by—and able to sustain—relationships based on mutual trust, respect, care and integrity." Teaching is a highly complex profession, involving not only the intellectual but also the physical and emotional. It is important that teachers prepare themselves for the rigorous demands of teaching. Research has identified resiliency as a key factor in promoting teacher persistence, acceptance to feedback, and professional development (Le Cornu, 2013; Day et al., 2011; Freeman et al., 2007; Bullough, 2005). What is resiliency and where does it come from? Is it something that is learned or is it something one is inherently born with? Le Cornu (2013) explains that resiliency is not inherent in the individual but rests in one's ability to make connections. Relational-cultural theory (Jordan, 2006) suggests that resilience resides not in the individual but in the capacity for connection. Jordan's (2006) model of relational resilience has its theoretical foundations in relational-cultural theory, which has as its core the belief that all psychological growth occurs in relationships.

Displeasure with the Test-Driven Environment

The former teachers also mentioned the displeasure with the test-driven environment as a reason for leaving teaching. The pressure of high stakes testing is placing a strain on our children and the teachers giving the lessons. Teachers feel pressured to teach only the material that is relevant to tests and the strategies that are approved by the administration. One teacher clarified,

> The administration set very low standards for student achievement but constantly wanted high results, which created a conflict. I also felt like the institution I worked for generally didn't value the work of teachers, and felt teachers were expendable. I also didn't like being in such a test driven environment, and most importantly, I wasn't teaching what and how I wanted to teach, given very little autonomy. There was a lack of support from administration, unwillingness to make necessary changes and nepotism within the organization.

The feeling of lack of control was a deterrent to stay in teaching. It was considered just another issue in a long list of problems that teachers experience and another issue that teachers feel is neglected by the administrators. One teacher bellowed, "The administration set very low standards…but constantly wanted high student results, which created a conflict." "There were no relevant P.D. sessions aimed at supporting teachers to better achieve student goals." Another teacher shared, "Administration was not very concerned with my development more or so due to the fact that my students wouldn't take statewide tests in the subject I taught." She believed that she was not able to make the type of difference that she wanted in public education. "I want to work with children of all ages and not be plagued by the politics of the education system." The expectation of students' success and the lack of the resources to help students' achievement led to discontent. If students were not performing to the expectation of the administration, it was considered to be a failure by the teacher. How can any campus leader expect students and teachers to succeed when these types of pressures pervade through the school? Where the early career teachers had access to ongoing professional learning opportunities and were supported in the development of their pedagogical beliefs, values, and practices, their confidence in their capabilities as a teacher were enhanced (Le Cornu, 2013).

As a campus leader, you have many tasks and obligations. It is easy to lose oneself in the mundane responsibilities and the mire of paperwork. However, one cannot forget that the most important vow a principal makes it to the children. One must do whatever they can to ensure students' achievement and success. The most important way to accomplish this is by safeguarding their teachers. It was through developing and nurturing relationships that were mutual, empowering, and encouraging and by being the recipient of relationships that had these attributes that the early career teachers' resilience appeared to be enhanced (Le Cornu, 2013).

Aspects of Resiliency

Mutuality

Mutuality is at the core of resilience (Le Cornu, 2013). Johnson et al. (2012) explain that mutuality resonates with the notion of reciprocity and reinforces many of the professional relationships that early career teachers engage in. Relationships with students and fellow teachers are significant for early career teachers and their resilience; teachers are both sustained and drained by the relationships that they develop with their students because they spend much time and effort trying to get to know their students and trying to form democratic relationships with them (Le Cornu, 2013). Hartling (2008) expresses that resilience can be strengthened through engagement in relationships that enhance one's sense of worth and sense of competence. Teachers also develop a stronger sense of resiliency when they feel a sense of connectedness and community with their fellow teachers; when they receive emotional and professional support from their peers, their sense of resiliency grows (Le Cornu, 2013). Teachers also feel a greater sense of validation professionally when their ideas are respected. When teachers feel that their ideas are respected and see those ideas being used by teachers who have been teaching longer than them, they feel that they are making contributions to their peers and that the relationship is not a one-way relationship (Le Cornu, 2013). Additionally, teachers feel affirmed by the feedback they receive from their support network and value feeling a part of a support group.

Empowerment

Another aspect of resiliency is empowerment. When early career teachers are able to establish trusting, respectful, and reciprocal relationships, they perceive themselves as more confident and competent, which enables them to feel more empowered (Le Cornu, 2013; Hartling, 2008). It is important that teachers form healthy relationships with their administrative leaders. Teachers' ability to form these types of relationships with administrative leaders, their peers, and themselves are important in establishing a teacher's resiliency (Le Cornu, 2013).

Courage

It is essential that teachers develop a sense of courage. Courage is defined as the capacity to move into situations when we feel fear or hesitation (Le Cornu, 2013). Teachers draw on the support of their peers and family to motivate them and to affirm them in their efforts to continue teaching. School leaders, mentors, and support staff such as education officers and advisory staff are also important in developing an early career teacher's courage in their abilities (Le Cornu, 2013). Family and peers provide the emotional support that teachers need to combat difficulties, while school administrators and staff provide the encouragement needed to feel competent in the classroom (Le Cornu, 2013). These relationships are important to forge for early career teachers. However, some early career teachers begin their careers in environments that suffer from high rates of teacher turnover, poor school climate and culture, and poor community support.

Promoting Resiliency in Teachers

The role of school leaders has emerged as a significant one for two reasons. First, in the relationships that school leaders establish with their early career teachers to encourage and support them directly, and second, with regard to the culture established in the school. Where leaders take the time to develop relationships based on respect, trust, care, and integrity, early career teachers appear to flourish (Le Cornu, 2013).

A culture that encourages reflection and professional dialogue among all members of the school community and provides both formal and informal opportunities for engagement promotes the building of a teacher's resilience (Le Cornu, 2013). As stated earlier, teachers also benefit from having strong connections to their fellow teachers. Pearce and Morrison (2011) suggest that personal identity takes shape during teacher's social exchanges and interactions with other members of the school community. Once a teacher develops his or her personal identity, it is important that he or she becomes confident enough to engage with other teachers in order to grow professionally. Teachers develop their ability to talk about teaching and interact in a professional way and value of receiving support from others who were going through a similar experience (Le Cornu, 2013). Although teachers receive validation from the affirmation and non-judgmental support that they receive from their peers, it is also important that they have an important relationship with themselves. The relationship that each early career teacher has with himself or herself, that is, how comfortable they feel as a person and in their role as a teacher, has emerged as a component of how well they are able to sustain themselves—and to contribute to sustaining others (Le Cornu, 2013).

Jackson (2012) explains that the more influence that individual teachers perceive they have over school policy, the more likely they are to remain in their school and the less likely they are to either transfer to a different school or leave teaching. Harper (2009) explains that teachers want school administrators who are eager to help a teacher when a need arises, active listeners, role models whose excitement for learning is contagious and spills over to teachers, and who know that teachers and students are in the school. School leaders concerned with increasing the stability of the school's teaching faculty should seek to cultivate opportunities for teachers in general to exercise influence over decision making in the school (Jackson, 2012). The stories that the teachers shared support findings from earlier research studies. Simon and Johnson (2013) suggest that the problems that influence teacher attrition rest with the schools, not the students. Johnson et al. (2012) report that teachers who leave high-poverty, high-minority schools reject the dysfunctional contexts of the schools rather than the students. Terry (2009) found that schools that were organized to support new teachers and provide them with collegial interactions and opportunities for growth were more likely to retain their teachers than schools that were not able to provide such resources for their new teachers. Brown and Schainker (2008) list the conditions and resources needed to support new teachers in their continuous learning, growth, and professional development; these include shared decision making on substantive issues, collaborative work with others to reach shared goals, and expanded teachers' leadership capacity.

New teachers who worked in schools that were organized to support them through collegial interaction and provided them with opportunities for growth, appropriate assignments, adequate resources, and school-wide structures supporting student learning were more likely to stay in those schools than teachers who were new and did not have such support (Simon & Johnson, 2013). Futernick (2007) states that teachers not only want their principals to be effective instructional leaders, but teachers also want them to create and maintain a safe working environment for them profession-ally. Johnson and Birkeland (2003) explain that schools' working conditions, including administrative support and collegiality, can help teachers achieve a "sense of success" and thus a commitment to remain in schools. If the teach-ers are not supported or they are burning out, the ones who suffer most are our children. By failing our teachers, we fail our children. How's that for "the one that got away"?

References

Aoki, T. (1990). Beyond the half-life of curriculum and pedagogy. *One World, 27*(20), 3–10.

Brown, K. M., & Schainker, S. A. (2008). Doing all the right things: Teacher retention issues. *Journal of Cases in Educational Leadership, 11*(1), 10–17.

Bullough, R. V. (2005). Teacher vulnerability and teachability: A case of a mentor and two interns. *Teacher Education Quarterly, 32*(2), 23–39.

Cress, C. M. (2008). Creating inclusive learning communities: The role of student-faculty relationships in mitigating negative campus climate. *Learning Inquiry, 2*(2), 95–111.

Day, C., Edwards, A., Griffiths, A., & Gu, Q. (2011). *Beyond survival: Teacher and resil-ience.* Nottingham, UK: University of Nottingham. Retrieved from https://www.nottingham.ac.uk/research/groups/crelm/documents/teachers-resilience/teachers-resilience.pdf.

Freeman, T. M., Leonard, L., & Lipari, J. (2007). The social contextual nature of resil-iency in schools. In D. M. Davis (Ed.), *Resiliency considered policy implications of the resiliency movement* (pp. 15–30). Charlotte, NC: Information Age Publishing.

Futernick, K. (2007). *A possible dream: Retaining California's teachers so all students can learn.* Sacramento, CA: California State University.

Harper, M. L. (2009). *An examination of teacher retention and attrition in school settings* (Doctoral Dissertation). Retrieved from the EBSCOhost Database. (Accession No. ED513696).

Hartling, L. M. (2008). Strengthening resilience in a risky world: It's all about relation-ships. *Women & Therapy, 31*(2–4), 51.

Jackson, K. M. (2012). Influence matters: The link between principal and teacher influ-ence over school policy and teacher turnover. *Journal of School Leadership, 22*(5), 875–901.

Johnson, B., Down, B., Le Cornu, R., Peters, J., Sullivan, A., Pearce, J., & Hunter, J. (2012). *Early career teachers: Stories of resilience.* Adelaide, Australia: University of South Australia.

Johnson, S. M., & Birkeland, S. E. (2003). Pursuing a "sense of success": New teachers explain their career decisions. *American Educational Research Journal, 40*(3), 581–617.

Johnson, S. M., Kraft, M., & Papay, J. P. (2012). How context matters in high-need schools: The effects of teacher's working conditions on their professional satisfaction and their student's achievement. *Teachers College Record, 114*(10), 1–39.

Jordan, J. (2006). Relational resilience in girls. In S. Goldstein & R. Brooks (Eds.), *Handbook of resilience in children*, New York: Springer.

Le Cornu, R. (2013). Building early career teacher resilience: The role of relationships. *Australian Journal of Teacher Education, 38*(4), 1.

Pearce, J., & Morrison, C. (2011). Teacher identity and early career resilience: Exploring the links. *Australian Journal of Teacher Education, 36*(1) 48–59.

Simon, N. S., & Moore Johnson, S. (2013). *Teacher turnover in high-poverty schools: What we know and can do.* Working Paper: Project on the Next Generation of Teachers. Cambridge, MA: Harvard Graduate School of Education.

Terry, K. (2009). Results from the 2009 teacher exit survey: What were the attitudes of [District] teachers exiting the district in regards to their teaching experiences? *Evaluation Brief 2*(2). Retrieved on October 5, 2011, from http://www.districtTEAisd.org/cms/lib2/TX01001591/Centricity/Domain/8269/PE_DistrictPrograms/2008%20Teacher%20Exit%20Sur.pdf.pdf.

2

A DARK PAST AND A PROMISING FUTURE

The Historical Reception of William Grant Still's *Troubled Island*

Gwendolyn D. Alfred

In 1949, 10 years after its completion, William Grant Still's opera *Troubled Island* earned its first main-stage production at the New York City Opera Company. It was the first time that a major American opera company produced a composition by an African-American composer. *Troubled Island* depicts the leader of the Haitian revolution, Jean Jacques Dessalines, whose corruption leads to his assassination. Greeted with mixed reviews, this piece is one that Still hoped would push him into mainstream recognition as a composer of serious music. However, his dreams failed to materialize, and *Troubled Island* remains a largely forgotten work.

Many scholars have discussed the reception of *Troubled Island*'s premiere performance. Tammy L. Kernodle, Beverly Soll, Wallace Cheatham, and Catherine Parsons Smith mention prejudiced views that could have led to *Troubled Island*'s poor reception. Tammy Kernodle states that Still "believed that the negative reviews resulted from a 'conspiracy' among the New York critics to thwart the success of an African American composer…[and] cold-war politics had affected some aspect of the opera's reception" (Kernodle, 1999). Similarly, Catherine Parsons Smith argues that "the noxious combination of racial prejudice…along with the continuing, more general prejudice against new 'American' operas was more than enough to sink *Troubled Island*" (Smith, 2008). Wallace Cheatham explores Still's feelings about the New York critics and describes these reviews as a "rejection of everything in which [Still] believed about an ultimate redemption of humanity" (Cheatham, 2006). With an unwavering effort to be recognized as not simply a "Negro" composer, Still believed that he was "divinely authorized" to use his gift as an agent for bringing about "integration, reconciliation, and understanding among the peoples of the world: the Black and Caucasian populations of the United States in particular" (Cheatham, 2006).

By closely examining the historical reception of *Troubled Island*, from its origin to recent revivals of the work, I hope to clarify some of the reasons for its present neglect. This study will include opinions of Still's compositional technique, the libretto, and its two productions to date. In such ways, this essay aims to reconsider the work's viability and importance in today's world.

Initially, Still's career as a professional popular musician held precedence over his experiences in the classical music field. After learning to play many instruments and mastering the art of arranging for ensembles, Still earned a job as an instrumentalist and arranger in local bands and orchestras. These ensembles were not merely limited to ragtime, two-steps, and jazz but also featured classical compositions such as opera overtures, waltzes, and marches. Hearing of his talent, W.C. Handy employed Still for 2 years as an arranger and band member for his touring ensemble based in Memphis. After this stint was over, Still landed a position as an oboist in the pit orchestra for the new all-black Broadway musical *Shuffle Along*, whose principal arranger was Will Vodery. After about 500 performances with the touring musical, Still sought further studies in composition and withdrew from the world of commercial music in favor of a concert career (Smith, 2008).

At the same time, Still's reputation in the commercial music field continued to earn him opportunities that were hard to reject completely. In 1929, he received a call from Paul Whiteman to be an arranger for his enormously popular orchestra. Like a symphony orchestra, "it featured large violin and woodwind sections, and both woodwinds and brasses were comfortable with jazz styles" (Smith, 2008). This move provided an important opportunity— one that may have functioned to bring Still's commercial and classical styles much closer together. After this assignment was done, Still soon moved to Los Angeles to pursue his career as an opera and symphonic composer.

Meanwhile, Still pursued formal lessons in composition. After completing three semesters of part-time study at Oberlin and leaving abruptly in the middle of the fourth to seek work as a performing musician, Still often commuted to the school for private lessons, though he was not officially enrolled. He also sought composition lessons at the New England Conservatory with George Chadwick while on tour with *Shuffle Along*. Formal training was a priority of Still, but it was not until later that he began his longest span of study with any composition instructor (Smith, 2008).

After receiving a letter from Edgard Varèse while on an arranging assignment with W.C. Handy, Still began 2 years of lessons with the French-American composer. Varèse encouraged Still to experiment with both form and content and to study such music as Stravinsky's *Petrushka* (Smith, 2008). More importantly, Varèse encouraged Still to find his own way and not imitate his teacher. Varèse also opened doors for Still to the world of concert performance by programming Still's music and introducing him to famous conductors, including Leopold Stokowski. Still's period of study with Varèse was a major breakthrough into a different world from that of night clubs, pit orchestras, and commercial arranging. It proved to be an important milestone in his career as a composer of serious music.

Troubled Island was derived from a play written by Harlem Renaissance poet Langston Hughes. Hughes's interest in Haiti began at a young age, and after completing college, he decided to incorporate the subject into theatrical settings. At the completion of his first Haitian play, *Mulatto*, he decided to write about the period when Haiti achieved its freedom, focusing on its great leader, Jean Jacques Dessalines. Hughes writes,

> Freedom early to me became a wonderful word, and I learned that the Haitians, on their little island in the West Indies, had fought for their freedom. To fight for freedom, I was taught, was a noble thing, as the United States had fought against the British, and the Haitians against the French. The American Revolution, the Haitian Revolution, the word revolution, was a good word in our house when I was a child. (Hughes, 1949)

After beginning his first sketches for the play and an outline, Hughes traveled to Haiti for 6 months to absorb the atmosphere. On his return, Elsie Roxborough presented Hughes's second Haitian play, *Drums of Haiti*, with the Roxanne Players in 1937.

Yet, even with the play's success, Hughes was still not satisfied with his product. He later detected mistakes in his script, added revisions, and renamed it the *Emperor of Haiti*. Hughes subsequently submitted the newly revised play to Broadway managers in hopes of its production in the commercial theater. However, due to production costs and lack of available actors for the lead roles, *Emperor of Haiti* was never produced on the Broadway stage.

Coincidentally, both Still and Hughes experienced similar disappointments at this time. While Still had been turned down by contemporary poets in his requests for operatic libretti, Hughes, similarly, had difficulties finding composers to set his works (Trotman, 1995). Nevertheless, it is not surprising that Still, who had previously set many of Hughes's poems to music, contacted him to create a libretto. Hughes then sent *Emperor of Haiti* to Still to consider as a possible basis for an opera. Still not only loved the play but also the idea of a collaboration with so prominent a writer. Hughes, who was also excited about the upcoming project, promised to transpose the text of the play into a more poetic form, "fashioning it to [Still's] liking" (Trotman, 1995). Meanwhile, Still began composing the music for a full-length grand opera in four acts with a large orchestra, chorus, and ballet—renaming it *Troubled Island*.

Many efforts commenced for the premiere production of *Troubled Island* in an operatic venue. Nevertheless, in 1947, after campaigns led by Stokowski to raise money for the production with an "all-Negro cast," major opera companies demurred. Still then agreed to allow the casting of white singers to portray the leading characters in blackface (Smith, 2008). Soon after, three performances were scheduled by the New York City Opera. The ecstatic opening night audience greeted the work with a standing ovation and numerous curtain calls; however, the attendance dwindled as the nights passed. Though there were critics who called the opera a "triumph," the negative response of the New York critics guaranteed that the opera would not succeed. Still and his wife, Verna Arvey, took these reviews as a personal attack against the composer. Arvey specifically stated in her memoirs that many New York critics plotted to "pan" the opera even before its premiere:

> At rehearsal, one of our friends came out with a startling statement. He warned Billy that plans were then afoot for "the boys" to pan the opera, even before they heard it. They must have been surprised when a Blue Ribbon audience gave it a tremendous ovation with many curtain calls on opening night. (Arvey, 1984)

After only three performances, *Troubled Island* closed and was never again produced by a major opera company. However, encouraged by the audience's response to *Troubled Island*, Still continued to compose operas and hoped to have another opera produced by a major company one day. Unfortunately, this never came to be.

Since its premiere, *Troubled Island*'s reputation has been defined by its initial reception. It is helpful to evaluate the critics' responses, including obscure reviews. Primarily, the African-American periodicals of the time tended to emphasize the positive qualities of the work. In the *Afro-American*'s article entitled "Critics Commend *Troubled Island*," the author specifically featured excerpts from reviews that merely comment on the positive characteristics of the opera as a whole. In particular, a segment of Olin Downes's review in the *New York Times* is included, as follows:

> There is enough that is broadly melodious, enough that supplies dramatic movement on the stage, enough of operatic architecture to make the opera as a whole entertaining and to justify, in all probability, a good number of repetitions before the season closes. (Downes, 1949)

Furthermore, Nora Holt's article in the *New York Amsterdam News* featured a detailed review of the opera. She specifically commended the singers for outstanding performances and proclaimed that Still "invests the score with music that pours from his soul." At the end of the article, Holt stated that "the opera is a stirring drama [with] gripping music and moving text, which should be seen to enjoy to the fullest" (Holt, 1949). In sum, African-American newspapers found it important to shed a positive light on *Troubled Island*, commending its compositional qualities and urging future productions.

In contrast, the articles found in the mainstream press contained specific remarks about the inadequacies of the work's libretto, music, and production. Many critics commented on the problems with Hughes's and Arvey's text. Cecil Smith's article in *The New Republic* described Hughes's libretto as "spotty and diffuse...lurch[ing] back and forth between the vernacular and the self-consciously poetic" (Smith, 1949). Also negatively criticizing the text was John Briggs of the *New York Post Home News*. Briggs felt that the text played an integral role in the opera's failure and remarked on the text's inability to "hold each act together and give the work overall unity" (Briggs, 1949). The libretto's unevenness may have been caused by Still's idea to incorporate Verna Arvey's text into certain sections of the score.

Still's compositional technique and inexperience with the operatic genre also came in for criticism. Critics questioned Still's use of popular musical elements. Overall, Francis D. Perkins presents a "middle-ground" opinion of the premiere performance. After commenting on the work's "straightforward presentation," Perkins stated in the *New York Herald Tribune*,

> The music suggested that Still had a flair for opera, but one that is not fully developed; it also suggested intentions not yet fully realized in a musical idiom for this form. As it was, it often told of the composer's musical individuality, but still gave a rather too revealing account of its various influences, which ranged from Delius on one hand to Gershwin on the other hand. (Perkins, 1949)

Perkins then elaborated on Still's use of hybrid musical qualities that are "reminiscent of the Broadway musical stage," combined with other sections of the piece, which contain a "flavor of lyric drama." He also felt that his rhythmic language lacked momentum. However, Perkins was satisfied with Still's emphasis on melodic themes in the score, specifically the "Haitian version of a French court ballet at the end of the second act." Perkins concluded by stating that the cast presented musical interpretations that were "well-balanced and earnest" (Perkins, 1949).

Time magazine noted Still's reactions to the premiere performance, which he attended in an up-front orchestra seat at a sold-out house. Still admitted his mistakes in the score and vowed to correct them in later productions. The critic gave his opinion of the work, stating,

> Still's music, sometimes lusciously scored, sometimes naively melodic, often had more prettiness than power. In all, *Troubled Island* had more of the soufflé of operetta than the soup bone of opera. With a little seasoning here and there, some listener's thought it could have been made into a Broadway hit. (*Time*, 1949b)

This particular review did not mention the work's incorporation of opera and operetta elements, as in other reviews, but simply considered it an operetta. The article reported that Still planned to keep on writing grand opera.

Troubled Island featured well-respected vocalists specifically known for their performances of American operatic repertoire at New York City Opera. To ensure the new work's success and encourage public appeal from a wider audience, Still utilized these same singers. However, due to the Haitian characters needed in the opera, these Caucasian singers were made up in blackface. Laszlo Halasz conducted the piece, Georges Balanchine and Jean Leon Destine provided choreography, and H.A. Condell designed the sets. Though it is pertinent to examine the critical response's to Still's compositional ability, one might also consider other occurrences that may have caused its mixed response—ones that may have been out of Still's control. Critics stated their opinions with regard to casting, choreography, costuming, and musical direction.

Newsweek felt that the singers performed well but objected to the decision to present the opera in blackface. Further, the review stated that the exaggeration of stage makeup on some singers proved to be unsuccessful, especially Marie Powers, who "was made-up to look a little too much like Aunt Jemima." The magazine's anonymous critic also stated,

> The company pulled a reverse twist and performed the world premiere of a Negro opera, which was written and composed by Negroes, but which had not one single Negro in a major role. Despite the obvious disadvantages of presenting grand opera in blackface, most of the cast performed rather well. (*Newsweek*, 1949a)

Additionally, due to the theater's limited size, staging choices were "not nearly as forceful and imaginative as it might have been." These limitations caused related problems, specifically "interfer[ing] with the effectiveness" of Jean Destine's voodoo scenes (*Newsweek*, 1949a).

All in all, the majority of the reviews from the premiere performance of *Troubled Island* proved to be especially critical of Still's compositional skills. Moreover, reviewers also believed that the dramatic subject, which had much potential, was not successfully realized in the libretto or the musical score. Also criticized was Still's hybrid style, which straddled the fence of operetta and grand opera. However, with all these factors in mind, one must recall Still's overall objective as a composer. He wanted to be different, for he believed that conforming to certain expectations showed weakness. This opportunity was wholeheartedly embodied in the score of *Troubled Island* and many other compositions by Still. Though *Troubled Island* was not universally praised at the time of its premiere, more recent critiques and performances shine a different light on the work and its controversial past.

Though *Troubled Island* was not universally praised at the time of its premiere, more recent critiques, presumably from the original cast recording, shine a different light on the work and its controversial past. Some music history texts have tended to treat Still and *Troubled Island* with considerable respect. Elise Kirk, author of *American Opera*, praised Still for his originality and accessible tunes. She further described Still's operatic works as "basically tonal, dissonant when the drama dictates, grand and eloquent in scope, and most important, flowing in supple melodic contour." She finds his approach to opera of special interest, which she claims is influenced by his experience in the film industry and shows a strategic use of symbolism and action. She states, "Still's stories seemed to work, perhaps because there is always a mystical, even chilling, irony about them." Also, the music that Still weaves into these tales is intriguing, "enliven[ing] and lighten[ing] them with grand, sweeping gestures." The music of Still's operas is the "ultimate protagonist," intensifying the diverse emotions of the characters (Kirk, 2001).

In her biography of William Grant Still, Catherine Parsons Smith discusses the composition and reception of *Troubled Island*, emphasizing Still's musical technique, which was motivated by African-American traditions, which "spoke in a genuinely new voice" and appealed to a "wide, multi-ethnic concert- and opera-going population." performance. She writes,

> Still chose to emphasize the "American" part of his contribution rather than the African American cultural elements that lent [*Troubled Island*] its distinctive character, making it easier for critics to miss the newness—as well as the "blackness"—of his musical speech. (Smith, 2008)

She then provides her own opinions about the opera:

> *Troubled Island* has some magnificent musical high points, among them "To the Hills," the chorus that closes the first act; Martel's "I Dream a World" and the love duet between the plotters in the second act; and, despite its unhappy positioning, Azelia's lament at the end of the opera. From a dramatic point of view, the singer playing Azelia found it impossibly difficult to hold the audience through the lament, for it comes after the action has ended, that is, after the murder of Dessalines and the departure of the plotters. In addition, the efforts at comic relief probably set up expectations that threw the audience (and maybe the performers as well) off balance. (Smith, 2008)

Recognizing his mistakes, Still made some revisions to the work after its premiere performance. He eliminated the elements of comic relief, according to Smith, and allowed Dessalines to survive long enough to exchange words with Azelia prior to her lament.

Lastly, Smith expands on Still's obliviousness regarding current political events, which may have clashed with the overall thematic makeup of *Troubled Island*. Still was very much aware of the political statement *Troubled Island* conveyed during a time period when grand opera was surrounded by aesthetic, intellectual, and political disputes. Writes Smith,

> The aftermath, like other aspects of Still's career, had much to do with contemporary political events, class issues associated with music, musical politics, and is so often the case in American culture. The opera's plot— about a revolution in which blacks killed their white erstwhile owners— may have become too radical for the moment when the opera actually reached the stage. (Smith, 2008)

The mostly white audience may have found it difficult to relate to a plot in which educated mixed-race characters use their skills to "systematically undermine the revolution of the proletariat" (Smith, 2008). Smith believed that Still's "outspoken political position" may have played a role, "right along with his musical decisions about style" in the declining interest in his music after 1949.

While many texts contain the previously cited reviews of the New York critics, the aforementioned historical texts provide a variety of personal opinions. Some authors commend Still's use of popular idioms, melodic themes, and accessible tunes, while others feel that these elements were directly associated with the work's lack of success. All in all, whether positive or negative, these authors view *Troubled Island* as an influential work that is an integral part of Still's musical career and American music history.

In 2013, after years of neglect, *Troubled Island* received a historic production by the South Shore Opera Company of Chicago. This single, sold-out performance employed an all-black cast and utilized a two-piano adaptation due to insufficient funding for a full orchestra. Leading roles included Kirk Walker as Dessalines, Gwendolyn Brown as Azelia, Dana Campbell as Claire, Antonio Watts as Stenio, and Cornelius V. Johnson III as Vuval. Andrew Patner of the *Chicago Sun Times* wrote a brief review about the opera's performance, stating,

> With a cast of 25, including a superb chorus prepared by Charles Hayes, director Amy Hutchinson, designers Shanna Philipson and Julian Pike, and eight dancers added for Kia Smith's strong choreography, South Shore made a handsome and convincing case for a production with full orchestra. Bravo to South Shore Opera Company for rescuing the collaborative work of these men [Still and Hughes], largely lost to history, and preparing the way for its wider rediscovery. (Patner, 2013)

In contrast with most of the critics in 1949, Patner spoke highly of the opera and expressed hope for future productions.

Similarly, Noah Kars of the *South Side Weekly* was convinced that the revival was a success and definitely "[gave] *Troubled Island* another shot after a rocky past." Kahrs recounts interviews with leading cast members, including Kirk Walker, who implied that being a part of such a historic production was a great experience. Cornelius Johnson was also excited to pay tribute to Still and an opportunity to perform what Johnson says is "[the composer's] crown lory." Also complimented was Gwendolyn Brown, whose portrayal of Azelia was "an integral part of [the] textural richness," introduced by the rich, jazz-based harmonies and extended chords. Brown's duet with Walker emphasized the work's jazz influences, "as the pair concluded their duet on a seventh chord" (Kars, 2013).

In 2014, Thee Black Swan Theatre and Opera Company, a company in the United Kingdom, presented excerpts from *Troubled Island* to a live studio audience, accompanied by keyboard. Director Joseph Charles introduced this work to a racially mixed audience and awaited their responses. Though the cast was racially mixed, black singers were strategically cast as the Haitian characters, whereas mulatto characters featured cast members from other races. Keel Watson appeared as Dessalines, Natasha Bain as Azelia, Andee-Louise Hypolite as Claire, Ronald Samm as Vuval, and Jake Gill as Stenio. Keel Watson spoke about his portrayal of Dessaline and the dichotomy of his character, stating,

> [Dessalines is an example] of how good men can be turned, but still have the good in them. Getting that feeling while you're acting that character, is difficult…it's challenging…but in a way its worthwhile to understand people like that. People that aren't bad, but the situation makes them bad. (People Pictures Media–Watson Interview, 2014e)

Ronald Samm spoke of the need for a full production of the opera with orchestra:

> There's some glorious moments in this opera, and we haven't heard it [with orchestra] yet. That is one aspect I really look forward to hearing…how it fits with the words and everything. The sections with drums and ballet…the contrast doesn't come through with the piano. But if [we] really had an orchestra it would be sensational. (People Pictures Media–Samm Interview, 2014d)

As the program came to a close, audience members gave their opinions of the work and production. Andre San Kouffer stated,

> I thought it was fantastic the way it was put together…and the way the story was told with the different twists. I've read about the characters in history books and it was nice to see them in a different dimension in the theater. (People Pictures Media–Kouffer interview, 2014c)

An anonymous member of the audience commented on the historical relevance of the work, stating,

> It's a fantastic production for black people, particularly young people, who don't have an idea of their history. I think this [opera] will help them, and help them get over their thoughts about it being an "opera," by viewing it in a wider context. I think it's superb! (People Pictures Media, audience interview, 2014a)

Yet another audience member, one who had never seen or even heard of *Troubled Island*, said,

> I think that it is an interesting opera and I think that it will be fantastic to see the whole thing...and for [the company] to receive funding so that [they] may be bring it to everybody. It's a really good production and a very interesting subject. (People Pictures Media, audience interview, 2014a)

After hearing feedback from the audience, Joseph Charles argued for a full-fledged production: "We [now] know there is an audience and we will provide great singers...that will produce the best for tomorrow" (People Pictures Media, Joseph Clark interview, 2014b). Thee Black Swan Theatre and Opera Company is currently working on a full production of *Troubled Island*, which is scheduled to make its debut in the near future.

Conclusion

William Grant Still's *Troubled Island* is a work that has been overlooked for many years due to the critics' reviews of the initial performance. Negative opinions of Still's compositional techniques and inexperience with the operatic genre overshadow the other elements of the opera that also received negative criticism. To address the possibility of racial bias in the criticism is beyond the scope of this study; however, *Troubled Island* was a work that clearly was premiered "before its time"—a time when its unique components were not particularly fashionably. And though the work might well have profited from some revision, no major opera company allowed Still another chance to rewrite this work or compose another.

In recent years, with its revivals, *Troubled Island* has shown itself to be a work worthy of a production and a place in the repertoire. Musicians, choreographers, vocalists, and audience members speak highly of the piece and its relevance. Given modern views on racial depictions, singers are now cast appropriately with regard to ethnicity, removing the negative connotation of cast members in blackface. Furthermore, the musical hybrid component of *Troubled Island* is a technique that is not only tolerated but very much accepted in today's world. Perhaps, with all these aforementioned factors taken into consideration, opera companies will see the validity of the work and decide to produce *Troubled Island* in the near future. Certainly, Still's opera should be remembered as an important landmark in the history of American opera.

References

Arvey, V. (1984). *In One Lifetime.* Fayetteville: The University of Arkansas, 143.

Briggs, J. (1949). Troubled Island has city center premiere. *New York Post Home News,* April 1.

Cheatham, W. (2006). William grant still and troubled Island. In J. A. Still & L. Headlee (Eds.), *Just tell the story: Troubled Island.* Vol. 32. Flagstaff, AZ: Master Player Library.

Critics commend Troubled Island. (1949). *Afro-American,* April 9.

Downes, O. (1949). Review, *New York Times,* April 7.

Holt, N. (1949). Freedom the theme in troubled Island. *New York Amsterdam News,* April 9.

Hughes, L. (1949). Troubled Island: The story of how an opera was created. *The Chicago Defender,* March 26.

Kars, N. (2013). Revolutionary revival: For one night, Troubled Island returned to life. *South Side Weekly,* October 22.

Kernodle, T. L. (1999). Arias, communists, and conspiracies: The history of still's "troubled Island." *The Musical Quarterly 83:* 487.

Kirk, E. (2001). *American Opera.* Chicago: University of Illinois Press. 203.

Patner, A. (2013). South shore opera company stages troubled Island. *Chicago Sun Times,* October 16.

People Pictures Media. (2014a). Audience interview.

People Pictures Media. (2014b). Joseph Clark interview.

People Pictures Media. (2014c). *Troubled Island: The journey begins.* YouTube video, 11:00, Andre San Kouffer interview, February 17, https://www.youtube.com/watch?v= nDwimN9bfZg.

People Pictures Media. (2014d). *Troubled Island: The journey begins.* YouTube video, 11:00, Ronald Samm interview, February 17. https://www.youtube.com/watch?v= nDwimN9bfZg.

People Pictures Media. (2014e). *Troubled Island: The journey begins.* YouTube video, 11:00, Keel Watson interview, February 17, https://www.youtube.com/watch?v= nDwimN9bfZg.

Perkins, F. D. (1949). Tragedy in Haiti. *New York Herald Tribune,* April 1.

Smith, C. (1949). Music: Operas, Haitian and Egyptian. *The New Republic,* May 2.

Smith, C. P. (2008). *William Grant Still.* Chicago: University of Illinois, 76.

Trotman, C. J. (1995). *Langston Hughes: The man, his art, and his continuing influence.* New York: Garland Publishing.

Troubled Opera (1949a). *Newsweek* 33, April 11.

Troubled Opera (1949b). *Times* 53, 73.

3

THE BLACK MALE TEACHER

America's Newest Slave Driver

Kevin B. Thompson

Introduction

With a focus on recruiting Black men, policymakers have attempted to diversify America's teacher workforce. Programs such as Call Me MISTER, the Honoré Center for Undergraduate Achievement, and the U.S. Department of Education's TEACH were designed with this purpose in mind. While achieving marginal success, our educational system has consistently failed to recruit and retain Black male teachers. Researchers have discovered some motivations for these occurrences. Scholars have identified the inability to facilitate change as a major reason for attrition. Lynn (2006) observes that regular experiences with the struggle of being Black and male in society allow Black men to think of teaching as "a form of social change." While the role of change agent is critical to the Black men's perception of teaching, education's preoccupation with standardized testing has regulated the implementation of culturally responsive practices and pedagogy by Black male teachers, suppressing the quintessence of Black male teachers' identity.

Researchers have identified a phenomenon within classrooms that has frustrated the mainstream for decades—Black male youth. Countless studies have dealt with American education's perceived inability to control the behavior of Black boys in classrooms. Numerous reports rank Black male youth at the bottom of educational achievement. Researchers have exposed the fact that Black boys receive discipline at higher rates within schools. In addition, current appraisals cite an over-relegation of Black boys to special education as compared with other ethnicities. The achievement gap is attributed to clear circumstances within the Black community, with the most popular being an increase in single-parent homes. Other researchers have ascribed the gap in achievement to the Black male youth's "uncontrollable" behavior. Teachers belonging to the predominant racial class have failed at identifying area(s) of disconnect between them and Black male youth. Theorists suggest that an extended absence of Black men in the home and classroom contributed to the behavioral misappraisal of children of color, especially Black boys.

America's current need for Black men is reminiscent of its former need for them during the dark ages of slavery. Slaveholders frequently exploited the physical prowess and intellect of Black men. Black men of certain physical and intellectual dispositions served as supervisors on plantations. In the spirit of American capitalism, these supervisors, or "drivers," were responsible for managing and increasing productivity among their fellow slaves. White supremacy sired America. White supremacy is seeking new slave drivers to manage the "education" of those typically unwilling to embrace European standards of learning and behavior—Black male youth.

To compare the function of a slave driver with that of a Black male teacher requires intellectual bravery. The comparison asks the reader and the writer to shed the comforts of familiarity in order to investigate the reason(s) for the American educational system's persistent interest in the recruitment of Black men along with its inability to connect with and educate children of color, in particular, Black male youth. Conversely, this investigation should prompt any Black man interested in teaching to consider and reconsider their motives prior to entering an American classroom as a teacher. Findings from this comparative inquiry along with additional research on the subject could severely affect minority recruitment programs, teacher education programs, and other initiatives "promoting" diversity within teacher recruitment. While this investigation warrants commentary, the dialogue should lead to action. In the words of Dr. Maulana Karenga, "knowledge is…important…because of its value and role in improving the human condition…" (Karenga, 2002). The writer's mission is couched within the Egyptian "activist-intellectual tradition." Within the ancient Egyptian era, according to Karenga, the "sesh" or the socially conscious and activist intellectuals of the day dedicated themselves to the service of the people (p. 7). It is the writer's intention to identify and expose any hegemony predicated on the destruction of Black people. The late Joe Kincheloe embodied this ideal. His work centered on critical pedagogy and its efforts at decimating suffering and marginalization caused by certain power structures within society. The notion that white supremacy undermines most areas of society is not new. However, analyses of its (white supremacy) motives and methods are rare and advertised as heretical. Kincheloe says that we should "…work to develop intellect and expose these power-related dynamics that prop up the status quo, undermine social mobility, and produce discourses, and ideologies…" that support oppression in any way (Kincheloe, 2008). This paper will draw a historical comparison between slave drivers with Black male teachers in an attempt to identify white supremacy's utilization of the Black male body to control the actions of other

Black bodies. Apprehensions associated with this comparison must be articulated due to the seemingly counterintuitive nature of the discussion. This comparison is not an argument against the presence of Black men in education. In fact, education would benefit from an increased presence of Black men as educators. However, this comparison assumes that the intentions of the American educational system are not as wholesome as advertised.

Identity Exploitation

The discussion's claim of white supremacy's interest in controlling Black bodies revolves around the educational system's failure to instruct children of color adequately, namely Black boys. The Schott Foundation's "50 State Report on Public Education and Black Males" illustrates disparities between Black men and other ethnicities. The report states that Black men "remain at the bottom of four-year high school graduation rates...evidence of a systemic problem impacting Black males..." (Schott Foundation, 2015). Bryan and Ford (2014) note, "...the lowest performing students in our nation's schools are Black males... (t)hey have the highest dropout rate, lowest graduation rate, highest suspension and expulsion rate, and lowest test scores." Therefore, the logical motivation for recruiting Black men would revolve around students' need. Brown supports the reasoning when he states, "the underlying assumption of this burgeoning discussion was that African American males hold special cultural knowledge...." A review of the literature associated with the attrition of Black male teachers along with an analysis of current Black male teachers' recruitment efforts indicates a sense of desperation regarding Black male youth within American education.

Equally, Black men within the community have sensed this desperation and have taken action. Many have resolved to counter this educational regression by becoming intimately involved in the teaching process. Lynn (2002) suggested, "Black men teachers were confident that their knowledge and experience in the community were important factors...." Lynn (2006) also commented, "Black men teachers are able to use their own experiences with oppression to understand...daily struggles with race and class oppression." This commentary establishes the notion of change as an integral part of the Black men's psyche. While the intentions of Black men are noble, agents of white supremacy have observed these aspirations and have devised methods to control the mental, physical, and spiritual trajectory of Black bodies. Yet, white supremacy has taken this unbridled passion for change and redirected its aim. Its principal method was the intentional neglect of culturally responsive practices. Black males who entered education came in with preconceived notions associated with expediting radical educational changes. To aid identifying white supremacy's interest in controlling Black bodies, one must familiarize themselves with one of white supremacy's greatest tools—slavery.

One of the first instances of cultural suppression occurred on the plantation. Hilliard advances this notion by stating that white supremacists (or "enforcers") "suppress the value of other cultures while glorifying and fabricating the history of themselves" (Hilliard, 2002). This cultural suppression served to replace positive images of African power, might, and intellect with those of inferiority and helplessness. Understanding the African's role in chattel slavery is pivotal in comprehending white supremacy's physical, mental, and spiritual positioning of Black men. According to Karenga, "the enslaved African was profitable on three basic levels: as a commodity to be sold; as an object of labor to be rented, and as a producer of cash products" (Karenga, 2002). Utilizing Karenga's definition of the African's role in slavery, one could assume that white supremacists with education seek to "rent" Black men to assist in the manufacturing of a certain product, well-behaved Black boys.

With emphasis on the terms "savior," "role model," and "father figure," white supremacy lures Black men into the classroom, ultimately exploiting the Black male's passion and enthusiasm. Shaw (1996) supports this thinking by stating, "…professional literature laments this scarcity of African American teachers, proposing numerous advantages to their presence in the classroom…the most often cited benefit is that Black teachers serve as role models for Black youth." While this view is ideal, it bears little merit. Cooper-Shaw rejects the course of the literature when she argues, "the role model lure, when offered as the primary inducement to enter teaching, is faulty in at least two…respects." She continues this thought by saying that the idea of Black men serving as role models within the classroom is "unrealistic" and that "Black students do not tend to identify their teachers as role models any more than White students do." To continue this point, Cooper-Shaw states, "the role model incentive contains a note of condescension and implies a cultural deficit view…." A suitable postulation would assert that once the veil of language is lifted, white supremacy's real need for Black male teachers would be revealed—behavior management.

Bristol (2015) articulates this sentiment plainly within his article on male teachers of color when he features a Black male teacher by the name of George Little. According to Little, he and his colleagues served "in more disciplinary roles when compared to his colleagues…duties such as monitoring or 'policing' the school door during dismissal…." Little advances this thought by mentioning his belief that administrators and colleagues viewed him "as a behavior manager first…teacher second." Observations of this nature support the discussion's investigation.

The Role of a Slave Driver

Examining these narratives draws a comparison of Black male teachers with slave drivers. To understand the connection between Black male teachers and slave drivers fully, the slave driver—his duties and his psyche—must be

placed within proper context. Before a slave became a driver, he was identified as a candidate for promotion. He had to possess particular qualities
in order to receive such responsibility. Prospects had to be "honest, indus-
trious, not too talkative..., a man of good sense...conform to instructions
notwithstanding the privations necessary, possess energy, ready intelligence
and satisfactory accountability...strength, working speed, and real or potential leadership ability" (Van DeBurg, 1979). Given the number of persons
on a plantation, maintaining visual contact was of the utmost importance.
The overseer was responsible for supervising all the work done in the fields.
The driver, a Black male slave typically, was charged with supervising groups
of slaves, encouraging compliance regarding plantation productivity measures. The driver had the authority to employ methods deemed necessary
to facilitate this increase in efficiency—even if it meant physically harming
their fellow slaves.

> (D)rivers had great responsibilities, superior privileges, and awesome dis-
> ciplinary powers. Within his memoir, Man's Search for Meaning, Frankl
> (1959) illustrates this power when he states, "Capos—prisoners who
> acted as trustees...were harder on the prisoners than were the guards, and
> beat them more cruelly than the SS men did." Some had virtually com-
> plete control of the plantation when the master or overseer was absent
> (Starobin, 1971)

Yet, Starobin argues that the thought of controlling their fellow bondsmen for
the benefit of their masters placed drivers in challenging positions. Starobin
supports this notion by mentioning a supposed luxury of drivers—contact with
field workers while maintaining their owner's trust. In return, the drivers were
responsible for "transmitting proper standards to the rest of the slaves." For years,
teachers have encountered problems in managing the behavior of Black boys
in the classroom. This discussion proposes that the reason for America's interest in recruiting Black male teachers deals with her desire to subdue Black
boys into a mental space of servitude. These individuals are viewed as practical
templates for white supremacy's agenda on Black male subjection. The only
entity perceived suitable enough for the job are individuals bearing a similar
resemblance—Black men.

White Supremacy's Intention

Identifying white supremacy's modus operandi is essential to understanding its
true intention for Black men. Welsing (1991) dedicated her life to examining
the impact of white supremacy's influence on people of color. Welsing postulates, "the goal of the white supremacy system is...the establishment, maintenance, expansion and refinement of world domination by members of a group

that classifies itself as the white 'race'." While remaining selectively open, white supremacy has mastered the art of hiding its true intentions, especially within education. The utilization of Black men within the classroom is a front for white supremacy's attempt to domesticate children of color, especially boys. In order to coerce Black male youth into cooperation, white supremacists employ Black men to serve as physical examples of proper behavior, speech, and dress, thereby modeling "good" behavior. Like slave drivers, Black male teachers are used to break the spirit of individuality among Black men and model conformity. Hilliard (2002) argued, "the enforcers of an oppressive system work to create cultural disorder among the oppressed." By facilitating an environment of conformity within the classroom, white supremacy inculcates impressionable minds to reject instinctive African behaviors for European behaviors. White supremacy has used Black male teachers to promote "proper" behavior. It is because of these policies (written and assumed), the inherent disrespect, and the underutilization of their skills and talent that most male teachers of color leave the classroom. The National Center for Education Statistics published its "Teacher Attrition and Mobility: Results From the 2012–2013 Teacher Follow-Up Survey First Look" report in September 2014. The report showed that America's teacher workforce was approximately 81% Caucasian, with 76% of these individuals identifying as female (Goldring et al., 2014). The report also highlighted the fact that Black teachers comprised approximately 7% of the teacher workforce, with Black men accounting for less than 2%. Quitting was an option unavailable to slave drivers because they were the property of the overseer. This is the only disparity between slave drivers and the bureaucratic intention for Black male teachers.

Conclusion

Black male teachers can be used as agents of white supremacy. King (1991) supports this notion with the following definition of dysconscious racism:

> Dysconscious racism is a form of racism that tacitly accepts dominant White norms and privileges. It is not the absence of consciousness (that is, not unconsciousness) but an impaired consciousness or distorted way of thinking about race as compared to, for example, critical consciousness. (p. 135)

Black male teachers are not there to immerse the students into the culture. They are there to regulate the new norm. Lynn (2002) states, "…schooling for non-whites became a process of deculturalization…if the aim of 'school' is to delegitimize the culture and history of Blacks…then teachers—even if they are Black—are forced to act as stewards of this detestable mission in the eyes of some community members." In essence, the role of Black male teacher was defined before the recruitment of Black male teacher. Brown (2012) supports this notion by stating the following:

> The Black male teacher has become constructed as what I call a pedagogical kind...a type of educator whose subjectivities, pedagogies, and expectations have been set in place prior to entering the classroom. In this sense, the Black male teacher has been situated directly in the context of the Black male student and received by the educational community to secure, administer, and govern the unruly Black boy in school. (p. 299)

As the writer mentioned previously, slave drivers were given specific responsibilities, and all on the plantation knew their duties explicitly. This is the same ideology for the basis of this paper. When a school hires a Black male teacher, his responsibilities are known throughout the school. Brown states "teachers share(d) the belief that Black male teachers are expected to be physically intimidating and capable of using their physical presence as a way to govern Black boys." While the Black man intends on making changes within his physical and mental presence, white supremacists have planned to utilize his (Black man's) presence to produce something conducive to the implementation of the white supremacist agenda—a docile, indoctrinated Black man.

References

Bristol, T. J. (2015). Male teachers of color take a lesson from each other. *Phi Delta Kappan, 97*(2), 36–41.

Brown, A. L. (2012) "On human kinds and role models: A critical discussion about the African American male teacher. *Educational Studies, 48*, 296–315.

Bryan, N., & Ford, Y. (2014). Recruiting and retaining Black male teachers in gifted education. *Gifted Child Today, 37*(3), 156–161.

Frankl, V. (1959). *Man's search for meaning.* New York: Simon & Schuster.

Goldring, R., Taie, S., & Riddles, M. (2014). Teacher attrition and mobility: Results from the 2012–2013 teacher follow-up survey. First Look. NCES 2014-077. National Center for Education Statistics.

Hilliard, A. (2002). *African power: Affirming African indigenous socialization in the face of the culture wars.* Gainesville: Makare Publishing Company.

Karenga, M. (2002). *Introduction to black studies.* Los Angeles: University of Sankore.

Kincheloe, J. (2008). *Critical pedagogy.* New York: Peter Lang.

King, J. E. (1991). Dysconscious racism: Ideology, identity, and the miseducation of teachers. *The Journal of Negro Education, 60*(2), 133–146.

Lynn, M. (2002). Critical race theory and the perspectives of Black men teachers in the Los Angeles public schools. *Equity and Excellence in Education, 35*(2), 119–130.

Lynn, M. (2006). Education for the community: Exploring the culturally relevant practices of Black male teachers. *Teachers College Record, 108*(12), 2497–2522.

Matter, B. L. (2015). *The Schott 50 state report on public education and black males.* Quincy: Schott Foundation for Public Education.

Shaw, C. (1996). The big picture: An inquiry into the motivations of African-American teacher education students to be or not to be teachers. *American Educational Research Journal, 33*(2), 327–354.

Starobin, R. S. (1971). Privileged bondsmen and the process of accommodation: The role of houseservants and drivers as seen in their own letters. *Journal of Social History, 5*(1), 46–70.

Van DeBurg, W. (1979). *The slave drivers: Black agricultural labor supervisors in the antebellum south.* Westport: Greenwood Press.

Welsing, F. C. (1991). *The Isis papers: The keys to the colors.* Washington, DC: C.W. Publishing.

4

CULTURED PEARLS

An Investigation of Culturally Responsive
Pedagogical Practices Used by White
Teachers in Urban Settings

*Jasmine Williams, Richard F. Price, Michara DeLaney,
Danielle Hairston-Green, Pamela R. Finley, Terence Finley,
and Lucian Yates, III*

Overview

Culturally relevant educational practices have been a part of the educational
lexicon for over four decades, beginning with Black student activism at
American colleges and universities in the 1960s (Claybrook, 2013; Rogers,
2012). There is wide consensus in the literature that an inclusive and diverse
curriculum is vital to the creation of educational environments that truly
meet the academic needs of all students (Bazron et al., 2005; Cholewa et al.,
2014; Gay, 2002). A culturally relevant curriculum is more important today,
juxtaposed with the 2014–2015 public school term, which marked the first
time when minority students outnumbered White students (Hefling &
Holland, 2014). Moreover, when the diverse student population is contrasted
with the predominately White female middle-class teaching force, a "cultural dissonance" occurs (Brown, 2007; Taylor, 2010). It is suggested that
this "dissonance" is in large measure responsible for the underachievement
of racially, ethically, linguistically diverse, non-White students (Brown,
2007; Gay, 2010; Taylor, 2010).

Related to culturally responsive educational practices is culturally relevant pedagogy. Culturally relevant pedagogy is conceptualized by Ladson-
Billings (1995) as teaching practices of opposition, whereby student outcomes
result in student empowerment. More specifically, Ladson-Billings (1995)
concluded that students emerge from the educational experience achieving academic success, developing and maintaining cultural competence,
and developing "a critical consciousness through which they challenge the
current status quo of the social order" (p. 160). Culturally relevant pedagogy represents the nexus of teaching styles and the home and community

culture of students in classrooms. Students' cultural experiences, values, and understandings must be integrated into the curriculum and the educational environment (Brown-Jeffy & Cooper, 2011). Preparing preservice teachers for an ever-increasing diverse student population is recognized as a priority by many in the educational community (Gay, 2013; Ladson-Billings, 1995; Martins-Shannon, 2012; Picower, 2009).

Courses that address culturally responsive pedagogy have been added to preservice programs, but scholars such as Gay (2010, 2013) indicated that insufficient attention given to the ingrained bias, attitudes, and beliefs of teacher candidates remains a major issue. Gay (2010) observed that culturally relevant pedagogy must be infused into teacher preparation programs at a level "of intensity, depth, and magnitude that far exceeded anything done before" (p. 1). However, in studies on primary and secondary school segregation, White students have been found to be the most racially isolated (Orfield & Lee, 2006; Reardon & Owens, 2014). A result of their racial and cultural isolation is that their susceptibility to myths and stereotypes proves resistant to change when they are introduced to culturally responsive course content as preservice teachers.

A review of literature underscores the challenges encountered in training teachers for diverse student populations. For example, Szabo and Anderson (2009) directed a study on teacher candidates' attitudes about cultural relevance before and after a one-semester course on the educational foundations of multiculturalism. The researchers used an instrument to measure the teacher candidates' sensitivity to and familiarity with multicultural issues to determine whether there was a positive effect on the candidates' awareness of multiculturalism. Their findings indicated that reliance on a single-semester course to increase a preservice teacher's multicultural awareness or change a preservice teacher's attitudes is an ambitious proposition.

Picower (2009) examined how the life experiences of White preservice teachers influenced their ability to navigate a multicultural education course when their attitudes and beliefs about race were challenged. Picower found that participants in the study adopted several responses that protected as well as reinforced mainstream understandings of race and racism. Rather than classify the responses as resistance, the researcher argued that the responses actually protected and preserved the dominant White culture. Picower (2009) stated, "The findings of this study argue that these privileges, ideologies, and stereotypes reinforce institutional hierarchies and the larger system of White supremacy" (p. 198). Although the studies conducted by Szabo and Anderson (2009) and Picower (2009) are not representative of all studies related to the cultural competence of White preservice teachers, few studies feature positive outcomes of culturally responsive pedagogy directed by non-African-American teachers who serve ethnically diverse student populations. The researchers in this study sought to explore this void.

Purpose of Study

The lack of diversity among teachers is a concern well represented among researchers and educational practitioners (Barnes, 2006; Chu, 2011; Gay, 2010; Ladson-Billings, 2005; Parameswaran, 2007; Saffold & Longwell-Grice, 2008; Szabo & Anderson, 2009; Taylor, 2010). As Parameswaran (2007) explained, "Traditional students in teacher training institutions are often unfamiliar with issues surrounding diversity and multicultural education" (p. 51). This unfamiliarity has serious implications for a majority of the estimated 50 million students in K-12 education (National Center for Education Statistics, 2014). As Barnes (2006) emphasized, "Many teacher education programs are still struggling to adequately prepare preservice teachers to successfully deal with the challenge of teaching a diverse student population" (p. 85). The role, therefore, of teacher preparation programs is immensely important in producing a workforce skilled in meeting the academic needs of all students (Frye & Vogt, 2010; Gay, 2010; Jett, 2012; Parameswaran, 2007; Prater & Devereaux, 2009). To this end, the purpose of this study was to discover the educational practices and techniques used by White teachers, who are graduates of a teacher preparation program, who taught in urban schools, and who are recognized for successfully infusing cultural relevant pedagogy into their curriculum. The following question guided this study: What are the educational practices and techniques used by culturally responsive White teachers who successfully infuse cultural relevant pedagogy into their curricula?

Theoretical Framework

The framework for this study, "centeredness," was adapted from the conceptualization of "Afrocentricity," as first coined by noted African-American scholar, Molefi Kete Asante (Mazama & Lundy, 2013). In the context of education, students are centered in the curriculum, or as Asante (2003) wrote, students experience education through the paradigm of their "interests, values, and perspectives" (p. 2). They are situated in the center of "familiar cultural and social references from their own historical settings" (Asante, 1992, p. 28).

The centeredness framework rests upon the premise that societies ultimately create institutions that are reflective of their cultural beliefs (Asante, 2003; Kunjufu, 1984; Williams, 2016). Relatedly, education must have meaning and relevance to one's life (Mazama & Lundy, 2013; Woodson, 1933). Centeredness, then, provides a critical lens through which to experience culturally relevant pedagogy embedded into the educational curriculum. In essence, centeredness and culturally responsive educational practices accomplish identical goals; both provide students with meaningful educational experiences relevant to who they are—students become participative, not mere bystanders. They are "centered" in cultural ways that make learning interesting and intimate (Asante, 1991). In this study, "centeredness" functioned as an authentic measuring stick of culturally relevant pedagogy embedded into the educational curriculum.

Research Design

The researchers focused this qualitative study on the experiences of two White female teachers of predominately African-American and Latino students who attended a teacher preparation program at a mid-South Historically Black University (HBU) and infused the K-12 educational curriculum with culturally relevant educational practices. This phenomenological approach was employed to ascertain the meaning of the lived experience of the study participants and to accept their reality as it was experienced (Jackson & Mazzei, 2012; Schram, 2006). This study was most suited for a phenomenological approach because it allowed the researchers to delve deep into understanding the experiences of the sample population (Fraenkel et al., 2012). The primary purpose of this study was to discover educational practices and techniques used by culturally responsive White teachers who infused cultural relevant pedagogy into the curriculum.

Data Collection

The sample population for this study was composed of two White teachers who completed a teacher preparation program at an HBU in the mid-South United States and subsequently taught in an urban school for at least a year. The participants were selected using a purposive sampling method in which the researchers determine the individuals to be included in the study (Creswell, 2013). The distance between the researchers and the study participants necessitated the use of email as the primary mode of communication. The interview protocol (Appendix A) consisted of 20 open-ended questions that were emailed to the participants, with a 10-day timeline to allow for in-depth responses; it was then returned to the research team.

Data Analysis

The NVivo-11 software was used to perform the analysis of the qualitative data and to identify themes through coding, which produced the following five premises: Developing Relationships, Education at an HBU, Unique Skills, Effective Lesson Planning, and Classroom Management. In addition, the researchers analyzed the data to identify pedagogical strategies that could benefit teachers, administrators, and, most important, students in the K-12 environment.

Participant Demographics

Participant one: Participant one was identified as a 30-year-old White female who graduated with a bachelor's degree in elementary education from Kentucky State University and, subsequently, master's degree in behavior and learning disabilities. She is currently completing the requirements for an education specialist degree, with principal certification from the University of Kentucky. She is the only person in her family to earn a master's degree and the first of her nuclear family to complete a college education. She was raised in a small town in the mid-South.

Participant two: Participant two was identified as a 31-year-old White woman who graduated with a bachelor's degree in elementary education from Kentucky State University and a master's degree in educational leadership from Eastern Kentucky University. In addition, she received rank I in reading and writing instruction from Eastern Kentucky University.

Results and Findings

The researchers formatted responses from the participants for auto coding in the NVivo-11 database. The data produced a total of 54 nodes and 108 references. Nodes are essentially a filing system to store data. In this research, the nodes were labeled to represent each question and subquestions. Additionally, the references represent how many times the participants' responses related to any one of those nodes or questions, which is also referred to as coding. In some cases, references can be stored in multiple nodes (Bazeley & Jackson, 2013). The researchers used the inductive reasoning process to establish the following themes and subthemes:

Theme 1: Developing Relationships

Subthemes: Cultural responsive pedagogy was critical in helping the educators to create relationships with their students and families.

Participants shared how important it was for them to connect with the students and their families. They indicated that trust was a big issue because the families noticed right away that racially the teachers did not represent their children. Participants expressed how important it was to submerge themselves into their student's community and connect to the things that the students enjoyed.

Participant one shared the belief that connecting to her students was critical to her success. She stated that she "[built] relationships so that students can openly and respectfully disagree with one another." She also stated that "Parents [did not] think that I related until I made connections with families. I was involved in every aspect I could be, and eventually

I earned the respect of parents and students. Most of the time they want to be heard—a simple hug and a lunch talk can do wonders."

Participant two stated, "All my students have problems that are similar and it is my job to learn what makes my students tick and what I can provide them to be successful." She further explained, "I took the time to get to know my students and their families and develop relationships with them. I make every effort to connect with all of my students and their life outside of school. Whether it be engaging in a hobby, talking about their home life with them, going to their basketball game or any extracurricular activity, sending home a postcard, the list goes on and on."

Theme 2: Education at an HBU

Subtheme: Participants did not believe that being an educated White woman gave them an advantage in relation to teaching in racially and ethnically diverse classrooms.

Both participants agreed that although they had an advantage that was different than their colleagues, the advantage was not due to the color of their skin. It was primarily due to their experiences at the Historically Black Colleges and Universities (HBCU), where they received their cultural responsiveness training. In fact, they believed they had to work harder because of the color of their skin to gain respect and trust from the families of the students they were charged with educating.

Participant one shared, "I [was not] given an advantage being [W]hite. These schools had high turnover rates with [W]hite females and I had to prove to my students that I was different." She added, "Most new teachers are placed in the lower achieving schools because those are the jobs that are open. It [does not] matter about your color. Being white never advanced me, because everyone around me was also [W]hite. Education advanced the people around me. The better your job, the better you lived"

Participant two indicated that she, "Will not classify [herself] as an educated [W]hite woman who has an advantage in relation to teaching in a racially and ethnically diverse classroom. I feel my experiences at an HBCU have helped me to become who I am."

Theme 3: Unique Skills

Subtheme: Culturally responsiveness gives an advantage in the school systems in which the participants are employed because they are the only individuals who understand the value and impact.

In reviewing the notes from the interviews, it was clear that the participants felt that their culturally responsive education received at the HBU provided them with the greatest advantage over their colleagues. According to both, they were able to gain a deeper and more meaningful connection with students in their classrooms. Their ability to establish relationships with the parents inside and outside of the classroom and to connect to the things that excited the students was essential in their classroom successes.

Participant one expressed her initial feelings upon entering the classroom for the first time. "I was scared. I can remember thinking... can I really do this? I felt that I [could not] make relationships because I [did not] have anything in common. But I soon realized that I [did not] have to have anything in common, I just had to be me." Additionally, when communicating with the parents, she believed, "The way to talk to parents also plays an important part in how they accept you. After a while, it [was not] about color—it was about the student."

Participant two shared, "I classify myself as a teacher who received and practices culturally responsive teaching with all students and because of that I have an advantage in my classroom with every student that walks into my classroom. I teach with many White women who know nothing about being culturally responsive. Many teachers have envied my connections with my students and their families." *Participant two* also discussed her experience as a first year teacher stating that "Teachers began telling me about my incoming students and I expressed to them that I was not trying to be rude but I did not want to develop any preconceived notions about my students."

Theme 4: Effective Lesson Planning

Subtheme: Designing and presenting lessons in class begins with using the foundation of what the students know and what things they can best connect to.

The participants were very open about how important it was for them to submerse the culture and the community in which their diverse student body and families lived, worked, and played. They believed that this submersion showed the students and the families that they cared for them outside of the school environment. They discussed instances of attending sporting activities, walking the neighborhoods, and even dining at the students' favorite community restaurants to deepen their cultural understanding and connection. This exposure helped them create a culturally appropriate educational environment for their students, where all students felt welcomed and respected. They created an environment in which each student believed they could achieve.

Participant one explained, "I accept all cultures and use them as teaching points. I build relationships so that students can openly and respectfully disagree with one another." In reference to designing lesson plans, she shared, "I begin with their background [in] mind—What they know and how they learn. Then I differentiate learning based on what they know." She also shared, "The center of my classroom is built around a learning environment that has relationships that are culturally responsive in every nature. Students should feel confident that their teacher cares and support[s] their learning."

Participant two shared, "When I present something new to my students I try to use something that I know will grab their attention. I may use a favorite cartoon, favorite food, favorite color, etc. to get through to my students. I find what makes them tick and go from there." She ensured that her students were respected and appreciated by establishing the rule of family earlier on. "My students know from the moment they walk into my classroom that we are family."

Theme 5: Classroom Management

Subtheme: Cultural Relevant training helped the educators to diffuse issues, problems, and poor attitudes in a productive manner.

One of the most difficult obstacles in any classroom is mastering appropriate techniques to diffuse problems and manage poor attitudes. Both participants believed that cultural responsiveness training provided them with the additional resources necessary to recognize and mitigate issues early and manage behavioral problems in the classroom. The educators believed that some of the behavioral issues were reflective of challenges unrelated to school. Their ability to engage students and their families, learn who they are, and understand their circumstances provided the added tools critical to successful classroom management.

Participant one shared, "This is the biggest difference in culturally responsive teaching for me. I have learned that the problem is rarely the problem. Students are usually mad about something else or are tired of the same thing happening over and over. When you have a close relationship with a student you can deescalate behaviors quickly." She also disclosed, "I teach my students that [it is] okay to be angry. And when I [am] upset I let them know and use strategies in front of them so that they understand that it happens to adults to."

Participant two expressed, "I have seen many teachers who do not know to handle students who display behavior issues in the classroom." She stated, "Through culturally relevant training I have learned how to diffuse issues before they begin or escalate."

Conclusion

Both participants shared similar passions for teaching and continuing to strengthen their cultural pedagogy. They attributed all of what they learned about cultural relevance to the HBU they attended and exposure to other students on campus during their academic journey and internships. The participants took similar paths: growing up in the same small county, being the first family member to earn a postsecondary degree, and attending an HBU, where they both received their culturally responsive training in the field of education. Participant one experienced an added obstacle; she battled with dyslexia as a young child. "Society restraints made [her] feel like [she] was never smart enough to become anything in life." As a result, participant one expressed, "I could not let even one student walk out of my door the same way they entered." While upon completion of her undergraduate degree, participant two, set out to "Save the world"; she started that process by working at a "district where [she] could make the biggest impact on students who needed [her]."

Both participants have very similar leadership philosophies (see Appendix B). Their focus, which scholars underscore as key to student success, is centered on the student (McLeod & Tanner, 2007). They believed that in order to successfully educate students, trusting, mutual, and respectful relationships must be established, not only with the students but also their families. They both believe that they have one of the most critical and influential positions as educators; that education does not begin and end in the classroom; and that it is their responsibility to provide the most productive, safe, culturally relevant experience that will equip students with the tools necessary to ensure success beyond the walls of K-12 classrooms.

Their advice for future educators who may be embarking on similar journey through a preservice program:

- Have an open mind
- Ask questions
- Research the latest trends in education
- Build a network
- Join groups on campus where you are the minority (one of the participants is a member of Sigma Gamma Rho, a predominately African-American sorority)
- Do not be afraid to be judged
- Create investigators and learners who are eager to learn
- Build relationships with your students, parents, and grandparents (learn their likes and dislikes)
- Make an investment in their culture and incorporate their cultures into lessons
- Do not try to be someone you are not
- Have compassion

Conclusion

Several scholars insist that the capabilities of White teachers to effectively meet the needs of minority students rest in the extent of their awareness of their own values, beliefs, and behaviors that may inhibit student learning (Chu, 2011; Gay, 2013).

"Teachers need both an intellectual understanding of schooling and inequality as well as self-reflective, transformative emotional growth experiences" (King, 1991, p. 134). However, it is difficult to engage in self-reflection if one does not believe that there is a reason to do so. Such reasoning brings into focus the undeniable importance of a culturally responsive pedagogy designed to improve the educational experience, and, by extension, the academic success, of all students. As such, the findings of this study suggest that a diverse public school population, in contrast to the racial and cultural composition of school leaders, most of whom enter the education profession unfamiliar with how to educate minority students (Orfield & Lee, 2006), can be improved through cultural responsiveness and embedding culturally responsive pedagogy into the K-12 curriculum.

> Within the context of U.S history, society, and education, race is one of the most powerful, pervasive, and problematic manifestations of human difference. Too many teachers try to dismiss or neutralize its significance by claiming that no pure races exist, and that race is a social construction. This may be true, *but a definitive feature of achievement gaps in U.S. schools is racial inequities* [emphasis by researchers]. (Gay, 2013, p. 61)

Another noteworthy finding from this study is that although race and inequities are intertwined, the participants asserted their ability to create equitable learning environments for historically marginalized students by the prominent positioning of the relationships between themselves, the students, and their families as a critical necessity for success. As McLeod and Tanner (2007) argued that classroom leaders whose cultural backgrounds differ from their students must "make connections" that "reach beyond environmental factors" (p. 101). The importance of establishing relationships with students and their families cannot be overstated and must undergird educator preparation programs for preservice teachers and staff development for current teachers.

Appendices

Appendix A: Interview Question Protocol

1. Tell me about you and about your background. Please include the following:
   a. Your current age
   b. Education of parents
   c. Education of siblings (if any)
   d. Community demographics
   e. Demographics of your elementary, middle, and high school.

2. Do you have an understanding of the theory of "White privilege"?
3. Do you feel that your status as an educated White woman gives you an advantage in relation to teaching in racially and ethnically diverse classrooms?

   a. If yes: What advantage(s) has that status seemingly afforded you?
   b. If no: Why do you feel that it has not afforded you an advantage?

4. Were you aware of any preconceived notions (cultural, racial, and socio-economic) that you may have held about your students before you began teaching in a diverse setting?
5. Please explain the notions and norms that you accepted previously and where they came from.
6. What experiences have you had that have either eradicated or solidified those beliefs?
7. How would you describe your educational philosophy?

   a. What experiences and beliefs shaped your philosophy?

8. Do you feel that your educational background has impacted how you attempt to reach your students—particularly your students of color?

   a. If yes: What type of impact was it (negative or positive)?

9. How did you feel, as a White female teacher entering a predominately Black and Latino campus, on the first day you entered your classroom?
10. What circumstances (personal choice, student-teacher program placement, etc.) led to you becoming a teacher on this particular campus?
11. Although your students originate from a different geographical and racial/ethnic than you, you have managed to establish positive relationships with them. What obstacles did you initially encounter when you were striving to develop this observable cohesiveness between you and your students?
12. Did you face any resistance from their parents?
13. What do you feel was the reaction of any Black and Latino teachers on your campus to the relationships that you have built with your students?
14. What has your campus done to assist/support you in relation to working with students from diverse populations?
15. Have you visited the community/residential zone from which your students originate from?

    a. If yes: How did that visit impact the manner in which you work with your students?

16. Prior to your training in cultural relevance, did you feel that urban Blacks, Latinos, and other minority groups value education less than Whites?

17. Are they aware of deficit model thinking and its impact on education?
18. What have you done in your classroom to ensure that the cultural contributions of your students are respected and appreciated?
19. How has your training on cultural relevance affected how you design and present lessons for your students?

    a. Has the training impacted how you handle student misbehavior in your classroom?

20. If you were invited to give a presentation to a group of teachers who have emanated from similar backgrounds as yourself and are beginning a cultural relevance preparation program, what advice would you give them?

Appendix B: Word Cloud (Participants One and Two)

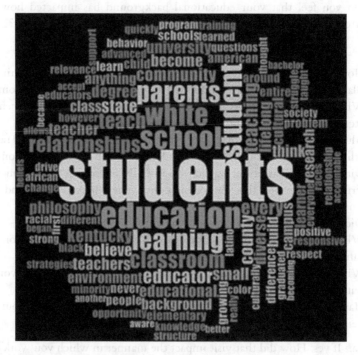

FIGURE 4.B.1 Participant one: The word query for this participant suggests that students, education, and parents were the most frequently occurring words throughout the interview

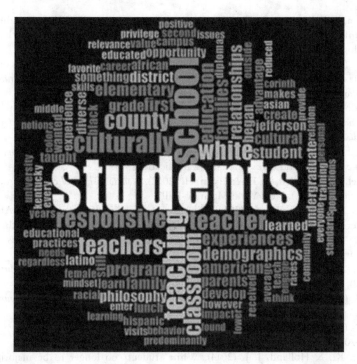

FIGURE 4.B.2   Participant two: The word query for this participant suggests that students, school, and teaching were the most frequently occurring words throughout the interview

References

Asante, M. K. (1991). The Afrocentric idea in education. *Journal of Negro Education*, *60*(2), 170–180.

Asante, M. K. (1992). Afrocentric curriculum. *Educational Leadership*, *94*(4), 28–31.

Asante, M. K. (2003). *Afrocentricity: The theory of social change (revised and expanded)*. Chicago, IL: African American Images.

Barnes, C. J. (2006). Preparing preservice teachers to teach in a culturally responsive way. *The Negro Educational Review*, *57*(1–2), 85–95.

Bazeley, P., & Jackson, K. (2013). *Qualitative data analysis with NVivo* (2nd ed.). London, UK: SAGE Publications.

Bazron, B., Osher, D., & Fleischman, S. (2005). Creating culturally responsive schools. *Educational Leadership*, *63*(1), 83–84.

Brown, M. R. (2007). Creating culturally responsive teachers, classrooms, and schools. *Exceptional Children*, *43*(1), 57–62.

Brown-Jeffy, S., & Cooper, J. E. (2011). Toward a conceptual framework of culturally relevant pedagogy: An overview of the conceptual and theoretical literature. *Teacher Education Quarterly*, *38*(1), 65–84.

Cholewa, B., Goodman, R. D., West-Olatunji, C., & Amatea, E. (2014). A qualitative examination of the impact of culturally responsive educational practices on the psychological well-being of students of color. *Urban Review, 46*(4), 574–596.

Chu, S. (2011). Perspectives in understanding the schooling and achievement of students from culturally and linguistically diverse backgrounds. *Journal of Instructional Psychology, 38*(3), 201–209.

Claybrook, M. K., Jr. (2013). Black power, black students, and the institutionalizing of change: Loyola Marymount University, 1968–1978. *The Journal of Pan African Studies, 5*(10), 1–19.

Creswell, J. W. (2013). *Qualitative inquiry & research design: Choosing among five approaches* (3rd ed.). Thousand Oaks, CA: SAGE Publications.

Fraenkel, J. R., Wallen, N. E., & Hyun, H. (2012). *How to design and evaluate research in education* (8th ed.). New York: McGraw-Hill.

Frye, B. J., & Vogt, H. A. (2010). The causes of underrepresentation of African American children in gifted programs and the need to address this problem through more culturally responsive teaching practices in teacher education programs. *Black History Bulletin, 73*(1), 11–17.

Gay, G. (2002). Preparing for culturally responsive teaching. *Journal of Teacher Education, 53*(2), 106–116.

Gay, G. (2010). Acting on beliefs in teacher education for cultural diversity. *Journal of Teacher Education, 63*(1–2), 143–152.

Gay, G. (2013). Teaching to and through cultural diversity. *Curriculum Inquiry, 43*(1), 48–70.

Hefling, K., & Holland, J. J. (2014). White students no longer to be majority in school. Retrieved from www.huffingtonpost.com/2014/09/03/student-teacher-demographics_n_5738888.html.

Jackson, A. Y., & Mazzei, L. A. (2012). *Thinking with theory in qualitative research: Viewing data across multiple perspectives.* New York: Routledge.

Jett, C. C. (2012). Let's produce culturally responsive pedagogues on deck. *Democracy & Education, 20*(2), 1–5.

King, J. E. (1991). Dyconscious racism: Ideology, identity, and the miseducation of teachers. *Journal of Negro Education, 60*(2), 133–146.

Kunjufu, J. (1984). *Developing positive self-images & discipline in black children* (1st ed.). Chicago, IL: African American Images.

Ladson-Billings, G. (1995). But that's just good teaching! The case for culturally relevant pedagogy. *Theory into Practice, 34*(3), 159–165.

Ladson-Billings, G. (2005). Is the team all right? Diversity and teacher education. *Journal of Teacher Education, 56*(3), 229–234.

Martins-Shannon, J. (2012). Support culturally responsive teaching! *Kappa Delta Pi Record, 48*(4–6), 4–6.

Mazama, A., & Lundy, G. (2013). African American homeschooling and the question of curricular cultural relevance. *The Journal of Negro Education, 82*(2), 123–138.

McLeod, K., & Tanner, T. (2007). Transitioning diverse classrooms toward educational equality: A new model of teacher dependence and independence. *The National Journal of Urban Education & Practice, 1*(1), 99–110.

National Center for Education Statistics. (2014). Digest of education statistics. Retrieved from www.nces.ed.gov/programs/digest/d13/tables/dt13_206.20.asp.

Orfield, G., & Lee, C. (2006). *Racial transformation and the changing nature of segregation.* Cambridge, MA: The Civil Rights Project at Harvard University.

Parameswaran, G. (2007). Enhancing diversity education. *Multicultural Education, 14*(3), 51–55.

Picower, B. (2009). The unexamined whiteness of teaching: How white teachers maintain and enact dominant racial ideologies. *Race Ethnicity and Education, 12*(2), 197–215.

Prater, M. A., & Devereaux, T. H. (2009). Culturally responsive training of teacher educators. *Action in Teacher Education, 31*(3), 19–27.

Reardon, S. F., & Owens, A. (2014). 60 years after *Brown:* Trends and consequences of school segregation. *Annual Review of Sociology, 40,* 199–218.

Rogers, I. (2012). The black campus movement and the institutionalization of black studies, 1965–1970. *Journal of African American Studies, 16*(1), 21–40.

Saffold, F., & Longwell-Grice, H. (2008). White women preparing to teach in urban schools: Looking for similarity and finding difference. *Urban Review, 40,* 186–209.

Schram, T. H. (2006). *Conceptualizing and proposing qualitative research* (2nd ed.). Upper Saddle River, NJ: Pearson Education.

Szabo, S., & Anderson, G. (2009). Helping teacher candidates examine their multicultural attitudes. *Educational Horizons, 87*(3), 190–197.

Taylor, R. W. (2010). The role of teacher education programs in creating culturally competent teachers. *Multicultural Education, 17*(3), 24–28.

Williams, J. (2016). Homeschoolers: Experiences of African American males. *Urban Education Research and Policy Annuals, 4*(1), 110–121.

Woodson, C. G. (1933). *The mis-education of the Negro.* Philadelphia, PA: Hakim's Publications.

5

AFRICAN AMERICANS IN HIGHER EDUCATION

Understanding the Significance of Culture, Identity and Media

TaNeisha R. Page

All over the country, individuals continuously make the decisions to further their education in hopes of advancing their position in life. Enrolling in and attending college is a step in unlocking a different life experience. Since everyone has different expectations when attending college, it is the task of teachers, administrators, and policy makers to make sure that students have positive outcomes. There has been countless research over the past few decades that highlights the African American experience in education. Isolation, discomfort, inequity, silencing, and various other systematic, cultural, and institutional barriers have all been identified as being reasons why African Americans' struggle during their time at college and ultimate reasons why they do not obtain their degrees (Ladson-Billings, 2000; Johnson, 2005; Harper & Hurtado, 2007; Harper et al., 2009; McDaniel, 2013; Gulati-Partee & Potapchuk, 2014; Naylor et al., 2015).

Higher-education institutions should be a place of progression and inclusion while serving as a foundation for every single student to have success at learning and obtaining their degrees. Yes, there have been changes made and there are more opportunities for African Americans in comparison with the past. However, this progress has been small, and there are still African Americans' experiences at college that are not positive. As Brannon et al. (2015) identified, educational settings that create a more inclusive multicultural environment can improve academic progress for African Americans. Everyone needs to be actively involved to ensure that African Americans are seen as partners in education and not as opponents.

This article will discuss how the various components of African American history and institutional standards create the foundation for African Americans to be treated differently. Educational institutions are a mirror of a larger social system in which they are situated (John-Steiner & Mahn, 1996). It is because of this social system that understanding the African American student population will help in understanding the dynamics. This article also seeks to magnify areas within education that are hindering African American students' educational experiences, thereby negatively impacting their advancement toward degree attainment.

Historical Context

African Americans were brought to this country as slaves and to be used for jobs nobody wanted to do. It was this action that started the creation of a racial hierarchy (Ladson-Billings, 2000). Racial hierarchies are referred to, in addressing the perception of ethnocentrism (Collins, 1998; Douglas, 2013). It is these hierarchies that are embedded into the way people approach and act in certain situations. For centuries, African Americans have been told and treated like they are inferior to others. This mindset and how we begin to move away from it will be the deciding factor on how we are able to change how African Americans are viewed in education. It was not until the late 1960s when breakthroughs for African Americans in education started the path of inclusive education (Duster, 2009). Since then, African American's have been entering higher-education environments at a higher rate, but the numbers are not as high for African Americans who are receiving their degrees. There are a multitude of reasons this can be happen, including but not limited to resources, accommodations, study habits, lack of support, not being prepared, social issues, expectations, and identity issues. Whatever the reason might be, it is important to understand how different societal factors impact African Americans remaining in higher education and how everyone has an active role in creating a successful positive environment.

The Impact of Culture

In order to understand the experiences of African Americans, the foundation of cultures needs to be discussed. Culture creates individual beliefs that will ultimately play a role in development of an identity and perspective. African American, Black, and dominant cultures all have to be considered. Carter (2003) identified the difference between African American culture and Black culture and how these two cultures work together and against each other in different scenarios within education. In consistency with sociocultural and social identity theory, each culture is important to understand because each plays a role in how identity is formed. Simply put, African American culture stems from the ancestors of African Americans and what slaves lived through and experienced (Carter, 2003). Some examples would be segregation, poverty, oppression, and lack of opportunity for personal and professional growth. Black culture refers to the retention and creation of continental ancestry memory (Carter, 2003). Examples would be music, clothing, dancing, language, and food, just to name a few. Each of these definitions is the opposite of the dominant culture, which provides a foundation of how many people get their understanding of how they fit into the world (Gulati-Partee & Potapchuk, 2014). The tone that is set through this dominant culture also reflects how people should behave and determines what is considered right and/or wrong. It is important to understand these three different cultures because depending on where a student falls within them can impact their development of their identity while they are going through their college experience.

Across various campuses, African American students come in contact with people who might not be aware of how African American culture or how Black culture impacts situations. However, the dominant culture is what is also painted as the standard, and it implies that it is a way that people should determine how they fit within that culture. With that being said, how can someone begin to understand when students come from a place of oppression or segregation? The reality is that a lot of African American learners enter into college settings fully aware of both African American and Black cultures and how these cultures impact their thought process and behaviors. Due to the concept of class, race, and gender, the ideas of social disparity are contextualized to describe and evaluate phenomena. However, just because African American students are aware of this does not mean other people are aware of it or even understand how that impacts them.

Brannon et al. (2015) conducted a study where they identified how African Americans can experience double consciousness as a psychological phenomenon and how it can impact educational settings. Similar to how African American culture and Black culture interact, double consciousness is reflective of deep complex influences that come from mainstream America, which is the dominate culture, and the African American ideas. The conclusions that were found in this study suggest that the ability to include African American culture into college campuses can be very resourceful and can address social and educational disparities (Brannon et al., 2015). Understanding African American culture, Black culture, and the dominant culture and how they all work together is important to bring together students of various backgrounds.

Identity Development Theories

Understanding the type of an identity with which a student enters into education can be the difference in that student being able to feel comfortable and settling into the environment. For African American learners, the development of their identities and how they evolve over time are an integral piece to understanding their perspectives as it relates to others. Each of the following two theories will illustrate how identities are formed and what impact this identify formation can have on African American learners and others who are within the educational social context. Sociocultural theory highlights how culture can be mixed with social factors to impact identities (Vygotsky, 1978). While social identity theory focuses on how individuals make sense of the works based on the identity of a social group that they feel is important (Samuel & Tenenbaum, 2011; Carlson & Donavan, 2013; Yukhymenko-Lescroart, 2014). There is a misperception that understanding a culture socially means you to understand a culture entirely. However, each of these theories speaks to the development of identity from a social and cultural perspective.

Sociocultural Theory

Lev Vygotsky's and his collaborators first introduced sociocultural approaches into learning in the 1920s and 1930s (John-Steiner & Mahn, 1996). Sociocultural theory highlights the impact of cultural context when mixed with social factors such as race, economics, psychology, and other social symbols (Vygotsky, 1978). This theory can be looked as a holistic approach to understanding an individual's foundation and perspective. Sociocultural theory takes into account both history and social situations of an individual in order to understand how identity can be constructed. As Vagan (2011) explained, learning in the sociocultural context happens with collaboration congruently between an individual and a group in a social context. During this process, the individual and people within the group are able to learn more information about how someone's historical culture impacts their social development. It is through this process of conversation and getting to understand someone, not only socially but also culturally, that individuals form identities. For African American learners, these conversations help when students are trying to find their comfort zones and figuring out where they fit into the educational environment.

Social Identity Theory

Since identities are dynamic by nature, being able to identify with some type of group consistently is important for African American students. Social identity theory is similar to sociocultural theory with regard to how social environments impact the development of identities. However, social identity highlights how three specific components of social environments impact the development of an individual's identity. These components are social comparison, social identity, and self-esteem (Trepte, 2006). How each of these components interacts with each other as well as the cohesion that an individual feels within a social group impact how identity is constructed with social identity theory. Look at this from the perspective of an African American student: if they are not able to identify with their classmates or other people around campus socially, then their social identity within that group will not be strong. This can ultimately be the reason for a student to disengage from a situation and in turn not obtain their degrees. Since social identities are predicated on status and have the ability to enhance self-esteem (Howard, 2000), it is important to make sure that students are in an environment where they can develop their identities. Not only is identifying with a social group important for a learner, but it is also important for teachers, peers, and institutions to know and identify with others through these social categories.

Construction of Identities

The focal piece of sociocultural theory and social identity theory is identifying and understanding how individuals develop their identity. Identities can be developed intrinsically by an individual, extrinsically by their teachers or peers, or a combination of both. It is the intrinsic identity that students will carry with them through their education and will be the basis for decisions and perspectives on topics in class. Depending on how someone identifies it can impact their comfortability and relatability to others in their environment. In an educational environment, one of the biggest challenges that African American's can face is trying to determine their identity. The complexity of African American history and culture, the portrayals in the media, and individuals experience are all factors that can impact the learning environment. Not only can an overall identity impact an individual, but it will also impact anyone who comes into contact with the individuals. However, in order to foster an environment of success and inclusivity, everyone must work diligently on not only identifying a particular identity but also on understanding how to relate to the identity.

Educational settings should be inviting, compassionate, and tolerable, but it can only be this way if everyone involved acknowledges, accepts, and works together to bridge the gap between differences. Identity evolves and constantly develops in various social practices (Park, 2015), and this is why understanding and respecting not only the developing but also the evolving of someone's identity is important at campus. The work of Tajfel and Turner on social identity theory (1979) and Vygotsky's research on sociocultural theory (1978) serve as a guide to understanding the path that students use to develop and understand themselves as well as to understand others in educational environments. Everywhere, people live in social networks, groups, and communities; this impacts their thoughts, feelings, and actions as well as the thoughts, feelings, and actions of others (Markus, 2008). Therefore, it is important to understand how identity can intersect with the experience of African Americans in higher-education environments.

Responsibilities of Higher Education

It is the institution's responsibility to make sure that students receive an adequate education and provide inclusion to all students. Due to the continuous achievement gaps for socially marginalized students, it is proven that more needs to be done in order to address educational problems. As Frazier and Goodman (2015) concluded, there are not only complications from individuals but also larger systematic factors that create undeniable challenges in education. Everyone who is a part of the educational environment can be a part of solving challenges. However, this cannot happen if everyone is not aware of the challenges and how those challenges impact learners. Learning occurs within a complex community of practice in which an individual gradually gains access (Vagan, 2011). It is these gradual gains that will have the most impact on African American learners.

Systematic Impact

One of the underlying strongholds on our educational institutional progression is the lack of attention that is given to systematic and institutional culture. When thinking about education, systematically consider how and where policies are made and who has a seat at the table or a voice in creating those decision. Systematically, educational institutions have an imbalance when it comes to people being in a position that has the most impact of a solution (Zambrana et al., 2015). A great example of systemic education is the idea that implementing learning technologies will positively impact higher-education outcomes. In August of 2013, the Obama Administration renewed a federal policy that involves higher-education information adopting technology to their learning environments (Soares, 2013). Sounds great in theory, but when you think about the cost of these technologies, the ever-growing population of non-traditional students re-entering school, and the negative impact that these technologies could have on students with disabilities, the question has to be asked, who was there to speak for these groups of people? Directly or indirectly, anyone who is disadvantaged with using technology will be directly impacted by its use. On the one hand, we are telling people to attend college and get education, but on the other hand, we are putting big barriers in front of them to impact their progression.

Education is not supposed to be a place where we begin to limit the goals of people because there are processes or systems in place or being implemented that work against them achieving their goals. Obtaining any type of degree is not an easy task, but there is a difference in coursework being challenging versus rules and regulations creating challenges. There are ways such as tutoring, changing majors, and even investing more time into coursework that can help students overcome the coursework challenges. However, handcuffing a group of learners systematically gives them a slimmer chance of trying to overcome those situations.

Institutional Culture

Institutional culture, or referred to some as university climate, is an important element of influence of African American learners (Dean, 2011). The amount of resources and attention that gets paid to this culture can be the difference in how students perceive their educational experience. It is important to have an institution provide support for all their students in order for students to feel like a part of the culture. For example, training programs for all college personnel and school organizations discussing topics in depth and unfiltered are a great start at providing support for students. African American students who do not attend Historically Black Colleges and Universities (HBCUs) find themselves in situations where their culture can be underrepresented or misrepresented, and this can present challenges (Huber & Solorzano, 2014). Similarly, college campuses have an obligation to prepare students for the world, and being accepting and integrative with diversity is an integral piece of this task.

Various studies have illustrated how African Americans are impacted by institutional culture (Gano-Phillips & Barnett, 2008; Duster, 2009; Dean, 2011; Huber & Solorzano, 2014). Each of these articles talks about the correlations between African Americans' struggles with institutional culture and obtaining their degrees. In order to ensure a consistent and dependable culture, it starts with the institution. There is not a blanket formula on how institutions can fix this problem. However, acknowledging how this negatively impacts students, bringing the right people to the table to work toward resolving these issues and getting a better understanding of the types of things students would like to see, should be a start. Institutional culture should not be a reason for any students to discontinue their studies, especially when these same institutions work so hard to get students enrolled.

Classroom Culture

What goes on around campuses is not the only aspect of institutional culture that matters. How classrooms are structured and operated is also an important piece of how the institutional culture is perceived. Teachers are pivotal to the classroom culture because they are seen, by the students, to be the "voice of the college." Students need to have a classroom where they feel safe to have class discussions about any topics, being able to add value to class discussions without fear, assignments that allow them to truly express themselves, and a supportive teacher through the process. McDaniel (2013) highlights how limiting what happens in a classroom can negatively impact students' learning and their sense of having a voice. Phrased another way, would be if a book report is an assignment, having a diverse group of authors or various topics, students could be allowed the topics of selection. Another restriction a teacher can put on their students is the choice of readings and options for students for their assignments. Having as much diversity where students are able to decide topics that they want to learn more about can have a tremendous impact on classroom culture.

Another way to improve classroom culture is by utilizing coalition pedagogy, which refers to instructors airing their identities and their perspectives in order for the student to understand their positioning (Pimentel & Pimentel, 2002).

This pedagogy is important for African American students because it will provide them an awareness to understand their instructors better. Within their study, they concluded that introducing coalition pedagogy would have a positive impact on how the students were able to relate to their students as well as students being able to relate to their teachers (Pimentel & Pimentel, 2002). This pedagogy is important because it gives everyone the opportunity to understanding different sides of a situation and be aware of the differences of others. It is a teacher's responsibility to reach all students, not just the students who look like them or might have the same thinking as them but also the ones that are different. African American students are one of the largest populations that are leaving higher-education institutions without obtaining their degree (Dean, 2011; Zambrana et al., 2015; Naylor et al., 2015). Providing a solution to this problem is imperative, and it starts with classrooms being more inclusive and adaptable to their African American students.

Media Impact in Higher Education

Whether we want to admit it or not, the media has an influence on how people are portrayed and stereotyped. If the media is constantly painting out criminals to look a certain way, that is something that we are watching and unconsciously absorbing. Depending on what side of the story you fall on, before you know it, the media can shape you into believing and following their narrative. How does this impact education? The way that African Americans are portrayed in the media leads people to formulate their opinions about African Americans.

Each of these four studies that have been conducted over a span of 6 years illustrates just how media impacts African Americans in education. Punyahunt-Carter (2008) conducted a study that included 412 undergraduate students. It revealed that what is shown on television impacts how they view African Americans. Similarly, Tan et al. (2009) included Chinese high school students in their study and found that the media portrayals of African Americans influence stereotypes. The Opportunity Agenda Group (2011) reported that African Americans are represented in news stories about poverty, which in turn paints negative pictures that reinforce stereotypes. Lastly, Scharrer and Ramasubramanian (2015) also concluded that the media does embody racial stereotypes.

Each of these studies emphasizes how the media's depiction of African Americans can have a tremendous impact on how they are viewed by their peers. With the media having this much influence when people do come in contact with African American students, there is a possibility, even before one word is spoken, that they have already made up their mind about this person's character. Similarly, for the African American student entering an environment where they are aware of how they are portrayed in the media, this impacts their ability to allow people to get to know who they are and what positive characteristics they can bring into an environment. The media single handedly has the ability to impact the environment of African Americans. At the very least, the media lays some type of stereotypical perspectives that leads to African Americans entering educational environments with a disadvantage before they even step a foot on campus.

Transforming the Future

The research that has been conducted about African American students in higher education has been consistent over the past 50 years. It is time to be innovative with our ideas to transform learning environments in order to connect with all students. We live in a society where we are constantly trying to find the next greatest idea or even the newest way to improve the way we do things on a regular basis. However, when we look at education, the question has to be asked, what are we doing to make a difference for all learners? The recurring themes in the literature suggests that we are aware of what is happening in higher education to African Americans, but change is still not happening. Everyone stands to gain by having African Americans obtain their degrees at higher rates, and it is time for educators, institutions, and students to lean into the uncomfortable or unfamiliar topics and conversations.

Ways to Transform the Future

Higher-education professional must allow for each student to have a voice throughout their learning process. Progress has certainly been made within higher education; however, the progress that has been made should not lead us to ignore the progress that still needs to be made. It is imperative that colleges implement consistent and focused strategies that are inclusive of everyone. Below are three important components that will help lay a foundation for unifying our educational environments.

Diverse Perspectives

Not having leaders such as faculty, administrators, and policy makers who are not diverse directly impacts the perception of African American learners (Vereen & Hill, 2008). Having people who can provide in-depth insight into how diversity impacts students and positive ways to make decisions that are created with all students in mind are significant. Zambrana et al. (2015) conducted a study outlining the positive impact that mentor can make in educational institutions. Having mentors who are able to help students overcome challenges will provide students a trustworthy ally. Zambrana et al. (2015) also mentions how having diverse perspectives being communicated to the student body is just as important. Similarly, Dean (2011) highlights how a diverse college faculty has an overall impact on campus climate. Infusing diverse perspectives and overall institutional diversity will help African American students in their educational development (Vereen & Hill, 2008). Making sure colleges have diverse teachers, leaders, administrators, and policy makers is imperative.

Tackling Race

For some reason, when race gets brought into a conversation, people often try to avoid the topic. However, avoiding race relations will not solve the solution. In our educational environments, making race a comfortable topic is a way to get rid of the elephant in the room. It is no secret that we all come from different backgrounds, and because of that, we all could have varying perspectives on topics. Gulati-Partee and Potapchuk (2014) detail the importance of engaging in race conversations and how these conversations provide an opportunity for more understanding and accountability. Attending college is not just about obtaining a degree but also about being able to have experiences, conversations, and learning about topics that would not otherwise happen. If we are not tackling the race conversation in colleges, how can we expect real sustainable change to happen? Harper and Hurtado (2007) classify race as a four-letter word and why being able to acknowledge and discuss what it means in our classrooms can help us move past the uncomfortability. By allowing these conversations to happen and be consistent, the institutional culture will seem more inviting and will positively impact overall institutional culture. It is important to note that having this conversation will not be easy, but having so many disparities or assumptions about race relations has created division and leaves more assumptions unanswered or resolved.

Comprehending All Identities

As individuals, we come into situations with assumptions that shape our views of the world. Because of this, it is important that we are able to understand our identities as well as others' identities, to understand how they impact our positions. Brannon et al. (2015) highlight the importance of understating identities and privileges that individuals bring into a classroom. This provides context to how and why things might be seen in a certain way. Oftentimes, our perceptions become reality, but that is only because we are only considering our own perceptions, or what we think we know to be true. However, investigating and communicating about identities is a step toward developing the skills that are needed in learning environments. Park (2015) details the influence that identity can have in a social context, while Lee et al. (2013) investigated identity to understand how the dominant culture has an impact on an individuals' identity. For African American learners, it is important that they are able to identify open and honestly, even if that means they might be in a position where they are in the minority. Overcoming the identity disparities will provide a sense of belonging and would go a long way toward eliminating biases.

Implementing these changes is not a quick fix and will take everyone involved to be committed to progress. There is plenty of ample evidence that supports the notion that educational environments are not inclusive of African American students and that it is time to make a change. More attention needs to be paid to the near misses and setbacks that are happening to African American students (Lareau, 2015). It is no secret that there are positions of privilege and power within our education systems. However, it is imperative that we view education as a place where everyone should be treated equal and given opportunities. When entering into educational settings, individuals should ask themselves questions similar to these: how can you positively impact a learning environment, what lens do you view situations through, and how will you show compassion to someone who has a conflicting viewpoint? Together, we have to wrap our arms around the situations African Americans find themselves in and become a fundamental part of the solution. The golden rule of treating someone how you want to be treated should be the foundation to how each and every student gets treated in our higher-education environments.

References

Agenda, O. (2011). Social science and literature review: Media representations and impact on the lives of black men and boys. *The Opportunity Agenda*, 13–55. https://www.racialequitytools.org/resourcefiles/Media-Impact-onLives-of-Black-Men-and-Boys-OppAgenda.pdf

Brannon, T. N., Markus, H. R., & Taylor, V. J. (2015). "Two souls, two thoughts" two self-schemas: Double consciousness can have positive academic consequences for African Americans. *Journal of Personality and Social Psychology, 108*(4), 586–609.

Carlson, D. B. & Donovan, T. D. (2013). Human brand in sport: Athletic brand personality and identification. *Journal of Sports Management, 27*, 193–206.

Carter, L. P. (2003). "Black" cultural capital, status positioning, and schooling conflicts for low-income African American youth. *Social Problems, 50*(1), 136–155.

Collins, P. H. (1998). It's all in the family: Intersections of gender, race, and nation. *Blackwell Publishing, 13*(3), 62–82.

Dean, J. (2011). The impact of campus climate and student involvement on students of color. *The Vermont Connection, 32*, 32–39.

Douglas, D. M. (2013). The surprising role of racial hierarchy in the civil rights jurisprudence of the first justice John Marshal Harlan. *Journal of Constitutional Law, 15*(4), 1037–1053.

Duster, T. (2009). The long path to higher education for African Americans. *The NEA Higher Education Journal*, 99–110. http://www.nea.org/assets/docs/HE/TA09PathHEDuster.pdf

Frazier, K. N., & Goodman, R. D. (2015). Traumatic stress and educational hegemony: A multi-level model to promote wellness and achievement among socially marginalized students. *The Practitioner Scholar: Journal of Counseling and Professional Psychology, 4*, 44–62.

Gano-Phillips, S., & Barnett, R. W. (2008). Against all odds: Transforming institutional culture. *Liberal Education, 94*(2), 36–41.

Gulati-Partee, G., & Potapchuk, M. (2014). Paying attention to white culture and privilege: A missing link to advancing racial equity. *The Foundation Review, 6*(1), 4.

Harper, S. R., & Hurtado, S. (2007). Nine themes in campus racial climates and implications for institutional transformation. *New Directions for Students Services, 120,* 7–24.

Harper, S. R., Patton, L. D., & Wooden, O. S. (2009). Access and equity for African American students in higher education: A critical race historical analysis of policy efforts. *The Journal of Higher Education, 80*(4), 388–414.

Howard, J. A. (2000). Social psychology of identities. *Annual Review Social, 26,* 367–393.

Huber, L. P., & Solorzano, D. G. (2015). Racial microaggressions as a tool for critical race research. *Race Ethnicity and Education, 18*(3), 297–320.

Johnson, A. M. (2005). Beyond higher education: The need for African Americans to be "knowledge producers." *The Modern American, 1,* 28–31.

John-Steiner, V., & Mahn, H. (1996). Sociocultural approaches to learning and development: A vygotskian framework. *Educational Psychologist, 31*(3–4), 191–206.

Ladson-Billings, G. (2000). Fighting for our lives: Preparing teachers to teach African American students. *Journal of Teacher Education, 51*(3), 206–214.

Lareau, A. (2015). Cultural knowledge and social inequity. *American Sociological Review, 80*(1), 1–27.

Lee, B. Y., Kozak, M. S., Nancoo, C. P., Chen, H., Middendorf, K., & Jerry, G. (2013). Exploring dominant discourses: Creating spaces to find voice and cultural identity, *Journal of Cultural Diversity, 20*(1), 21–29.

Markus, H. R. (2008). Pride, prejudice, and ambivalence: Toward a unified theory of race and ethnicity. *American Psychologist, 63*(8), 651–670.

McDaniel, G. (2013). Creating a more successful college experience for black students. *Diverse Issues in Higher Education,* Retrieved From: http://diverseeducation.com/article/52011/.

Naylor, L. A., Wyatt-Nichol, H., & Brown, S. L. (2015). Inequality: Underrepresentation of African American males in U.S. higher education. *Journal of Public Affairs Education, 21*(4), 523–538.

Park, H. (2015). Learning identity a sociocultural perspective, *Adult Education Research Conference,* Paper 41 Retrieved at: http://newprairiepress.org/aerc/2015/papers/41.

Pimentel, C., & Pimentel, O. (2002). Coalition pedagogy: Building bonds between instructors and students of color. In S. B. Fowler & V. Villanueva (Eds.), *Included in English studies: Learning climates that cultivate racial & ethnic diversity.* Merrifield, VA: AAHE Publications. Eric Document Reproduction Service No. ED470332.

Punyahunt-Carter, N. M. (2008). The perceived realism of African American portrayals on television. *The Howard Journal of Communications, 19,* 241–257.

Samuel, R. D., & Tenenbaum, G. (2011). The role of change in athletes' careers: A scheme of change for sport psychology practice. *The Sport Psychologist, 25,* 233–252.

Scharrer, E., & Ramasubramanian, S. (2015). Intervening in the media's influence on stereotypes of race and ethnicity: The role of media literacy education. *Journal of Social Issues, 71*(1), 171–185.

Soares, L. (2013). Creating an environment for learning technologies: Toward a generative model of state policy and institutional practice. *Educause Review, 48*(5), 70–75.

Tajfel, H., & Turner, J. (1979). An integrative theory of inter-group conflict. In J. A. Williams & D. Worchel (Eds.), *The social psychology of inter-group relations,* pp. 33–47. Belmont, CA: Wadsworth.

Tan, A., Zhang, Y., Zhang, L., & Dalisay, F. (2009). Stereotypes of African Americans and media use among Chinese high school students. *The Howard Journal of Communications, 20,* 260–275.

Trepte, S. (2006) Social identity theory. In J. Bryant & P. Vorderer (Eds.), *Psychology of entertainment.* Mahwah, NJ: Lawrence Erlbaum Associates Publishers.

Vagan, A. (2011). Towards a sociocultural perspective on identity formation in education. *Mind, Culture and Activity, 18,* 43–57.

Vereen, L. G. (2008). African American faculty and student-oriented challenges: Transforming the student culture in higher education from multiple perspectives. *Journal of Thought, 43*(3–4), 83–100.

Vygotsky, L. S. (1978). *Mind in society.* Cambridge, MA: Harvard University Press.

Yukhymenko-Lescroart, M. A. (2014). Student and athletes? Development of the academic and athletic identity scale (AAIS). *Sport, Exercise and Performance Psychology, 3*(2), 89–101.

Zambrana, E. R., Ray, R., Espino, M. M., Choen, B. D., & Elison, J. (2015). "Don't leave us behind": The importance of mentoring for underrepresented minority faculty. *American Education Research Journal, 52*(1), 40–72.

6

KEMET-kA

The African Spirit in Sport

Drew D. Brown

Introduction

The agency of African people can be described as their ability to create and produce things based on their own will. Historically and presently, this agency is exhibited through sports. When Africana people (continental and diaspora) perform sport, both the participants and the sport are wrapped in African cultural elements and ethos. It is true that countless cultural components of African culture were lost during the Maafa, and Blacks were kept out of Euro-American-run sports for the better part of 400 years.[1] Yet, still, there remains a heavy presence of African culture in contemporary sports that can be traced back to early Egyptian civilizations. Aesthetic customs are one of the most significant things that Africans were able to maintain through their vicious removal from Africa and displacement in the Americas (Holland, 2002). Some folks in general society will often refer to the display of African cultural elements in sport as a "Black style." For example, Willie Mays' famous basket catch, Michael Jordan's improvisation under the basket, Florence Griffith Joyner's harmonious balance of power and grace, and Muhammad Ali's quick rhythmic timing all exude the traditions found in Africana cultural aesthetics. The continuity of African culture in sport is affirmed by Afrocentric theorist Molefi K. Asante, who claims, "Almost all Africans share cultural similarities with the ancient Egyptians" (1985, p. 6). In addition to the aesthetics, there are other African cultural elements that remain present in contemporary sport. There exists a social significance of sport to the Black community and a utilization of sports to strengthen and unite the Black community. The impact of sport on the Africana community has created heroes, leaders, and role models. The social influence and heroic platform provided to athletes allow sport to carry a reciprocal relationship with the community. In this essay, I identify African elements found in the function and performance of sport by introducing "Kemet-kA," which identifies a sporting style and function that are unique to people of African descent. Although Kemet-kA could be used to analyze any sport that involves people of African descent, in this essay, I focus on Africans in America who I identify as "Blacks." Exploring the similarities between the sporting traditions found in historical African culture and those found in contemporary Black culture allows for a more critical understanding of the influence that "pre-colonial" African culture has had on the world.

Kemet-kA

Kemet is the great civilization in ancient Egypt, where many of our modern roots in mathematics, philosophy, spirituality, technology, and architecture can be traced, well before the emergence of Greek civilization. The ancient Egyptian word "Kemet" means "the land of the Blacks" (Asante, 2000, p. 11), while the term "kA" is the ancient Egyptian term for spirit or life energy (Asante & Mazama, 2009, p. 359). Therefore, "Kemet-kA" literally means Black spirit. It can be identified in the sporting practices, behavioral patterns, actions, and physical manifestations of African people within the aesthetics, influence, and function of sport. The major elements of Kemet-kA are African aesthetics, community relationship, and cultural heroism. All the tenets of Kemet-kA are interconnected; one rarely functions alone. For example, the community-sport relationship has an effect on cultural heroism, and inversely, African aesthetics is connected to the community relationship. Heavily characterized with an emphasis on non-verbal communication, creativity, balance, rhythm, improvisation, resistance, and inspiration, it is often associated with Black athletes such as Willie Mays, Muhammad Ali, Florence Griffith Joyner, Michael Jordan, and Allen Iverson. Kemet-kA is the theoretical framework by which the performance of sport by Africana people is analyzed and the authentic African cultural presence is identified.

Even though it is not always measurable or seen, Kemet-kA is always present. According to Africana Studies scholar Marimba Ani (p.k.a. Dona Richards), "this (African) spirit will not and cannot die" (Welsh-Asante, 1994, p. 13). Therefore, it is not a matter of whether one has it but how much one utilizes it.

Theoretical Framework

If one is to embark on the task of identifying the function and uniqueness of sport performed by Africana people, he/she must understand and comprehend African aesthetics, culture, and sport. This essay reveals the consistent presence of Kemet-kA among both ancient Egyptians and contemporary Blacks in sport. Scholars of the seventeenth and eighteenth centuries suggest that Greece was the sole civilization participating in organized competition (Crowther, 2007). Egyptian historian Cheihk Ante Diop (1989) was one of the first to scientifically model and study the connection between ancient Egyptians and contemporary Blacks. He debunks the idea that the Greeks were the first to develop the major tenets of societies by arguing that ancient Egyptians were Black and participated in many things, including sports, well before the Greeks (Crowther, 2007; Decker, 1992). The literature surrounding ancient Egyptian sports is very limited. The Ancient Egyptian civilization must be studied as a whole in order to draw conclusions about the significance of sports in it. The short list of literary works on ancient Egyptian sports makes this a difficult study.

There are few English texts (Crowther, 2007; Decker, 1992) that focus on, or devote more than one or two chapters to, ancient Egyptian sports. Wolfgang Decker is the primary writer on the subject. He renders a thorough look at ancient Egyptian sports by using Egyptian sources such as ancient equipment, temple walls, and written accounts. Decker incorporates a range of non-English texts into his book *Sports and Games of Ancient Egypt*.

The examination of African aesthetics found in sport comes from the study of African aesthetical traditions outlined in Kariamu Welsh-Asante's text *African Aesthetics*. Welsh-Asante outlines the characteristics and traditions of African aesthetics through her Nzuri model.

The Nzuri model is an Afrocentric theory used to demarcate the production and products of African aesthetics. The major components of the Nzuri model (spirit, rhythm, and creativity) function as the source and axiological premise of African aesthetics. The Nzuri model also contains seven operational aspects: method, form, meaning, ethos, function, mode, and motif (Welsh-Asante, 1994, p. 10). By looking at the Nzuri model, previously mentioned texts, and additional literature, I was able to extract information regarding the characteristics of African sport from within the Ancient Egyptian civilization and the contemporary world of sports.

This study utilizes an Afrocentricity framework and furthers the developments of Diop by centralizing this study around an African perspective and cosmology. My approach to examining the African spiritual presence in sport involves identifying the most influential yet distinctive characteristics of the Kemet-kA tradition, some of which are born out of survival (Thompson, 1983). Kemet-kA is a working definition of African spiritual presence in sport and carries some of the aspects of Welsh-Asante's Nzuri model of artistic manifestation (1994). While Welsh-Asante places much emphasis on aesthetics, relegates "meaning" as secondary to "creativity," and does not mention "heroism" as a primary component, Kemet-KA adds emphasis to "meaning" by focusing on the reciprocal relationship between sport and the community, in addition to focusing on the importance of cultural heroism. Thus, aesthetics, communalism, and heroism are the major elements of Kemet-kA.

What Is Sport?

The definition of "sport" has changed over time and has carried various meanings in different societies. In fact, "sport" is a fairly recent term. It emerged roughly two centuries ago (Crowther, 2007). During the ancient periods, sports were known merely as competitions. A common definition of sports is "institutionalized competitive activities that involve rigorous physical exertion or the use of relatively complex physical skills by participants motivated by internal and external rewards" (Coakley, 2007, p. 6). Physical exertion is a key component that separates sport from other games. Board games were a popular form of competition in many ancient Egyptian societies but do not fit into the common definition of sport. The physical movement involved in sport produces a display of aesthetic and, therefore, can be appropriately examined by the Kemet-kA theory of analysis.

Other terms, such as recreation and leisure, are often associated with sport. The function of leisure, as defined by Holland, is to provoke enjoyment (2002). Just as African tradition does not embrace art for art's sake, Africans do not preform and embrace sport for its own sake. Thus, leisure or play that is "for its own sake" could be considered a Western idea, much like the concept of "art for its own sake." Sport has a didactic function that serves Africana communities by teaching social norms and determining leadership. It often functions as a pedagogical device for imparting morals, traditions, and beliefs. The combination of these forces accounts for the laws of culture (Tylor, 1958). In ancient Egypt, sport was closely aligned with the ideologies of the monarch than with the entertainment of the people (Crowther, 2007, p. 26). According to Holland, recreation is "free" or "unobligated" time meant for relaxation or regeneration (2002). Given the lack of freedom afforded to enslaved Africans, who were forced to perform sport (Holland, 2002; Rhoden, 2004), and the social pressures placed on contemporary Blacks to engage in sport (Coakley, 2007; Hoberman, 1997; Sailes, 2003), the concept of recreation is often inapplicable to Blacks and therefore not associated with the concept of sport used in this essay.

The Historical Presence of Sport in Ancient Egypt

Since the recording of history, sport has been a significant part of African societies. There is not much evidence of sports earlier than ancient Egypt such as Nubia, but this is no indication that sport was not present. Many sports competitions occurred in Ancient Egyptian civilization. Statues of wrestlers and female acrobats have been discovered and can be traced to ancient Egypt (Decker, 1992, p. 12). Tombs and wall drawings contain written sources and miniature display—scenes of competition also provide evidence of sports. In the temple of Ramesses III, from the twentieth dynasty, there are pictures of a sports contest between the Egyptians and another group; in it, the pharaoh is participating in a sport with horses (Decker, 1992, p. 12). The gravesite of Prince Min shows him instructing Amenophis II in archery. The site also depicts scenes of fishing and bird hunting. In addition, inscriptions were often found alongside visual representations of sports. Inscriptions accompanied the sports scenes in the tomb of Ramesses III.

The types of sports presented in ancient Egypt were similar to those of contemporary times. The prevalence of visual representations and inscriptions would suggest that archery was the most illustrated sport. The bow predates the written history of Egypt (Decker, 1992, p. 34). It was used as a hunting tool and weapon and utilized by the Egyptian army in practicing their marksmanship. The master of archery was Amenophis II, whose great athletic skills can be traced from his childhood. He may have possessed the greatest athletic abilities out of all the Egyptian kings and queens (Decker, 1992, p. 36). Egyptian chariots and equestrians arrived in the second millennium B.C. It re-emerged in Greece, mainly in the Olympic Games, but it was the Egyptians who first made it an artistic sport (Decker, 1992, p. 47). The combat sports, such as wrestling, have also been significant and remain imbedded in most cultures of Africa. Egyptian wrestling is the most visually documented sport. The overall presence of sport in ancient Egypt was a significant aspect of culture. Just as the countless traditions and cultural practices of Africa have been passed down from generation to generation, so has Kemet-kA.

The Impact of Colonization on African Culture

The common presence of Kemet-kA throughout the culture of over 1000 African ethnic groups shows the cultural similarities that they carried irrespective of their differences. Asante states, "African ethnic groups are culture, not rigid or fixed, but related history and experience. Culture can vary over time, but in the case of the African culture, it will always be articulated in a similar way" (Asante, 1985, p. 5). Marimba Ani estimates that up to 150 million Africans were forcefully removed from Africa over a 300-year period (Asante, 1985, p. 11). Still, the African style remained present within sport throughout the diaspora. Evidence of this exist in Desch-Obi's text *Fighting For Honor* (2008), where he documents the continuation of African styles of fighting in diaspora communities.

To say that slavery has had an effect on Africans' culture and sporting performance would be a gross understatement; some might say it would be insulting. The enslavement and oppression of Black people heavily altered their performance of sport by denying them the right to freely express themselves through sport, in their own way. According to Vernon Andrews, American sports society continues to police Black cultural expression even today by penalizing it on and off the field of play (Andrews, 2015).

In addition, like Jazz, visual art, and other forms of cultural aesthetics, the corporate heads of sports leagues have misappropriated and exploited the stylistic displays of Kemet-kA. They have used the style and physical prowess of African athletes to entertain spectators. It cannot be overlooked that the wealth, visibility, and social access awarded to many Black athletes has greatly increased the incentive for participating in sport.

Oppression has transformed the dimension of community relationship in Kemet-kA. The colonization of Africa and Africans has left Blacks suffering from the symptoms of oppression even today. As a result of oppression through slavery, Jim Crowism, and the overall white supremacy, they experience nihilism, suboppression, and a low of self-esteem. The colonization of Africans has diminished the practice of maintaining unity between the individual athlete and the community around him/her. Instead, a more selfish approach has been adopted from Eurocentric ideology. Black athletes are often socialized to disassociate with their Africanity and take up a more individual and materialistic agenda. This benefits the capital oligarchies that financially profit from the detachment of the Black athlete from the Black community. Thus, discouraging Black athletes from utilizing their political voice to fight against injustices that damage the Black community is a way to control not only the Blacks in sports but also the communities from which they influence. But the one aspect of Blacks in sport that is least controllable and was not lost through enslavement is aesthetics of the body. Black athletes have mastered the dexterity of their bodies and are able to artistically utilize their bodies in sport through various African traditions of aesthetics and spirit, Kemet-kA.

Aesthetics

Africans have been dynamic in their aesthetic expressions (Holland, 2002, p. 46; Welsh-Asante, 1985). Scholars such as Addison Gayle (1971) and DuBois (1926) have laid a foundation for viewing African aesthetics (Welsh-Asante, 1994, p. 81; Judy, 1994). From their work, several concepts of African aesthetics exist. But, it is Walsh-Asante's (1994) Nzuri model that is heavily relied upon to describe the aesthetics of Kemet-kA. When African athletes perform sport, they carry a distinct form, feeling, and rhythm that can be attributed to culture and memory (Welsh-Asante, 1994; Neal, 1972). Welsh-Asante describes in more detail,

> Epic memory. There is a spiritual dimension to this concept of experience. This spirituality is another manifestation of the epic memory. It flows into and overlaps with experience, preceding, feeding, and imprinting the African aesthetic qualities. It is not religious by definition, but can involve ritual; it is the conscious and subconscious calling upon the ancestors, gods, and mind, to permit the flow of energy so that the artist can create. (1985, p. 80)

According to Welsh-Asante's Nzuri model, the aesthetic spirit (*Kra*) in African athletes is linked, through the power of Nommo, to the life force (*Ntu*), which guides their rhythm and allows them to enact their creativity through artistic

movement (Welsh-Asante, 1994, p. 11). Just as with soul music, break dancing, spoken word, and religious preaching, sport carries a unique cultural style
when performed by Africans. Rhythm is one of the most important aspects of
African aesthetics and carries two functions in Kemet-kA, just as there are in
the Nzuri model (Welsh-Asante, 1994, p. 2). The first is the individual expressions of rhythm that harmonizes the body, mind, and soul, so that they all act
as one. The style of body movement and athleticism among African athletes
is a manifestation of the aesthetic spirit in Kemet-kA. Wilma Rudolph, the
first American woman to win three gold medals at one Olympics, embodied
this manifestation. The Kemet-kA in her gave her a smooth and eloquent look
when she ran. William Rhoden describes her as a runner with "willow grace
and speed" (Rhoden, 2004, p. 152). The second is the rhythm of the collective
or community. Welsh says, "this complexity of rhythm generates multi-layered,
multi-leveled, multi-existence so that it is possible for people to respond to different layers, levels and planes and still be in harmony with the framework
of the rhythms and with each other" (Welsh-Asante, 1994). This means that
rhythm works to keep everything, including people, in harmony. The concept
of harmony is exemplified and imperative in Kemet-kA.

Whether it is music, dance, martial arts, or sport, the rhythmic elements of
African aesthetics are identifiable in all art forms. In sport, it remains present
within the limitations of rules, strategies, and physical boundaries. For example,
the quick rhythmic steps of Muhammad Ali, Barry Sanders, and Rudolph are
examples of an inner rhythm within an external structure. The polyrhythms of
a timed step and movement within the inner-moving rhythm of the changing
play is much like the creative movement of a trumpet player within a jazz set
(Welsh-Asante, 1985, p. 78). These examples also demonstrate the significance
of repetition, which is one of the most significant elements of African aesthetics
(Welsh-Asante, 1985, p. 80). Repetition includes a slight modification for every
recurrence. Therefore, the replication and intensification of one movement
allows for athletes to transition toward the desired goal without losing their
rhythmic flow. Another great example of repetition is found in the emergence
of the crossover. Players bounce the basketball a number of times at the same
speed but change the direction of the ball with each bounce. This causes the
dribbler to change direction while maintaining balance and control of the ball.

The presence of creativity in Kemet-kA is a material and easily identifiable manifestation of African aesthetics. It is used, simultaneously, for offense
and defense to overcome anything that threatens the goals of the community.
It is the manifestation of spirit from both the individual and the community.
It serves both the community and the individual by using creativity and purpose to act in line with and toward the "Ultimate Goal" (Welsh-Asante, 1994,
p. 13). For instance, in Richard Major's book *Cool Pose*, he writes about how
Black men have been emasculated by the race ideologies that hinder and dis-
able their ability to obtain the European characteristics for manhood: protector,

provider, and procreator (Major & Billson, 1992). Therefore, Black men have had to portray a "cool pose" that renders the bravado of unemotional and unaffected carelessness toward their social degradation. The cool pose is a defense mechanism that allows oppressed Black men to protect their dignity and self-respect against social emasculation. This creativeness has constructed new characteristics of Black manhood. Kemet-kA embraces the cool pose through a dimension of community relationship, and athletes now reproduce the cool pose in their style of play and posture.

African rituals have been passed down generation after generation through cultural expression, such as sports and dance (Andrews, 2015). The Black athletes introduced, established, and advanced dancing rituals in sports such as basketball and football. Elmo Wright was a Black wide receiver who first started finishing off his touchdown receptions with celebratory end-zone dances in the early 1970s (Andrews, 2015). The end-zone dance in football has continued the celebratory traditions of African culture. It allows the spirit of excitement to be released while also allowing others to join in on the celebration from wherever they are. It is certainly a communal event. Most of the dances have become modes of communication that have symbolic meaning and coded messages often decoded in hip-hop culture. The ability of hip-hop (in its essence) to speak to the experiences of Black people has created a form of communication that even athletes can communicate through end-zone dances. In addition to the end-zone dances, there are additional displays of Kemet-kA found in the creative celebrations initiated by Blacks. In fact, Blacks are responsible for the innovation of most celebratory actions, including the butt slap, chest bump, high-five, low-five, fist bump, crowd baiting, spiking the football into the turf, booty-shaking, dirty bird, and Lambeau leap. In addition, they are the innovators of sports moves such as the alley-oop, spin move, and dunking.

Spontaneity is another important aspect of African aesthetics that manifests through sport. The intuitive improvisations displayed by many Black athletes dazzle fans and frustrate opponents. The holistic creativity exhibited by Black athletes functions as an arsenal of tools appropriately used according to the situation or environment. Spontaneous movements such as arm waving and head jerks have been used to distract or misdirect defenders. Robert Thompson cites Richard Alan Waterman, who says, "An African learns to be conscious mentally of every instrument employed in an African orchestra and this has a tremendous influence on his dance. All the various muscles of the body act differently to the rhythms of the instruments" (Welsh-Asante, 1985, p. 75). He calls this dancing ability "multi-metrically." When looking at the phenomenon of the Black quarterbacks in the NFL, many of them have been multi-metrical in their ability to harmoniously think, run, and pass. According to Thabiti Lewis, Black quarterbacks have a wide range of weapons in their arsenal, making them harder to defend. He states, "these new school quarterbacks have changed the game with their quick wits, fleet feet, and rocket arms"

(Lewis, 2010, p. 130). Although the aesthetical aspect of Kemet-kA is an important one, by no means it is the only aspect. The connection between Africana sport and athletes exhibits a virtue communalism that functions within African cosmology. It also represents another important aspect of Kemet-kA.

The Black Athlete and the Black Community

The objective of Kemet-kA is to contribute to the harmony of the community. It works as a form of pedagogy for cultural norms and beliefs. Conversely, the community beliefs and norms manifest in sports. The concept of African aesthetics shows that art cannot be divorced from life; it is a part of life (Asante, 1985, p. 8). One of the best representations of the Black community, specifically urban-youth life and culture, is former NBA player Allen Iverson. When asked how Michael Jordan impacted their attraction to sports, one former Black NFL prospect responded, "I wanted to be more like [Iverson]." Iverson represented the Black men who were "unrefined" or not adequately assimilated by white social standards. He was a figure of success, yet he looked, talked, and carried himself similar to many of the Black men who were rendered invisible or silenced by society. As hip-hop was beginning to dominate the marketing world, Iverson was hip-hop's athlete; he was a baller. Sean Powell argues that the marketing attention Iverson's baller image received contributed to the desire of Black men to emulate it. Powell states, "Iverson represents the black men that are in the media and who companies endorse and affirm, not David Robinson. Therefore, Iverson, the 'thug,' is the more desirable image to emulate based on the response it receives" (Powell, 2008, pp. 92–116). The "thug" image of Iverson gave him "street credibility." In other words, he represents what Katina Stapleton calls "an authentic street culture" that mirrored Black youth experience (Stapleton, 1998, p. 228). While at Georgetown, Iverson made the first cover of *Slam*, an up-and-coming basketball magazine. It was in 1999 when Iverson made the cover for the third time. This time, he donned an Afro, diamond earrings, platinum jewelry, and many tattoos. Iverson's image, along with *Slam* magazine, became a representation of Black culture in sports. Powell explains,

> Any basketball player who did not exude the "hood was treated by Slam [magazine] as a badminton player. And neither Page nor Slam make any apologies for the urban slang and Ebonics prose that flow through many of the feature stories." (Powell, 2008, p. 197)

The relationship that Iverson had with the Black community was strengthened by the ban that the NBA put on his "urban" style of dress. The NBA attempted to extract any visual relationship that Iverson or any other Black player shared with the Black community by implementing a dress code that made players look more like businessmen and less like urban youth. We see the result of the dress code as most players in the NBA and NFL dress professionally on game day when not in uniform. But hip-hop culture is not the only aspect of the Black community that is represented in sports. Sporting events are a space where cultural behaviors are learned and practiced.

The relationship between the Black community and Black sport is a reciprocal one, defined by the heavy influence that each has over the other. Kemet-kA is the spirit that causes sport to learn from the community and simultaneously the community learns from sport. Welsh-Asante describes the influence of the community on art when she states, "The value system and religious ethos normally provide and stimulate the creative setting for 'stylized art'" (1985, p. 72). *Ma'at was the initial belief system of ancient Egypt that worked to right all wrongs and maintain moral order. Asante describes it as, "the inevitability of good overcoming evil, of harmony replacing disharmony, and order taking the place of disorder"* (Asante, 2014, p. 25). The philosopher Maulana Karenga suggests that Ma'at is a physical concept (Karenga, 2004, p. 6). The cultural ethos of the Black community has set the style of play among Black athletes. The physical prowess and individual or community's mastery of sport are the acquisition of Ma'at. Sport then becomes a manifestation or example of Ma'at and is useful in teaching the beliefs of Ma'at: truth, righteousness, justice, order, balance, harmony, and reciprocity.

Similar to contemporary Black communities, sports in ancient Egyptian communities were as much a part of the society and culture as any other aspect. Many jobs and responsibilities were awarded to the most athletic individuals. Sport was used to select political leaders and prepare people for duties of war. Additionally, the performance of sport was used to teach lessons and model certain character traits. Sports were used to determine social class. The aristocrat charioteers would use their chariot as a badge of their social class and displayed it as a status symbol (Decker, 1992, p. 46). Many of the participants who competed in sports were also competing for prestigious social roles. Excellent runners had the natural talent to hold many roles in ancient Egyptian societies. Hunters and nomads were excellent runners (Decker, 1992, p. 61). Egyptian messengers were also great runners. Similar to the Secret Service agents who protect the president of United States, private escorts of prominent men were often the best runners. The high officials traveled by chariot, and the escorts were required to run fast enough to keep pace with them. Many Africans used combat-sports training as an enjoyable way to prepare for war. Crowther agrees, "Training for war found an outlet in sports" (Crowther, 2007, p. 26). They included wrestling, boxing, and stick fighting. Today, sport functions as one of the few spaces in the Black community, where Blacks, especially men, teach and learn cultural values, morals, and behaviors. Coakley (2007) suggests that sports are connected to important ideas, beliefs, and major fields of Blacks' social life such as the family, religion, and education (p. 21). In addition, sports are also linked to the non-physical realms of the community. In Welsh-Asante's *African Aesthetics*, Zadia Ife describes the social mode of Nommo in theater arts as "the moral tenets of the people, those laws that unify the collective vision of the community, and those images of people that will assure the blessings of the ancestors who sustain the progress of the race for future generations" (Ife, 1993). The collective spirit of Kemet-kA is similar to the Ife's Nommo spirit in theater arts. The collective spirit is not limited to the Africans who presently exist on Earth, but also includes the living spirits of African ancestors who are also a part of the African community. Therefore, Kemet-kA is a spiritual energy that is found in the African culture and reaches beyond time and space to bind the African community.

Heroes of Hope and Resistance

Michael Eric Dyson, a scholar of Black life and culture, argues that sports often include a heroic dimension (2004, p. 463). This is true in ancient Egyptian communities, where some of the greatest leaders were also great athletes. Amneophis II and Tutankhmon are great examples of this. Other kings used sports to show their ability to provide. In order to publicize himself as a great ruler, the king projected himself as a great warrior, hunter, and athlete. The purpose of this run was for leaders to display their physical ability to rule. The killing of a hippopotamus was a testimony of a king who was able to provide for his people (Decker, 1992, p. 149). The "Jubilee Run" was a run performed by the pharaohs on the thirtieth anniversary of their leadership and every 3 years after that (Crowther, 2007, p. 26). Both kings and queens took part in this run. For successful athletes who show prowess in sports, the collective spirit of Kemet-kA provides them with social influence and a platform of leadership. This is especially important among the oppressed Black communities, where the development of successful individuals outside of sports has been limited.

Kemet-kA functions as a spirit of hope and is produced by the Black athletes' triumph over physical, mental, and social obstacles. Jack Johnson, the first Black heavyweight-boxing champion of the world, was one of the first images of a financially successful Black athlete. For many Blacks, Jack Johnson was "a source of racial pride" (Hoberman, 1997, p. 14). His physical domination over the white boxing champion Tommy Burns and succeeding defeat of the Great White Hope, Jim Jefferies, did more for Blacks than if he outwitted Albert Einstein (Hoberman). Joe Louis increased racial pride among Blacks during his career. After he won the heavyweight championship on June 22, 1937, Blacks celebrated in the streets throughout the night (Caponi-Tabery, 2002). Louis' triumph was an example of what Black people could accomplish when given a fair chance. Muhammad Ali stood up to the colonial imperialism. By refusing to enroll in the military after being drafted, he set an example of resistance for many Blacks in the political struggle for human liberation. Had Ali not been a major Black athlete, his resistance would have most likely been unknown to the general public. Yet, his participation in sport gave him a platform to influence the community with his refusal to fight for an oppressive government. The opportunities for Blacks in America have always been uneven compared with Whites, both in and outside of sports. The way in which athletes have overcome the barriers set before them in sports works as a metaphor that inspires oppressed, Black people. Kemet-kA energizes the community around those like Johnson, Louis, and Ali, who have overcome obstacles and leave oppressed people with a strengthened sense of hope.

The historical backdrop of social, political, and economic oppression toward Black people has helped produce sporting icons. The Africana community often celebrates athletes who embrace the opportunity for political resistance and hold them as beacons of possibility and hope. These athletes transcend the confines of their specific sport and its boundaries to become, as Dyson states, "symbolic figures who embodied social possibilities of success denied to other people of color" (Dyson, 2004, p. 463). The unspoken (or covertly spoken) sociopolitical styles of many Black athletes were often described as having an attitude. According to sports historian and journalist William Rhode, Willie Mays once executed an extremely difficult over-the-shoulder catch. But what was equally intriguing was what he did after. Rhoden says that Mays "nonchalantly picked the ball out of his glove, tossed it back to the infield, coolly walked back to center field, flicked his sunglasses back up, and waited for the next play" (Rhoden, 2004, p. 148). Similarly, both the Michigan "fab five" basketball team and Miami University football teams during the 1990s carried a style of play that was filled with sociopolitical coded body language and playing style (Rhoden, 2004). The emotional end-zone celebrations were not simply expressions of joy but also the "in-yo-face" psychological warfare that allowed Blacks to emphasize their success on the playing field when they were unable to do so outside of sports. Andrews explains,

> Historically, taunting was evident on the streets of any Southern city on any given day when whites disagreed with black behavior, however humble blacks might appear. So many years later we took our expression to the arena, the only place we would be allowed to stand up to White folks.

The dancing, taunting, and trash talking exhibit a political spirit of resistance and victory. It allows the collective Black community to fight vicariously through Black athletes. Oftentimes, Black athletes represent the collective Black community in their athletic matches. Joe Louis and Serena Williams have had an entire community of Black people cheering and rooting for them, regardless of their opponent. It was as if their victory increased the pride that Black people held. But it is the "in-yo-face" style of many Black athletes that, in its own way, is a direct response and resistance to the invisibility and social hindrances that fill the Blacks' experience. This form of resistance that fills the sporting style of Black athletes remains a major aspect of Kemet-kA.

Conclusion

The uniqueness of sport performed by Africans carries immense cultural traditions that enable Africans to successfully navigate through this world and any other world in which they reside. Kemet-kA is the mechanism that guides these traditions in the realm of sports. The study of ancient Egyptian culture is filled with pictures, stories, and artifacts that support Decker's claim that sport was a major mechanism by which cultural norms, traditions, and beliefs were taught. Sport was the tool used to exemplify the character and morals of Ma'at. This is also true in contemporary Black culture. The three major characteristics of Kemet-kA, aesthetics, community relationships, and cultural heroism, provide a framework for analyzing participation in sport by people of African descent. African aesthetics have been deeply outlined in the Nzuri model and work through rhythm and character to create the style that is beautifully displayed in the performance of Black athletes.

The function of sport has always been, for Africans, to be a representation of the community and its ideals. Kemet-kA aligns athletes and sport with rhythms of the community. The creative power of Kemet-kA works for the individual and community, not as merely a form of beauty but also as a function to defend off that goes against Ma'at. Through the perseverance, work, communalism, joy, and tenacity of Black athletes, the Black community has hope. The ways in which sport mirrors the world allow athletes to emerge as cultural heroes. However, the constant strangle of colonization has altered Black cultural heroes by stripping them of integrity and diminishing their moral consciousness. Kemet-kA is always present. Black athletes performing contemporary sports must bolster more of their Kemet-kA in order to better align with Ma'at, the rhythm of the community, and the ancestral legacy of African heritage, which they represent.

This chapter outlines an early form of Kemet-kA. Future studies that explore ancient Egyptian sports further are needed to expand the knowledge of Kemet-kA in them. Also, a more critical look at the tenets of Kemet-kA allows for a stronger definition of and identification for each of them. Until then, Kemet-kA, as it stands, should be used to study the phenomenon of sport and people of African descent.

Note

1 "Maafa" is a term often used to describe the enslavement of African people. It is a term that derived from a Kiswahili word meaning disaster or great tragedy.

References

Andrews, V. (2015). The control of Black expression in American sport & society. January 15.

Asante, M. K. (1985). Afrocentricity and culture. In M. K. Asante & K. Welsh-Asante (Eds.), *African culture: The rhythms of unity*, pp. 3–12. Westport: Praeger Pub Text.

Asante, M. K. (1987). *The Afrocentric idea*. Philadelphia, PA: Temple Press.

Asante, M. K. (2000). *The Egyptian philosophers: Ancient African voices from Imhotep to Akhenaten*. Chicago: African American Images.

Asante, M. K. (2007). *The history of Africa*. New York: Routledge.

Asante, M. K. (2014). *Facing south to Africa: Toward an Afrocentric critical orientation*. Lanham: Lexington.

Asante, M. K., & Mazama, A. (Eds.). (2009). *Encyclopedia of African religion* (Vol. 1). New York: Sage Publications.

Caponi-Tabery, G. (2002). Jump For joy: Jump blues, dance, and basketball in 1930s African America. In J. Bloom & M. N. Willard (Eds.), *Sports matters: Race recreation and culture*. New York: New York University Press.

Coakley, J. (2007). *Sports in society* (9th ed.). New York: McGraw-Hill.

Crowther, N. B. (2007). *Sport in ancient times*. Westport, CT: Praeger Publishers.

Decker, W. (1992). *Sports and games of ancient Egypt*. Binghamton, NY: Vail-Ballou Press.

Desch-Obi, M. T. (2008). *Fighting for honor: The history of African martial art traditions in the Atlantic world*. Columbia: University of South Carolina Press.

Diop, C. A. (1989). *The African origin of civilization: Myth or reality*. Chicago: Chicago Review Press.

Dubois, W. E. (1926). Criteria for negro art. *The crises: A record of the darker races, 32*, 295–296.

Dyson, M. E. (2004). *The Michael Eric Dyson reader*. New York: Basic Books.

Gayle, A. (1971). *The black aesthetic*. New York: Doubleday Books.

Hoberman, J. (1997). *Darwin's athletes how sports has damaged black America and preserved the myth of race*. New York: Houghton Mifflin Company.

Holland, J. W. (2002). *Black recreation: A historical perspective*. Chicago: Burnham Inc. Publisher.

Ife, Z. (1993). The African diasporian ritual mode. In K. Welsh-Asante (Ed.), *The African aesthetic: Keeper of the tradition*, pp. 31–51. West Port, CT: Praeger Publisher.

Judy, R. A. (1994). The new black aesthetic and WEB Du Bois, or Hephaestus, limping. *The Massachusetts Review, 35*(2), 249–282.

Karenga, M. (2004). *Maat: The Moral Ideal in Ancient Egypt: A Study in Classical African Ethics*. New York: Routledge.

Lewis, T. (2010). *Ballers of the new school*. Chicago: Third World Press.

Major, R., & Billson, J. M. (1992). *Cool pose*. New York: Lexington Books.

Neal, L. (1972). Some reflections on the Black aesthetic. In A. Gayle (Ed.), *The black aesthetic*, pp. 12–15. New York: Anchor Books.

Powell, S. (2008). *Souled out?—How Blacks are winning and losing in sports*. Champaign: Human Kinetics.

Rhoden, W. (2004). *Forty million dollar slaves*. New York: Random House.

Sailes, G. A. (Ed.). (2003). *African Americans in sport*. New Brunswick: Transaction Publisher.

Stapleton, K. R. (1998). From the margins to mainstream: The political power of hip-hop. *Media, Culture & Society, 20*(2), 219–234.

Thompson, R. F. (1983). *Flash of the spirit*. New York: Vintage Books.

Tylor, E. (1958). *Primitive vulture*. New York: Harper and Row.

Welsh-Asante, K. (1985). Commonalities in African dance: An aesthetic foundation. In M. K. Asante & K. Welsh-Asante (Eds.), *African culture: The rhythms of unity*, pp. 71–82. Westport: Praeger Pub Text.

Welsh-Asante, K. (Ed.). (1994). *African aesthetics: Keeper of traditions*. Westport, CT: Praeger.

7

FEMINIST STANDPOINT THEORY AND WOMEN'S SEXUALITY

Implications for HIV Prevention

Grace A. Loudd

Introduction

The World Health Organization (WHO, 2006) conceptualizes sexuality as optimal sexual health that goes beyond the absence of disease, with an expectation of pleasurable sexual experiences (p. 4). However, when considering that approximately 51% of individuals identify as women (U.S. Census Bureau 2012) and the overall impact of HIV in the United States, this conceptualization begins to fade into the shadows. Currently, there are over 1.2 million people living with HIV in the U.S. and one of every four are women the Centers for Disease Control and Prevention [CDC, 2016a], "HIV in the United States". The situation becomes even more alarming when assessing the impact of HIV among the different groups of women. In 2013, among all women diagnosed with HIV/AIDS, 61% were black compared with 34% white and Hispanic women (CDC, 2016a, "HIV in the United States"). Surveillance reports indicate that women are more likely to contract the disease during sexual contact as a result of infected semen, vaginal secretions, and/or blood (CDC 2015b, "HIV Surveillance Report"; Yarber et al., 2010). These numbers suggest that there is no mistaking women are seriously impacted by the HIV/AIDS epidemic in the U.S. and there is much more work to be done to address this issue.

Compared with when HIV first became a public health concern, we, as a collective, are in a much better position than before with regard to slowing the disease's progression down while improving the life span of diagnosed individuals. Nonetheless, we have taken a more circuitous public health approach to getting to where we are today, which has not consistently resulted in promoting an overall positive sexual discourse. A review of HIV prevention literature would lead one to believe that optimal sexual health and HIV prevention are two distinct concepts, when, in fact, they are one and the same. Several HIV prevention programs designed for use with women of unknown or HIV-negative serostatus primarily focus on some variation of increasing sexual knowledge, demonstrating proper condom use, strengthening sexual negotiation skills, and providing resources and referrals (CDC, 2015a, "Effective Interventions"). Many of these programs are funded at the governmental level and primarily implemented through non-profit organizations and local health departments, with mixed reviews. Some studies report that HIV prevention programs incorporating techniques such as role playing, group dialogue, and empowerment are effective in targeting certain sexual behaviors (Johnson et al., 2009) whereas others suggest that the protective gains reported do not sufficiently modify sexual behaviors in the long term (Adimora et al., 2002). For HIV-positive women, prevention programs follow a similar format but also include content that builds on abstinence, avoiding reinfection, distinguishing between healthy and unhealthy relationships, and substance use (CDC, 2015, "Effective Interventions"). What is particularly interesting about all these different prevention programs for both groups of women is that they often do not take into account the full complexity of various environmental contexts and how each one's unique dynamics shape sexual outcomes and decision making (Shapiro & Ray, 2007).

At first glance, the prevention literature and subsequent behavioral efforts appear to be a reasonable social response to an increase in sexually transmitted infections. However, it is just as reasonable that what we are learning about the state of our public health, and how we go about responding to it may be more a reflection of our dominant values toward sexuality. In the early 1980s, our collective preconceived sexual biases are what allowed the greater population to initially believe that HIV was a white, gay, male disease for far longer than what the evidence suggested. Sexual abstinence is routinely injected into our national sexual discourse despite 41%–54% of U.S. teenagers reporting having had sexual intercourse, much of which is unprotected (CDC, 2016b; ReCAPP, 2016). An HIV diagnosis among women often renders sexual wants and/or desires to have children invisible (Shapiro & Ray, 2007, p. 68). It appears that instead of allowing the real-life circumstances and evidence lead our sexual discourse, we are being led by dominant notions of what is right and appropriate regarding sexuality. This paper proposes that the manner in which the knowledge of HIV/AIDS has been and is produced, interpreted, and disseminated in the U.S. is consistent with a dominant negative sexual discourse that fails to consider the potential burden that its structure imposes upon a significant portion of its population—women. More specifically, this type of knowledge production strengthens social marginalization, perpetuates stigma (Herek & Capitanio, 1993), and restricts female sexual agency (Brown & McNair, 1995). A different analysis could potentially yield a different interpretation that not only promotes a more accurate public health discourse but also affirms those traditionally marginalized and frequently unheard.

The Public Health Trajectory

The current U.S. public health approach to disease prevention and epidemic control combines varying methods of education, as well as punishment, to achieve its goal of reducing and/or eliminating infectious disease. The approach developed out of the contagion theory, which essentially rests on a biological explanation of infection (Chan & Reidpath, 2003). A biological explanation focuses solely on the progression of the disease being passed from an infected individual to an uninfected individual. This perspective is in direct contrast to the miasma theory, prominent until the early nineteenth century, which assumed that infectious disease was the result of one's exposure to "bad airs" (UCLA, University of California at Los Angeles, "Competing Theories" Frerichs, 2001). In many respects, public health is greatly improved because a disease cannot be eradicated if we do not know how it actually operates. However, what is important here are the extent and manner in which each prominent perspective influences our social obligations to one another.

The miasma theory is no longer useful as a source guiding public health knowledge. Nonetheless, it is important to note that its basic premise would not support holding individuals accountable as to how a disease progresses, because the problem was viewed as beyond an individual's control. It is reasonable to believe that subsequent behavioral efforts addressing disease during this time followed a similar course, because anyone could be exposed to "bad air." In the contagion theory, the government's role in disease prevention and control is predicated on identifying those individuals who are infected (case identification), identifying those with whom they have been in contact (contact tracing), and testing and/ or isolating the case and subsequent contacts to contain further spreading of the disease (Chan & Reidpath, 2003). Once these individuals are properly identified, the assumption is that they will make rational choices to protect themselves and others from further spreading the disease. For those who refuse to act rationally, imprisonment and/or quarantine is readily available. The implicit message associated with such punitive measures suggests that individuals who place others at risk are irresponsible and should be punished.

Shifting the larger societal perspective for disease progression from the social environment to the individual makes it that much easier to exclusively associate morality with behavior. In light of the HIV/AIDS discourse over the years, the concept of morality becomes even more pronounced depending on a disease's etiology. In today's climate, it is safe to say that an individual diagnosed with terminal cancer, no matter whether it is a result of poor lifestyle choices or a genetic predisposition, is more likely to get a better reception than an individual disclosing he/she is HIV positive. The varying responses to the two scenarios are partially a reflection as to how public health knowledge is mass produced, interpreted, and disseminated. It also reflects the behavioral morality component in that, for all intents and purposes, cancer is not typically spread from one person to another, whereas HIV is predominantly spread through sexual contact.

Feminist Standpoint Theory

Theorist Sandra Harding (2008) is better known for conceptualizing the feminist standpoint theory (FST) as an epistemology critiquing traditionally dominant modes of knowledge production. These dominant modes, consisting of supposedly objective and rational approaches, are what traditionally became accepted as authoritative Western science. The FST builds on Hegel's reflections and Marx's insights in that there is valuable epistemological knowledge to be gained in starting from the position of often-marginalized groups. The marginalization, albeit a social outcome typically associated with one's race, class, gender, and/or sexuality, comprises all different types of social locations intricately shaping the day-to-day experiences of individuals living outside the dominant norms. The marginalization is what obscures these types of experiences out of the mainstream discourse, practically rendering them invisible. The FST's value culminates as based on two primary assumptions: the first being that one's social location is relevant to what types of knowledge can and cannot be known and the second being that, in some instances, certain social locations as a starting point for generating knowledge are preferred over others.

Since Harding's initial writings, introduced over two decades earlier, the FST's primary assumptions have been challenged and criticized. It has been charged with encouraging false dichotomies and an inability to accommodate diversity (Hekman, 1997) and erroneously promoting biological essentialism and relativism (Landau, 2008). Harding (2008); in addition, other FST proponents Nancy Harstock (as cited in Kokushkin, 2014) and Dorothy Smith (1997) responded to these claims coalescing around the fact that an alternative approach to knowledge production makes room for various aspects of social relationships that would otherwise be overlooked because certain behaviors would not meet traditional androcentric standards for examination. For the sake of clarity, it should be made clear that the FST does not imply that all individuals within a marginalized group have the same experiences or respond in like fashion. Similarly, it does not suggest that every marginalized perspective is more valuable than the next. However, the FST is an alternative to the positivist tradition and commonly accepted modes of epistemic inquiry (Harding, 2008), which is often criticized for devaluing other ways of knowing, as it determines which assumptions are made, the questions asked, and how those questions are answered and interpreted (Intemann, 2010).

Marginalization is a reflection of unfavorable implicit and explicit socially constructed power structures. To observe subdued aspects of social relationships inclined to go unnoticed, it is best to start with where power is exerted and how knowledge is produced and disseminated. Revealing and evaluating these power structures and their associated outcomes while supporting collective critical consciousness are the standpoint (Intemann, 2010). Rolin (2009) supports this perspective in acknowledging power structures as having the ability to suppress, distort, and limit access to knowledge arising from non-dominant sources of knowledge. Likewise, the lack of critical consciousness necessary for recognizing a standpoint can lead to a plethora of negative emotions such as disgust, shame, anger, and stigma (Rolin, 2009). Earnshaw and Chaudoir (2009) proposed that these negative emotions and their resultant outcomes depend on one's social location and the psychological responses activated to address them. In the case of HIV, uninfected individuals are more likely to engage in psychological responses that allow distancing from the devalued attribute through coping techniques such as stereotypes, perpetuating prejudicial beliefs, and even engaging in discriminative acts (Earnshaw & Chaudoir, 2009). Herek and Capitanio's (1993) study aligns with this knowledge, validating that during the early epidemic years, the general public harbored morally punitive views about persons living with HIV/AIDS (PLWHAs) to the point that they even supported separating and quarantining affected individuals from the larger population. A decade later, similar attitudes were again reported in that both whites and blacks continued to associate HIV with same-sex orientations, perceptions of HIV-related sexual transmission as the most heinous route, espousing exaggerated fears regarding physical contact with PLWHAs, and an overall negative evaluation in general (Herek & Capitanio, 1999).

Feminist Standpoint Theory and Women's Sexuality

Sexuality, as a significant social power structure, influences how individuals perceive and are perceived by the world, shapes the partnering process, guides interpretation of laws and social mores, influences interpersonal interactions, and even motivates media consumption. Sexuality is everywhere, yet we have a cultural collective history of pretending that it is not. When it is acknowledged, it is typically viewed and/or transmitted within a greater context of psychopathology and/or deviance as a way to suppress and/or distort that existing outside the mainstream. Corrêa et al. (2008) note for this reason that sexuality has long been recognized as controversial, observed most visibly at the macro level, and in part an effort to establish governmental legitimacy. Legitimacy being large organizations, similar to the WHO and the CDC, defining what sexuality is, the Supreme Court deciding how sexuality should be understood, the legislature determining who gets tax dollars to meet their sexual needs, and scholars that get to say what "proper" sexual behavior actually is.

The political progression for sexual legitimacy aligns itself with Michel Foucault's (1978) interpretation of what he refers to as deployments of alliance and sexuality (as cited in Baker, Wininger, & Elliston, 407). In this work, he argues the physical act of sex itself is what gave rise to the deployment of alliance. This alliance, he speaks, is a reference to social and legal rules, such as marriage, kinship, and the transfer of wealth and resources, that are inherently designed to maintain social order, perpetuate norms, and be reproduced. From a systemic perspective, the deployment of alliance is the pattern maintenance that regulates proper and improper sexual interactions most easily observed through legal statutes. With the advent of an increasingly more complex society, the rules that once made the deployment of alliance predictable are now less tenable. Foucault posits that, in response to this, power became increasingly executed through another knowledge mechanism, deployment of sexuality. The deployment of sexuality is similar to the former in that it is also linked to the economy, yet it is different, because its underlying goal is not to encourage reproduction but to control and penetrate the body.

Foucault's (1978) work is largely analytical; however, his use of the word penetration is a deliberate and powerful metaphor. Classical antiquity scholar David Halperin (1978) (as cited in Baker, Wininger, & Elliston, 416) puts Foucault's conceptualization to work in his analysis of ancient Athenian culture. His review supports the conception in that within this society, the physical sexual act distinguished itself along the lines of social status. Citizens, being the premier status, were expected to engage in sex with people of lower status such as women of all ages, foreigners and slaves (both male and female), and free boys who had yet reached the point of becoming citizens. To be a citizen or a non-citizen came with different sexual roles akin to the penetrator as dominant (citizen) and the penetrated as submissive (non-citizen). In other words, sexuality in Athenian culture was a social construction and functional for maintaining control. This preoccupation with sex continued well into the eighteenth century, as demonstrated by four dominant sexual paradigms recognized as (1) a hysterization of women's bodies, (2) a pedagogization of children's sex, (3) a socialization of procreative behavior, and (4) a psychiatrization of perverse pleasure (Foucault, 1989) (as cited in Baker, Wininger, & Elliston, 406). Within each of these paradigms, factors associated with women, children, and men's sex were used to validate knowledge and justify strategies and techniques to control and/or regulate a larger socially constructed sexuality. According to Foucault (1989), the deployment of sexuality did not supplant the deployment of alliance, but it built upon it, most notably through the use of families (as cited in Baker, Wininger, and Elliston, 408). He proposes that families are the units that bind sexuality and sexual behavior to both deployments of alliance and sexuality. Through interaction with a family's suprasystem, sexuality is promulgated by legal statute (alliance) and kept in check through privilege (sexuality).

One way to better view this type of abstract sexual insidiousness is through science and knowledge production regarding various aspects associated with women's sexuality. Housh's (2011) work traces a pervasive trend all the way back to Aristotle's time, when it was thought that women's lower body heat was a defective trait and the main reason why some embryos were female rather than male. She further points out that in the nineteenth century, Charles Darwin contributed to this line of thinking when he proposed that pre-historic men commonly chased after women and as a result they gradually developed a more acute mental capacity. This supposedly gave men an intellectual advantage because women did not chase men; thus, women were less intellectually evolved in comparison.

Today, most would consider this type of knowledge absurd; yet, it also suggests the deployment of sexuality has been and is still alive and well. Lest we not forget that it was not until 1973 that the American Psychiatric Association removed homosexuality as a mental disorder from the *Diagnostic Statistical Manual* (Drescher, 2015), thus loosening the stronghold of organizationally sanctioned sexual-related stigma. A related example of the deployment of sexuality involves our current position regarding paid sex work. Indian writer and filmmaker Bishakha Datta suggests that the problem with women in sex work is not the selling of sex but the stigma attached to sex work, which is greatly compounded by our perception of sexuality (New Internationalist, 2013). She argues that whether we morally agree with prostitution or not, the fact remains that consenting adults engaging in sex work should be recognized as an accepted form of work, just like we do when working with any other part of our body. One study analyzed the relationship between legal positions about prostitution, personal attitudes, and beliefs (Valor-Segura et al., 2011). Among their findings, they learned that people in favor of prohibiting prostitution were also more likely to engage in hostile sexism via victim blaming toward sex workers and the profession itself. They argue that sexist ideologies, practices, and beliefs situated in a patriarchal culture are what reinforce negative responses to sex work, thus further stigmatizing sexuality among women working in this profession. From a pop cultural perspective, we are repeatedly inundated with sexual scripts of good girls, strong men, virgins, whores, studs, dykes, gays, freaks, hoes, and fuckboys (Stephens & Phillips, 2003), which influence sexual stereotypes while reinforcing a dominant negative sexual discourse. All these sexual scripts are meaningless without sexual constructions, and they are the deployments of sexuality that bind us.

The traditionally unspoken aspects of social relationships impacting women, as they relate to HIV and prevention, intersect at a point between sexual agency and environmental context. Although believing in one's own capability and knowing public health facts are important, there are a myriad of other factors at play that must also be considered in HIV prevention efforts. Women's sexuality is often inhibited in situations where women are relegated to using sex as a means of survival to pay their bills or to take care of their children (Forna et al., 2006). This is typically a situation where women lack power in sexual relationships and oftentimes may not be in a position to insist on protective measures. Schwartz et al. (2014) analyzed a gender-based violence sample of both HIV-positive and -negative women enrolled in the Women's Interagency HIV Study conducted in three cities in the U.S. This study found that both groups reported similar rates of lifetime gender-based violence (over 58%) and child sexual abuse (over 22%), suggesting that the sample's con-textual factors might share many similar characteristics. However, they differed in that HIV-negative women were more likely to engage in heavy drinking and non-injection drug use and be married or living with a partner, whereas HIV-positive women were more likely to be older, unemployed, and with lower income. Despite these behavioral differences, the primary factors distinguish-ing them were experiencing gender-based violence and/or child sexual assault and subsequent poor mental health and substance use outcomes. These findings clearly indicate that for many women, early-life experiences at the hands of others are just as important, if not more, when assessing contextual factors that impact one's sexual health.

Individual-level behavioral factors such as accessing medical care, getting tested, and knowing your partner's status are pieces to combating and defend-ing oneself against the spread of HIV (CDC, "HIV in the United States"), but none of these behaviors can be successfully completed without compliance or availability of an outside entity. Where a woman lives affects how she has to behave or adapt, and sexual vulnerability is severely impacted by poverty (Gentry et al., 2005). An overall higher prevalence rate of sexually transmitted infections, violence and drug use (CDC, "HIV Surveillance Report") within many geographic communities where elevated levels of HIV saturation means a woman living there is more likely to come into contact with an infected sexual partner (Adimora et al., 2009).

Women's sexual vulnerability is also impacted by the norms associated with marriage or long-term relationships (Soler et al., 2000). Marriage or long-term commitment is generally understood to be a protective factor, but the evidence suggest that assumption no longer serves our best interests. Renwick (2002) conducted a study among international HIV-positive women and reported 80% of them having gotten the disease while in a long-term relationship with a stable partner. Furthermore, for those women who are married or are in com-mitted relationships and use a condom may be perceived as contrary to their concept of monogamy and fidelity even if they or their partner are suspected of having sex with others outside the relationship (Maia et al., 2008; Rosenthal et al., 1991).

A similar connection can also be made regarding the various labels ascribed to those who at first glance appear not to conform to what are perceived as moral behaviors. Public health labels such as at-risk and high-risk add another layer of implicit immorality, creating more social barriers for those most affected as well as those who care about them. Chan and Reidpath (2003) note a perspective as such that relies heavily on labels results in individuals being essentially treated as if "they are independent of the socio-economic contexts in which they live," (p. 40) ultimately increasing the complexity of efficient and socially responsible disease control and prevention.

From a public health perspective, the use of such labels might be especially beneficial for epidemiologists, but from the perspective of social relationships, they only serve to shift our attention from what is really important—that the face of HIV can look like anyone. Sociologist Quinn Gentry's (2012) in-depth ethnographic studies of black women living in a "high-risk" inner city community revealed that "the factors leading to [one's] risk are as different as the diverse faces" (p. 6) we are likely to encounter. The at-risk discourse is yet another power structure embedded within dominant notions of sexuality, thus distorting the evidence.

Shifting the Paradigm: A Sex-Positive Framework

A sex-positive framework encompasses an understanding and dissemination of sexuality that works to establish values, attitudes, and beliefs that go beyond disease prevention and reproduction to include satisfaction, pleasure, and well-being for everyone (Gubrium & Shafer, 2014; Williams et al., 2013). Similarly, a sex-positive framework focuses on healthy sexual outcomes such as appropriate experimentation, affirming sensuality, attaining sexual competence through the ability to give and receive sexual pleasure, and setting sexual boundaries based on what one prefers and knows is safe and responsible (Robinson et al., 2005). This framework is consistent with findings from a qualitative study that assessed women's own understanding of what women's sexuality meant to them. In this study, women stated that sexuality is not one monolithic fixed characteristic but a multifaceted one representing your mind as well as how you present yourself to the world (Bellamy et al., 2011). This leads one to believe that a woman's perception of her sexuality is closely aligned with how much autonomy she exhibits over the activities she engages in with her own body.

Destigmatizing pleasure is a critical component of sex positivity. Bowman (2014) attempted to do this in her study that assessed the function and meaning of masturbation for women. Among her sample, she found that the majority of women (87.6%) reported masturbating in the previous 3 months, and their top two reasons for doing so were for sexual pleasure and to learn about their bodies. Similarly, the women who engage in masturbation for pleasure and educational purposes were also more likely to report self-empowerment due to higher genital self-image and sexual self-efficacy (Bowman, 2014). This suggests at the individual level, in addition to being informed about health and safer sex practices, that women should also learn and routinely incorporate what it means to affirm your body and genitals as well as enhance one's capacity for self-pleasuring.

Additional individual-level factors supporting a sex-positive framework might consist of more open sexual communication and education and affirming a comprehensive range of sexual diversity. Gubrium and Shafer (2014) piloted a sexual education program with young female parents that included sensory content using the arts to help them connect what they should know about sexuality (negotiation, safe sexual practices, etc.) with what they actually experience in day-to-day life. The authors suggest couching safe sex messages in the various senses not only to increase protective factors but also to simultaneously encourage women to be active participants rather than passive recipients when it comes to sexual matters.

At the societal level, a sex-positive framework should consist of reframing our philosophical approach to capturing, interpreting, and disseminating knowledge about sexuality. Williams et al. (2013) suggest that one way to do this is to honestly reevaluate how we view and/or categorize alternative erotic preferences. They argue that due to our overall perception of sex and sexuality, many health clinicians demonstrate heterosexist and normative biases against individuals engaging in non-traditional or non-dominantly approved sexual activities. This has grave implications for moving toward concerted efforts such as routine HIV testing during medical examinations and/or integrating pre-exposure prophylaxis as standard components of public health efforts thus eventually leading us toward a more integrated and comprehensive holistic sexual perspective.

Conclusion

It is next to impossible to underestimate the influence of knowledge contributing to larger societal values regarding sexuality. In light of the prevalence of HIV among U.S. women, we are socially obligated to seriously consider all knowledge that might work toward improving long-term sexual outcomes. A large component of our public health knowledge and discourse is propelled by epistemological frameworks tainted by moral assumptions. A socially negative sexual discourse hinders our ability to acknowledge, recognize, and accurately respond to public health, sexual diversity, and related contextual factors within social relationships. Positive sexuality, as a broad sexual rights perspective, promotes providing access to a full range of sexual services, affirming pleasure, and encouraging the right to sexual diversity for all women. This framework is important because it should apply to all, but most notably, it must apply to women—women categorized as supposedly high-risk as well as women living in reportedly high-risk communities. A sex-positive framework becomes all the more important for women and anyone else living with HIV or any other sexually related condition because it supports approaching these diseases as population concerns that affect everyone rather than subsets of groups leading to marginalization. Assessing women's sexuality starting with their day-to-day lives means that we are seeking their truth in hopes of bringing their experiences back into the mainstream.

References

Adimora, A. A., Schoenbach, V. J., & Doherty, I. A. (2002). Concurrent sexual partnerships among women in the United States. *Epidemiology 13*(3), 320–327.

Adimora, A. A., Schoenbach, V. J., & Floris-Moore, M. A. (2009). Ending the epidemic of heterosexual HIV transmission among African Americans. *American Journal of Preventive Medicine 37*(5), 468–471.

Bellamy, G., Gott, M., Hinchliff, S., & Nicolson, P. (2011). Contemporary women's understandings of female sexuality: Findings from an in-depth interview study. *Sexual and Relationship Therapy 26*(1), 84–95.

Bowman, C. P. (2014). Women's masturbation experiences of sexual empowerment in a primarily sex-positive sample. *Psychology of Women Quarterly 38*(3), 363–378.

Brown, S., & McNair, L. (1995). Black women's sexual sense of self: Implications for AIDS prevention. *The Womanist 1*(2), 1–5.

Centers for Disease Control and Prevention [CDC]. (2016a). *Effective Interventions: HIV Prevention That Work*; 2015.

Centers for Disease Control and Prevention. (2015b). *HIV Surveillance Report*, 2014; vol. 26, December.

Centers for Disease Control and Prevention. (2016a). *HIV in the United States: At a Glance*; June.

Centers for Disease Control and Prevention. (2016b). *Sexual Risk Behaviors: HIV, STD, & Teen Pregnancy Prevention*, July.

Chan, K. Y., & Reidpath, D. D. (2003). "Typhoid Mary" and "HIV Jane": Responsibility, agency and disease prevention. *Reproductive Health Matters 11*(22), 40–50.

Corrêa, S., Petchesky, R., & Parker, R. (2008). *Sexuality, health and human rights*. New York: Routledge.

Drescher, J. (2015). Out of DSM: Depathologizing homosexuality. *Behavioral Sciences 5*(4), 565–575.

Earnshaw, V. A., & Chaudoir, S. R. (2009). From conceptualizing to measuring HIV stigma: A review of HIV stigma mechanism measures. *AIDS and Behavior 13*(6), 1160–1177.

Forna, F. M., Fitzpatrick, L., Adimora, A. A., McLellan-Lemal, E., Leone, P., Brooks, J. T., Marks, G., & Greenberg, A. (2006). A case-control study of factors associated with HIV infection among black women. *Journal of the National Medical Association 98*(11), 1798.

Foucault, M. (1989). Domain. In R. Baker, K. Wininger, & F. Elliston (Eds.), *Philosophy and sex* (pp. 405–412). New York: Prometheus Books.

Frerichs, R. (2001). *Competing theories of Cholera*. UCLA Fielding School of Public Health Department of Epidemiology. Retrieved from http://www.ph.ucla.edu/epi/snow/choleratheories.html.

Gentry, Q. (2012). *Black women's risk for HIV: Rough living*. New York: Routledge.

Gentry, Q. M., Elifson, K., & Sterk, C. (2005). Aiming for more relevant HIV risk reduction: A black feminist perspective for enhancing HIV intervention for low-income African American women. *AIDS Education & Prevention 17*(3), 238–252.

Gubrium, A. C., & Shafer, M. B. (2014). Sensual sexuality education with young parenting women. *Health Education Research 29*(4), 649–661.

Halperin, D. M. (1989). Is there a history of sexuality? In R. Baker, K. Wininger, & F. Elliston (Eds.), *Philosophy and sex* (pp. 413–431). New York: Prometheus Books.

Harding, S. (2008). Borderlands epistemologies: Two problematic epistemological strategies. In A. Jaggar (Ed.), *Just methods: An interdisciplinary feminist reader* (pp. 331–341). Colorado: Paradigm.

Hekman, S. (1997). Truth and method: Feminist standpoint theory revisited. *Signs* 22(2), 341–365.

Herek, G. M., & Capitanio, J. P. (1993). Public reactions to AIDS in the United States: A second decade of stigma. *American Journal of Public Health 83*(4), 574–577.

Herek, G. M., & Capitanio, J. P. (1999). AIDS stigma and sexual prejudice. *American Behavioral Scientist 42*(7), 1130–1147.

Housh, K. (2011). Different but equal-inequalities in the workplace, the nature-based narrative, and the title vii prohibition on the masculinization of the ideal worker. *Tex. J. on CL & CR 17*, 117.

Intemann, K. (2010). 25 years of feminist empiricism and standpoint theory: Where are we now? *Hypatia 25*(4), 778–796.

Johnson, B. T., Scott-Sheldon, L. A. J., Smoak, N. D., LaCroix, J. M., Anderson, J. R., & Carey, M. P. (2009). Behavioral interventions for African-Americans to reduce sexual risk of HIV: A meta-analysis of randomized controlled trials. *Journal of Acquired Immune Deficiency Syndromes 51*(4), 492.

Kokushkin, M. (2014). Standpoint theory is dead, long live standpoint theory! Why standpoint thinking should be embraced by scholars who do not identify as feminists? *Journal of Arts and Humanities 3*(7), 8.

Landau, I. (2008). Problems with feminist standpoint theory in science education. *Science & Education 17*(10), 1081–1088.

Maia, C., Guilhem, D., & Freitas, D. (2008). Vulnerability to HIV/AIDS in married heterosexual people or people in a common-law marriage. *Revista de Saúde Pública 42*(2), 242–248.

New Internationalist. (2013, April 1). *Should prostitution be legalized?* Retrieved from https://newint.org/features/2013/04/01/should-prostitution-be-legalized-argument.

ReCAPP, Resource Center for Adolescent Pregnancy Prevention. (2016). *Statistics: Sexual activity* Retrieved from http://recapp.etr.org/recapp/index.cfm?fuseaction=pages.StatisticsDetail&PageID=555.

Renwick, N. (2002). The "nameless fever": The HIV/AIDS pandemic and China's women. *Third World Quarterly 23*(2), 377–393.

Robinson, B. E., Scheltema, K., & Cherry, T. (2005). Risky sexual behavior in low-income African American women: The impact of sexual health variables. *Journal of Sex Research 42*(3), 224–237.

Rolin, K. (2009). Standpoint theory as a methodology for the study of power relations. *Hypatia 24*(4), 218–226.

Rosenthal, D., Moore, S., & Flynn, I. (1991). Adolescent self-efficacy, self-esteem and sexual risk-taking. *Journal of Community & Applied Social Psychology 1*(2), 77–88.

Schwartz, R. M., Weber, K. M., Schechter, G. E., Connors, N. C., Gousse, Y., Young, M. A., & Cohen, M. H. (2014). Psychosocial correlates of gender-based violence among HIV-Infected and HIV-uninfected women in three US cities. *AIDS Patient Care & Stds 28*(5), 260–267.

Shapiro, K., & Ray, S. (2007). Sexual health for people living with HIV. *Reproductive Health Matters 15*(29), 67–92.

Smith, D. (1997). Comment on Hekman's "Truth and method: Feminist standpoint theory revisited": Truth or justice? *Signs*, 367–374.

Soler, H., et al. (2000). Relationship dynamics, ethnicity, and condom use among low-income women. *Family Planning Perspectives, 32*(2), 82–101.

Stephens, D. P., & Phillips, L. D. (2003). Freaks, gold diggers, divas, and dykes: The sociohistorical development of adolescent African American women's sexual scripts. *Sexuality and Culture* 7(1), 3–49.

U.S. Census Bureau. (2012). *2010 Census Summary File 1* [Tables P12, P13, and PCT 12]. Retrieved from https://factfinder.census.gov/faces/tableservices/jsf/pages/product-view.xhtml?pid=DEC_10_SF1_QTP1&prodType=table.

Valor-Segura, I., Expósito, F., & Moya Morales, M. C. (2011). Attitudes toward prostitution: Is it an ideological issue? *The European Journal of Psychology Applied to Legal Context* 3(2), 159–176.

Williams, D. J., Prior, E., & Wegner, J. (2013). Resolving social problems associated with sexuality: Can a "sex-positive" approach help? *Social Work* 58(3), 273–276.

World Health Organization. (2006). *Defining sexual health: Report of a technical consultation on sexual health, 28–31 January 2002, Geneva.* Geneva, Switzerland.

Yarber, W. L., Sayad, B. W., & Strong, B. (2010). *Human sexuality: Diversity in Contemporary America.* New York: McGraw-Hill.

8

EVALUATION OF THE RELATIONSHIP AMONG MORAL FOUNDATIONS, CRIMINAL JUSTICE, AND PERCEPTIONS OF TERRORISM IN COLLEGE STUDENTS ATTENDING HISTORICALLY BLACK COLLEGE AND UNIVERSITY

Derek Wilson, Courtney Bryant, and Aisha Asby

Statement of the Problem

According to Miller and Jensen (2015) of the National Consortium for the Study of Terrorism and Responses to Terrorism (START), there were 256 terrorist attacks on American soil between 2000 and 2014. Since the September 11 attacks, there has been a growing concern about future attacks, resulting in hyper-vigilance, fear, and, to some degree, discrimination toward individuals who share similar ethnic/racial and cultural backgrounds of the attackers (UDHS). Statistics gathered by UDHS revealed that 73% of the attacks in the United States were from groups such as the Earth Liberation Front and the Animal Liberation Front. Other attempts by individuals affiliated with al-Qaida in the Arabian Peninsula and Tehrik-i-Taliban in Pakistan have been successfully pre-empted. In addition, 40% of terrorist attacks in the United States involved individuals with little association to known radical factions. However, there are still many who may empathize with the attackers; they may view the attacks on the U.S. soil as being justified and in turn feel the need to embrace "the cause." Should mass killings also be considered acts of terrorism? Since 2006, there have been more than 200 mass killings in the United States alone. The Federal Bureau of Investigation revealed from 2006 to 2012 172 cases of mass killings (Overberg et al., 2013). Most famous incidents are the images from Newtown, Aurora, and Virginia Tech. These incidents may also be viewed as terroristic acts. What is not known is African Americans' view of terroristic acts and behaviors. Recent attacks on African Americans have reminded many of the Civil Rights era of the 1950s and 1960s.

The history of Africans in America parallels to that of targeted groups who experienced terroristic acts and behaviors and psychopathic racial personality emanating from white European cultural ethos. This was common given that African Americans have been the most attacked group since the founding of America and its history of slavery. The historical precedent of acts of violence against African Americans has been committed by individuals who do not fit the profile of contemporary terrorist image (e.g., hate groups, police officers, and Tea Party). The most recent acts of terrorism against Blacks have been played out in the police shootings and killing of unarmed Black boys, men, and women. The fatality of Blacks at the hands of the police was identified as high as 37% being unarmed, 1 in 3, in 2015 despite black people being only 13% of the total U.S. population. For instance, police killed at least 102 unarmed Black people in 2015, nearly two deaths for each week of the year. Unarmed Black people were killed at five times the rate of unarmed whites in 2015. Not so surprising is that only 9 of the 102 cases resulted in officer(s) being charged with a crime (Mapping Police Violence, 2016). While social justice has yet to adequately address this issue, the current political climate in which African Americans live reveal no research to date being conducted on their perceptions of terrorism. The research question for this study is: How are moral foundation, comprehensive justice, and perception of terrorism associated within African American population?

Based on the research supporting moral foundation, it is the assumption that a person's morality plays a significant role in the way they perceive justice and terrorism. Past terroristic acts such as 9/11 and more current events such as the 2009 shooting at Ft. Hood and the South Carolina massacre in 2015 can be viewed differently, depending on the person's definition of justice and view of terrorism. Yet, the review of the current literature provides very little insight concerning African American's view of individual attitudes about crime and justice and perceptions about terrorism. Therefore, this study will begin the initial exploration of the relationship among the aforementioned factors that may play a role in African Americans' perception of terrorism. This study will also attempt to explain what role moral foundation and comprehensive justice play on perceptions of terrorism and the mediating effect of an individual's political affiliation. As suggested by the intergroup emotion theory (IET) and systemic justification theory (SJT), moral foundation and comprehensive justice, as informed by one's political affiliation, will provide some insight about an individual's views of perception of terrorism. More importantly, the examination of these variables within an African American population may shed light into this particular population's take on the perception of terrorism, moral foundation, and comprehensive justice. It is predicted that moral foundation and comprehensive justice will be related to the perception of terrorism within African American population. The hypotheses for this study are as follow:

H1:There will be a relationship among moral foundation, comprehensive justice, and perceptions of terrorism within African American college students.

H2: Different aspects of terroristic perceptions (target, fear/worry, alerts, anger, faith, mental illness, and skillfulness) will be impacted by dimensions of moral foundation and comprehensive justice within African American college students.

Theoretical Framework

When explaining fear of terrorism, there are many theories associated with cognitive appraisals, terror management, behavioral responses, and group emotion. Many theories exist, explaining such fear as appraisal-tendency (Lerner et al., 2003), terror management theory (Greenberg, Solomon, & Pyszczynski, 1997), theory of planned behavior (Ajzen, 1985), situational theory of publics (Grunig, 1992), the protection motivation theory (Rogers, 1975), and the extended parallel process model (Witte, 1992) to name a few. These theories hypothesize that emotion, cognitive appraisal, and protection from threats play a role in our perception of terrorism. One theory of note is that of the IET (Seger et al., 2009), which will be used to examine groundwork for understanding the perception of terrorism in relation to moral foundation and comprehensive justice.

The IET was developed to explain how intergroup relations determine motivation forces elicited by emotions that group members feel about other groups in relation to themselves. According to Mackie et al. (2008),

Intergroup emotions are generated by belonging to, and by deriving identity from, one social group rather than another. They are shaped by the very different ways in which different groups see the world, and they come, with time and repetition, to be part and parcel of group membership itself. Once incited, such intergroup emotions direct intergroup behavior. It is the anger, anxiety, pride, and guilt that other groups evoke in us that drive our social, political, and physical responses to them, and it is only by changing such emotions that intergroup behavior can change. (p. 1867)

The breadth and depth of how one identifies with a group may impact their emotional responses, and the interplay with the group impacts the emotions of the group and behavior. The IET postulates that worldview shapes our emotions due to similar group identification. This suggests that belonging to a group serves as a psychological concept more than just demographic. Individuals who self-categorize engage in a process of transitioning from the individual self to group identified self or group membership (Mackie et al., 2008). Furthermore, it is within this group membership that individuals develop the capacity to distinguish significant meaning in attitude and beliefs associated with the group. These attitudes and beliefs, associated with group memberships, serve to foster a sense of collective emotions.

While we are all affiliated to multiple groups (i.e., professional, fraternities, ethnic, class, and or sociopolitical), some groups hold more weight and more importance than others; it is those groups that appear to be more salient to have impact on our emotional connection (Mackie et al., 2008). As captured by Mackie et al. (2008) and earlier revealed by Tajfel and Turner (1986), "the more central and important the group is to the self, the more an individual identifies with, or derives his or her identity from, it" (p. 1868).

While this theory emphasizes the way in which people self-identify within groups, the condition for which that group occupies on a sociopolitical level directs our affective pathways that are more in line with the group, notwithstanding the worldview. This suggests that if you identify with a collective identity group, you may then engage in more egalitarian value system, where your emotional sense is guided by traditional justice. However, if you identify with more individualistic value-laden group identity, then your emotional tone will be that of more repressive value and may see the world in a progressive sense. More importantly, African Americans status in the United States has been acrimonious at least and oppressed and marginalized at best. Based on the IET, due to their sociopolitical status as African Americans, their political ideology may reflect a collective emotional tone as a group informing their moral values and sense of comprehensive justice, thus shaping their perception of terrorism. Initial application of the IET may offer some understanding in how African Americans perceive terrorism.

What Is Terrorism?

Terrorism, as defined, means to frighten, deriving from the Latin verb terrere. Different U.S. governmental agencies have different definitions. The US Department of State defines terrorism to be *"premeditated politically-motivated violence perpetrated against non-combatant targets by sub-national groups or clandestine agents, usually intended to influence an audience."* The FBI uses this definition: *"Terrorism is the unlawful use of force and violence against persons or property to intimidate or coerce a government, the civilian population, or any segment thereof, in furtherance of political or social objectives."* The U.S. Department of Defense (2010) defines terrorism as *"the calculated use of unlawful violence or threat of unlawful violence to inculcate fear; intended to coerce or to intimidate governments or societies in the pursuit of goals that are generally political, religious, or ideological."* Within these definitions are the elements of violence, fear, and intimidation—and each element produces terror in its victims. Additionally, anti-terrorism policies illustrate the decisions and political attitudes in combating terrorism (Huddy et al., 2005). Overall, these attempts underscore the significance of government's need to counteract threats of terrorism and the development of effectual interference intended at eradicating negative counteraction to terrorism (Kowoll, 2012).

Research indicates that worry, individual preparedness, and avoidance behavior (Lee & Lemyre, 2009) suggest that individuals rely more on government officials. However, the fear that is instilled since 9/11 attacks has individuals in the United States believing that the government does not have the capacity to protect them (Richman et al., 2008), revealing inconsistencies for reducing fear of terrorism. Situational theory applies to a variety of studies assessing a variety of public events and universal public response to natural disasters (Major & Atwood, 2004) and now the need to fear terrorism. The situational theory of publics gives meaning to rise of Black Lives Matter movement due to the number of killings of unarmed Black men. However, the applicability of these theories has yet to be examined with African American population. Other studies reviewed recognize the connection between political attitudes and fear and further retorts to terrorism.

Continued Terrorism

While political motivations may be the root of the current climate for which African Americans are required to live under, mass killings have also been a part of the cultural psychology of today. For example, 2015 mass church killing in Charleston, South Carolina, saw a white man brutally shoot and kill nine members in a historical Black church for what has been deemed a hate crime. Right wing terrorism is just as fatal for African Americans as mass killings have been for typical white America. The ideological attributes contributed to political conservatism, right wingers, have linked fear of terrorism to increase avoidance behavior and information seeking (Nellis, 2009) and amplified fear (Wilcox et al., 2006). Such political affiliations have also been associated with terroristic attitudes, as engendered in Western countries, including the United States, Canada, Australia, and Europe. Terroristic acts have not only been attributed to right wingers, racists, and nationalists but also to Islamic terrorists operating in Western countries. Nevertheless, white supremist individuals, who adhere to a range of ideologies, including White racial superiority, anti-abortion extremists and social dominance orientation (Graham et al., 2012) in contemporary times, exhibit the image of terrorism, which includes environmentalist and Islamist extremists, as normative political undertones. In short, given the recent lethal attacks, which include 2009 shooting at Ft. Hood in Killeen, Texas, Colorado, and Louisiana movie shootings, to 2015 San Bernadino and South Carolina church shootings, it is important to understand those factors that motivate such behavior. What contributes to the evolution of an individual crossing the line into "terrorism" is when the young person becomes involved in a group and becomes "a different person"

(Goodwin et al., 2005). While understanding the motivation for engaging in terroristic acts is important, it is beyond the scope of this discussion. More importantly is the need to understand what may impact our fear of terrorism.

Fear of Terrorism

Fear of terrorism can arrest a society and have debilitating effects on psychosocial atmosphere. While the chances of becoming a victim of a terrorist attack are very low, psychosocial strain and unrealistic biases can increase risk perceptions (Kowoll, 2012). Researchers have investigated reactions to the fear of terrorism (Lerner et al., 2003) and acknowledge its need in its determinants. Terrorism is a value and politically laden concept. As is generally noted, one person's terrorist is another person's freedom fighter. Today's terrorists can become tomorrow's heroes, respected statesmen or women, and heads of governments. Many, therefore, perceive terrorism as a violent act, with political ramifications undertaken to protect or advance group ideological, religious, social, or political interests, as against ordinary crimes undertaken by individuals or group of individuals for economic or personal aggrandizement. Another disturbing trend is that terrorism is increasingly viewed as having a religious character (White, 2011). Marshall (2007, p. 373) observed that the "proportion of known terrorist organizations claiming a religious identity has increased sharply in the last two decades, and the use of religious language to describe their deeds is commonplace." Hudson (1999, p. 9) states that "unlike the average political or social terrorist, who has a defined mission that is somewhat measurable in terms of media attention or government reaction, the religious terrorist can justify most heinous acts, in the name of 'God, Jesus Christ or Allah' for example." Researchers Sinclair and LoCicero (2006) have developed a questionnaire utilizing eight main constructs that they suggest will aid in differentiating the different perceptions of terrorism. The eight constructs included are (1) extent to which people think they will be a target of a future terrorist attack; (2) fear/worry about another terrorist attack; (3) personal impact when terror alerts are issued by the government; (4) feelings of anger toward terrorism and less tolerant of others from different cultural backgrounds; (5) desire to understand the reasons for terrorism; (6) faith in the government to protect them from terrorism; (7) perception of terrorist as being mental illness; and (8) skillfully capacity of carrying out such threats (Sinclair & LoCicero, 2006).

The IET may allow for more accurate examination of perception of terrorism, as it requires one to examine their emotional response to acts of terrorism, which may impact their level of fear and its deterministic view in relation to group self. The current study will examine specific cognitive traits of moralistic views in relation to the perception of terrorism. Since certain emotional reactions can be dictated by specific group membership (Seger et al., 2009), the question is how does our moral foundations inform our emotional response?

Moral Foundation

The establishment of moral values and character was first established by Kohlberg (1969) with his moral psychology theory. Expanding on Piaget's (1965) work, moral development is culturally bound and motivated by onward flowing progression of cognitive development of justice (Graham et al., 2012). The deficiencies of Kohlberg's moral development theory as challenged by Gilligan (1982) revealed gender differences in that girls matured from an ethic of care and an ethic of justice (Kohlberg et al., 1983). Other developmental theorist (Turiel, 1983) accounted for more widely acceptable description for moral development as "prescriptive judgments of justice, rights, and welfare pertaining to how people ought to relate to each other." Overall, morality should be seen as interpersonal way of relating to respect and protection between individuals (Graham et al., 2012; Gilligan, 1982; Kohlberg, 1969; Turiel, 1983).

As with all theories, the question of culture brings to light ontological foundation inherent within the theory. For instance, it has been argued that current cognitive-developmental theories reflect traditional secular Western societal views (Shweder, 1990). Researchers Shweder et al. (1997) revealed how culture determined moral structure through ethos of harm, human rights, and fairness protecting autonomous individuals; the ethos of community as sense of duty, admiration, and loyalty, as determined by organizations and social order; and the ethos of spirituality, as governed by the notions of sacredness and wholesomeness; and transgressions, as defined by ontological principles of being (Graham et al., 2012).

While morality may be directly related to culture, the challenge to offer universal explanation remains (Schwartz & Bilsky, 1990). While Brown (1991) presented an inventory of human imperatives within moral psychology. Haidt (2007, 2012) has begun to formulate his moral foundations theory (MFT). Haidt (2007, 2012) purports that the humans are prepared to learn values, norms, and behaviors in accordance to a diverse set of circumstances. His nativists view sees the human mind as an innate organism designed in advance of experience and shaped by its adaptive ability due to evolution. Haidt (2007, 2012) described moral foundation as composed of five factors: (1) harm/care, which is the ability that individuals possess to have compassion toward others; (2) fairness/reciprocity, related to reciprocal altruism; (3) ingroup/loyalty, the loyalty of individuals to their inner group and the mistrust they have of other group members; (4) authority/respect, the respect for leadership; and (5) purity/sanctity, the holding on to traditions. Haidt's (2007) theory on moral foundation has been established and examined.

Initial research has demonstrated differentiation on political ideology between liberals and conservatives, as determined by dogmatic viewpoints. Aforementioned political and ideological views have been identified as precursor to overt beliefs of terroristic ideations. Graham and colleagues (2011) revealed that conservatives more likely than not valued power, faithfulness, and sacredness, whereas liberals constantly valued concern and equality. Additionally, political orientation establishes nationwide and cultural contexts, informing trend, and degree. While African Americans have been classically conditioned to display racial political ideological stance on non-violent principles, the social justice system has not awarded this population the belief that equal justice exists, whether republican or democratic affiliation. Haidt (2007) describes his research on moral foundation to be both a cultural-psychological theory and a nativist theory—innate means organized in advance of experience—in supporting his findings that morals change based on culture, social structure, and how adults within the culture inculcate these morals into their children (Haidt & Graham, 2007). While the novelty of this research examining views of moral foundation has been captured as a cultural phenomenon, African Americans ideals of moral foundation have not been captured.

Comprehensive Justice

African Americans have unique experience when it comes to their sociopolitical status and identity. While recent history would classify that most African Americans take on democratic political stance, large numbers of African Americans continue to adhere to very conservative values. This identity conflict and variability in political ideology have grave impact on group-centered policy agendas and have not come without African Americans understanding their place in society. As within all societies, there is a system of justification that forms the basic interplay between those in society and how society influences views of justice on particular groups of people. For instance, comprehensive justice can be seen as either traditional forms of being or taking a less progressive stance for our existence. To understand this difference is to recognize the contrasting points of view of man's existence in the world and his society. *Progressives* tend to take on the tabula rasa view that man comes into this world as a blank slate. Man is then required to create the values that, whatever society sets for it, will bring about desired goals for the people it serves. For progressives, individual advantages are more important than equality, care, and total liberation (Kalb, 2014). The axiom for progressives is to question everything, rebel against authority, and liberate one's self from societal uncertainty. Whereas, traditionalists see morality in society as normal and natural way of our existence, not entirely man-made (Kalb, 2014). Man is a social being. Interpersonal relating forms the fabric of society and morality in order to assist him in being who he truly is. Much like Ubuntu, "I am human due to other's humanity" (Wilson & Williams, 2013). Man comes into the world with goodness, and the world is seen as productively good, and to act socially and morally is to realize one's own nature, being human, by interaction and judgment. So, the loyalty and authority that create a social world and make us part of it are natural to man and necessary for a good life. Increased disparities in the criminal justice system in the United States continue to be influenced by conservative opinion (Luttig 2013; Trump & White, 2015). For African Americans, this system of justice is at best acrimonious, engendering variability in sociopolitical attitudes.

One framework to evaluate comprehensive justice is that of the SJT. System justification is defined as "the psychological process by which existing social arrangements are legitimized, even at the expense of personal and group interest" (Jost & Banaji, 1994, p. 2). This process originates in a psychological need to believe that social arrangements, including one's social system at large, are fair and justified. For instance, history has captured that African Americans face insurmountable odds in dealing with the criminal justice system. The SJT (Jost & Banaji, 1994, Jost et al., 2004) offers a vital construction for an indulgent view of comprehensive justice. The end goal is the management of uncertainty, psychological threats real or imagined, and interpersonal coordination of relationships (Kowoll, 2012). While SJT helps to explain socioeconomic and political identification, it also gives meaning to the rise of Black Lives Matter movement due to the number of killings of unarmed Black males and the lack of criminal charges/indictments of those who kill. For instance, while African Americans face insurmountable odds in dealing with the criminal justice system, they are often required to engage in cognitive dissonance when dealing with unequal protection societal laws. This contraindicates progressive views in that all men are not treated equally. In addition, their ideological political views are often challenged when the system operates from White racial superiority and institutional discrimination. This often results in African Americans having to engage in ideological dissonance, resulting in various psychological outcomes. Perhaps when African Americans have strong Black identity consciousness, they are more likely to endorse reform, traditionalist views, and garner the psychological need to assist disadvantage and negative association with system justification. More importantly, based on the limited literature on the SJT, this theory informs the explanation of comprehensive justice for African Americans sociopolitical attitudes. One can suspect that Blacks may endorse more comprehensive view of justice that is reflective of their unique status and beliefs about how their racial group has been politicized and exploited within the United States. In every nation, society establishes itself based on its take of traditional or progressive views.

Methodology

Sample

Participants consisted of $N = 323$ undergraduates college students; 18% males ($n = 58$) and 79% females ($n = 254$), attending a Southwestern university. Current academic classification consists of freshman = 23.5%, sophomore = 27.6%, juniors = 16.1%, seniors = 23.2%, 5-plus years = 6.2%, and not classified = 3.4%.

Thirteen (4%) were identified as international students and 296 (91.6%) non-international students. Political affiliation for this sample consisted of 72.9% (*n* = 231) identified as democrat, 6% (*n* = 19) as republican, 16% (*n* = 51) as other, and 5% (*n* = 16) did not indicate their political affiliation. The sample largely fell between middle-class and lower-middle-class range, with 74% of the sample falling below $74,000. Majority of participants classified as protestant (e.g., Baptist, Presbyterian, Methodist, Nondenominational, Holiness, and Pentecostal) = 51.7%, and other Christian = 23.5%.

Measures

Demographic questionnaire: A demographic questionnaire was created for the current study and administered to each participant. The measure is composed of eight items that obtained information pertaining to the participants' gender, classification, annual income, ethnicity, and political and religious affiliation. Participants' income was assessed in close-ended format in which participants chose the most accurate estimate of their annual income. Responses were coded as 1 = under $10,000, 2 = $10,000 to $29,000, 3 = $30,000 to $74,000, 4 = $75,000 to $149,000, 5 = $150,000 to $249,000, 6 = $250,000 and above, and 7 = don't know. Education was assessed by asking participants to identify number of years in college. This demographic questionnaire is not a standardized measure; it was created for the current study.

The Moral Foundations Questionnaire (MFQ; Graham et al., 2009): It is a 30-item questionnaire that examines participants' conceptions of moral judgment/ reasoning and seeks to understand how varying patterns of intuition underlie human morality. Specifically, this measure assessed the five foundations of moral intuition that exist across cultures and emerged in human evolution to regulate group life, harm/care, fairness/reciprocity, in-group/loyalty, authority/respect, and purity/sanctity. Two of these foundations have been labeled the individualizing foundations: harm/care and fairness/equality. Harm/care refers to the protection of individuals, while fairness/equality refers to broader concerns about justice, and three of these foundations are considered the binding foundations: in-group/ loyalty, authority/respect, and purity/sanctity in their approach to morality (Graham et al., 2009). The MFQ is divided into two parts: part 1—*moral relevance* (15 items) and part 2—*moral judgments* (11 items). For part 1, participants respond to items using a seven-point Likert response format, ranging from 1 = not at all important, 2 = very unimportant, 3 = somewhat unimportant, 4 = neither important or unimportant, 5 = somewhat important, 6 = very important, and 7 = extremely important. Example question, "*Whether or not someone suffered emotionally.*" For part 2, participants respond to items using a six-point Likert response format, ranging from 1 = strongly disagree, 2 = moderately disagree, 3 = slightly disagree, 4 = slightly agree, 5 = moderately agree, and 6 = strongly agree. Example question, "*Compassion for those who are suffering is the most crucial virtue.*"

Ideally, with the use of published scales, it is not considered wise practice to arbitrarily change the response format or the set of questions, as this may throw some doubt on the psychometric properties and could further strain the comparison with other studies. However, for purposes of this study, we used two existing subtests with different scale systems, adapted to fit a 7-point Likert scale for part 1 (individualizing foundations) and 6-point Likert scale for part 2 (binding foundations). After the scale change and standardization of scale scores, the internal consistency for individualizing foundations' total subscale in the current sample was excellent (α = 0.943). The internal consistency for binding foundations' total subscale in the current sample was good (α = 0.852). Combined internal consistency for this study was excellent (α = 0.943).

Comprehensive Justice Survey (Haidt, Darley, & Gromet, unpublished manuscript): It is a 28-item Likert-format questionnaire (1 = strongly agree to 6 = strongly disagree) that measures attitudes toward crime and punishment on whether someone takes a more traditional standpoint versus a progressive alternative to punishment. Example item, "The legal system should try to do more to help the victims of crime find closure and satisfaction." Possible scores range from 21 to 147. The Comprehensive Justice Survey was utilized in the current study and demonstrated excellent internal consistency within the study sample (α = 0.96).

Perception of Terrorism Questionnaire–Short Form (PTQ-SF; Sinclair & LoCicero, 2006): It is a 25-item measure that assesses an individual's perception of and reaction to terroristic act. Items ask respondents to give his or opinion as to why people become terrorists, why are certain groups targets of terrorism, and what type of terroristic behavior is most feared. Participants respond to items using a 6-point Likert scale, ranging from 1 = not at all to 6 = extremely. The PTQ-SF identifies eight constructs: (1) perceptions of terrorists as having mental illness, (2) terrorists being skilled at or possibly carrying out further attacks, (3) the impact of terror alerts, (4) anger or lack of tolerance toward others from a varied cultural background due to acts of terrorism, (5) the perceived threat that terrorism poses, (6) a desire to understand terrorism rationales, (7) faith in the government to protect its citizens from further attacks, and (8) the extent to which an individual believes he or she will be the victim of possible terror attacks (Sinclair & LoCicero, 2006). For each construct or subscale, scores are derived by transforming raw scores to a 0–100 metric score; higher values suggest "greater degree of the construct" (p. 19). The Perception of Terrorism Questionnaire–Short Form was utilized in the current study, and it demonstrated good internal consistency within the study sample (α = 0.865).

Procedures

Students were recruited from various departments within the university by contacting department heads and faculty, primarily in the College of Arts and Science and College of Criminal Justice and Psychology. Information letters along with flyers were distributed, announcing the study and providing a link to complete the survey online via Qualtrics. Online surveys included an information sheet that identified the nature of the study, limits to confidentiality, and contact information for the principal investigators. On completion of the study, participants were provided with a reference sheet with the contact information to the on-campus counseling services as well as mental health clinics in the surrounding area of each campus.

Students were also given the option to complete paper-and-pencil versions of the survey, facilitated by a graduate research assistant. On receiving consent, each participant was given a survey packet that included measures of moral foundation, perceptions of terrorism, and comprehensive justice. Once data was collected, it was entered into SPSS without any personal identifiable markers.

Data Analysis

Associations among demographic variables, moral foundation, comprehensive justice, and perception of terrorism were determined by Pearson correlation analysis to examine the relationships among harm/care, fairness/reciprocity, ingroup/loyalty, authority/respect, and purity/sanctity to target, fear/worry, alerts, anger, tolerance, faith, mental illness, and skillfulness, with a 95% confidence interval (CI). Internal consistency among all scales was examined by Cronbach's alpha statistic. The t test analyses were conducted to compare mean scores between gender. Analysis of variance was conducted to examine variant effect of moral foundation subscales and comprehensive justice (traditional and progressive) on perception of terrorism.

Results

Descriptive Statistics and Bivariate Pearson Correlations

Descriptive statistics are presented in Tables 8.1 and 8.2.

Given the breath of literature, there was no suggestion of gender effects on moral foundation, comprehensive justice, and perception of terrorism; descriptive statistics were compared between males and females in the current study. While male participants tended to endorse less terroristic perceptions (fear/worry, alerts, target, faith, mental illness, and skillfulness) and comprehensive justice, they endorsed greater moral foundation scores (harm/care, fairness, ingroup/loyalty, authority, purity, traditional, and progressive) than females in the current study. Independent sample t tests revealed significant differences between the genders on comprehensive justice and perceptions of terrorism (fear/worry, alertness, and skillfulness). Overall, participants' scores were inconsistent with previous literature. For example, the mean harm/care scores in the current study were inverse, with males having higher mean scores ($M = 64.1$, $SD = 35.1$) than females ($M = 63.2$, $SD = 35.8$). This is intriguing, since more women are perceived as being more intuitive due to their child-raising skills to

TABLE 8.1 Correlations

	Comprehensive justice	Moral foundation	3	4	5	6	7	8	9	10
1. Perception of terrorism	0.464*	0.231*	—							
2. Fear/worry	0.448*	0.487*	0.627*	—						
3. Alert	0.570*	0.159*	0.727*	0.653*	—					
4. Anger tolerance	0.465*	0.566*	0.528*	0.822*	0.577*	—				
5. Target	0.522*	0.191*	0.720*	0.578*	0.823*	0.555*	—			
6. Faith	0.509*	0.247*	0.715*	0.606*	0.782*	0.634*	0.720*	—		
7. Mentally ill	0.539*	0.180*	0.756*	0.593*	0.828*	0.586*	0.781*	0.816*	—	
8. Skillfulness	0.465*	0.146*	0.632*	0.532*	0.743*	0.494*	0.685*	0.701*	0.785*	—

* Correlation is significant at the 0.01 level (two-tailed).

TABLE 8.2 Significant univariate effects for fairness and ideological justice

Source	Dependent variable	Type III sum of squares	Df	Mean square	F	Significance
FairnessR	Target	91.100	2	45.550	4.676	0.010
HiLoTraditional	Fear/worry	608.322	1	608.322	3.753	0.054
	Alert	111.043	1	111.043	4.384	0.038
	Anger tolerance	584.854	1	584.854	4.108	0.044
HiLoProgressive	Faith	86.083	1	86.083	8.195	0.005
	Mentally ill	192.227	1	192.227	4.612	0.033
	Skillfulness	53.853	1	53.853	4.293	0.040

detect signs of suffering, distress, or neediness (Graham et al., 2012). In addition, when political affiliation was controlled for participants, scores were consistent with previous literature. For example, those who identified as republican had lower mean scores for overall moral foundation ($M = 372.5$, $SD = 30.1$) than those identified as democratic ($M = 380.0$, $SD = 21.3$), and for perception of terrorist as skill, republican ($M = 8.1$, $SD = 2.56$) versus democratic ($M = 8.5$, $SD = 2.37$). Since politics inform perception, the beliefs about conservatives valuing care and fairness are consistent with prior research. It is safe to say that it can be predicted when participants self-report their political ideology; their implicit political identities will reveal their moral foundation-related judgments.

Independent-sample t tests were conducted to compare means for moral foundation, comprehensive justice, and perception of terrorism between males and females and political affiliation. There was significant difference in mean scores for comprehensive justice for males ($M = 33.4$, $SD = 10.9$) and females ($M = 36.8$, $SD = 8.4$); $t(239) = -2.97$, $p < 0.05$; and political affiliation, republicans ($M = 41.2$, $SD = 6.4$) and democrats ($M = 36.2$, $SD = 8.7$); $t(189) = 2.05$, $p < 0.05$. There was also a significant difference in mean scores for fear/worry between males' ($M = 23.9$, $SD = 6.9$) and females' ($M = 27.6$, $SD = 5.2$) conditions; $t(168) = -2.7$, $p < 0.01$. This pattern continues in that significant difference in mean scores occurred on being alert to perception of terrorism for males' ($M = 9.6$, $SD = 3.5$) and for females' ($M = 10.9$, $SD = 3.9$) conditions; $t(224) = -1.95$, $p = 0.05$. Lastly, there was a significant difference in mean scores on perception of terrorists as being skillful, for males' ($M = 7.89$, $SD = 2.41$) and females' ($M = 8.74$, $SD = 2.39$) conditions; $t(323) = -2.2$, $p < 0.05$.

Different patterns emerged for political affiliation. There was significant difference in mean scores for perception of being targeted for republicans ($M = 8.1$, $SD = 2.3$) and democrats ($M = 6.5$, $SD = 2.4$); $t(177) = 2.44$, $p < 0.05$. Also, significant difference in mean scores was identified for perception of fear by political affiliation, for republicans ($M = 8.6$, $SD = 1.8$) and democrats ($M = 7.30$,

$SD = 2.78$); $t(175) = 2.05$, $p < 0.05$. The t test analyses reveal significant differences on psychosocial variables gender and political affiliation, indicating that female had higher scores for perception of terrorism and overall comprehensive justice than males; for political affiliation, republicans had higher overall comprehensive justice and perceived threat that terrorism poses and faith in the government to protect its citizens from further attacks. Results counter previous research on gender differences but remain similar on political affiliation. The typical conservatives endorse loyalty, authority, and sanctity, and the typical liberals endorse Care and Fairness.

In examining the first hypothesis, there will be a relationship among moral foundation, comprehensive justice, and perceptions of terrorism. Pearson product correlation analysis was conducted. Consistent with the pattern of results in the literature, Table 8.3 shows significant relationship between perception of terroristic behaviors, ideological justice, and moral foundation. A positive significant correlation occurred between comprehensive justice and moral foundation. In addition, correlation analyses reveal significant associations among *comprehensive justice, moral foundations,* fear, alert, anger, target, mental illness, and skillfulness.

To test the second hypothesis, different aspects of terroristic perceptions (target, fear/worry, alerts, anger, faith, mental illness, and skillfulness) will be impacted by dimensions of moral foundation and comprehensive justice; a multivariate analysis of variance (MANOVA) was conducted. Comprehensive justice and morality dimensions were entered into a MANOVA with the dependent variables of terroristic perceptions. Significant univariate effects were found on six dependent-variable scales and three independent-variable subscales (Table 8.4).

Pairwise comparisons showed that for the scale of feeling targeted, those with lower levels of fairness had significantly higher scores than those with higher level of fairness (Table 8.4). On the scales of fear/worry, alerts, and anger, those with lower traditional scores had lower mean scores than those with higher level of traditional beliefs (Table 8.5). On the subscales of faith, mental illness, and skillfulness, those lower in progressive thinking had lower means scores than higher progressives. Overall, the MANOVA showed variant

TABLE 8.3 Fairness

Dependent variable	FairnessR	Mean	Standard error	95% confidence interval	
				Lower bound	Upper bound
Feeling target	1.00	6.556	0.666	5.241	7.870
	2.00	5.446	0.249	4.954	5.938

TABLE 8.4 Traditional

			Standard	95% confidence interval	
Dependent variable	HiLo Traditional	Mean	error	Lower bound	Upper bound
Dimension0 Fear/	Dimension1 1.00	18.562	2.763	13.112	24.012
worry	2.00	22.183	2.970	16.324	28.042
Alert	Dimension1 1.00	7.833	1.092	5.678	9.987
	2.00	9.380	1.174	7.063	11.696
Anger	Dimension1 1.00	21.784	2.589	16.676	26.892
tolerance	2.00	25.335	2.784	19.843	30.826

TABLE 8.5 Progressive

			Standard	95% confidence interval	
Dependent variable	HiLoProgressive	Mean	error	Lower bound	Upper bound
Faith	Dimension1 1.00	5.189	0.708	3.791	6.586
	2.00	6.635	0.761	5.134	8.136
Mentally ill	Dimension1 1.00	10.301	1.411	7.518	13.084
	2.00	12.462	1.516	9.472	15.453
Skillfulness	Dimension1 1.00	6.165	0.774	4.639	7.692
	2.00	7.309	0.832	5.669	8.950

effect of moral foundation (fairness/reciprocity) and comprehensive justice (traditional and progressive) as significant in perception of terrorism. The variables moral foundations and political ideology have implications for how people perceive and make judgments about the perception of terrorism.

Discussion

The current study investigated the relationships between moral foundation, comprehensive justice, and perception of terrorism in a sample of African American college students. Results suggest that African Americans' perception of terrorism may be associated with their attitude toward justice beliefs and issues of morality. Similar to previous studies, researchers' (Haidt, 2012) examination of the role between morality and emotion showed care/harm or justice impacted judgment but not disgust. While comprehensive justice measures attitudes toward crime and punishment for this research, latent factors embedded within ideological view of justice were related to taking a more *traditional stance* on crime versus *progressive* alternative view to punishment. With regard to morality, varying patterns endemic to underlying human mores may center around five moral clauses that may exist across cultures. Two of these foundations are seen as *harm/care*, which refers to the protection of individuals, while *fairness/equality* refers to broader concerns about justice. The axiom is that nothing happens outside culture; nobody doubts that cultural learning is a part of moral development. One would suspect that for African Americans, their attitudes about equal protection under the law are beliefs that they hold due to their cultural ontological self "survival for the group" as American citizens. This study advances the line of inquiry by examining the psychological effects that terrorism has on young African American population and determines whether different morality types and ideological justice influence their perception of terroristic behavior. While Kohlberg's (1969) "conventional" moral judgment has been evaluated varying by culture, Turiel (1983) argues the universality of morality development. Both theories find support for intergroup emotion theory, alleging that morality can be identified from social interactions with others, aided by the process of political affiliation.

Hypothesis one was supported in that there was significant positive correlation among intrinsic mores, ideological justice, and perception of terroristic behaviors. In line with previous research, conservatives who endorse all facets within moral foundation would be expected to have increase association with traditional justice. Previous research by Inbar, Pizarro, Iyer, and Haidt (2012) showed that self-identified conservatives, both in the United States and around the world, reported greater propensity toward feeling contamination disgust and that disgust sensitivity predicted voting patterns in the United States. Interestingly, Jarudi (2009) found that conservatives were more sensitive to purity concerns about sex but not about food (harm/care). African Americans have been known to adhere to conservative standards, particularly those in the South. The pattern of positive associations occurred among all scales. Thus, indicating that those who demonstrated greater moral affiliation and traditionalist views of justice had higher perceptions of terroristic threats and group solidarity.

Do the relations between moral foundations and political ideology have implications for how people perceive and make judgments about groups and individuals? Do people recognize the moral differences between liberals and conservatives? Do liberal and conservative moral profiles predict what characteristics they will view favorably in others? Hypothesis two was partially supported in that there appears to be particular pathways toward understanding of psychological impacts of terrorism. For instance, perception may be influenced by individualized, binding moral values and traditionalist views, versus progressive justice. In contrast to previous research on conservatives adoption of all five moral foundations of fairness/reciprocity, harm/care, ingroup/loyalty, authority/respect, and purity/sanctity in their approach to morality, this research demonstrated that, for this African American population, only fairness and reciprocity had a main effect on

the psychological impact of terrorism. Haidt (2012) suggest that moral foundation may have overestimated the role of cultural learning and downplayed self-
consciousness for care and fairness. Perhaps this may be due to the high number of
participants who identified their political affiliation as more democratic or liberal.
It has often been said that politics is perception. Do the relations between moral
foundations and political ideology have implications for how people perceive and
make judgments about groups and individuals? Liberals tend to be primarily concerned with the two *individualizing* morality constructs, placing greater emphasis
on fairness/equality and harm/care, and this may contextualize their feeling less
targeted by acts of terrorism. In prior research, Tamborini et al. (2012) indicated
that those with increased care scores also had higher perceptions of more graphic
violence as less appealing. It can also be said that traditionalist view, in this case
more conservative standpoint of justice, would place greater emphasis on group-
related psychosocial terroristic acts. It was revealed that those with higher traditionalist views had higher scores on fear of future attacks, alerts, anger, or lack of
tolerance. This is similar to the research by Lerner et al. (2003) in that emotional
responses to acts of terrorism are frequently disproportionate to the concrete
risk, and it is much more common for men to respond with anger, while women
display more fear to such events. However, those who were more progressive had
higher perceptions of terrorists as having mental illness, being skilled at carrying
out attacks, and faith in the government to protect its citizens. One acceptable
critic to the MFT by Janoff-Bulman and Carnes' (2013) inclusion of different
contexts (intrapersonal, interpersonal, intragroup, and even intergroup) echoes the
critique by Rai and Fiske (2010) that the MFT doesn't pay enough attention to
relational context. Perhaps gender differences among participants impacted psychological perceptions of terrorist acts. Since females tend to assess risk estimates
at higher rates than males, similar patterns appeared for risks within this population of African Americans (e.g., concern for mental capacity, capable of carrying
out attacks, and reliance in the government to protect its citizens). The gender patterns make sense in light of previous research on moral foundation, that is, harm,
fairness, and purity, with greater endorsement by females. Females are more likely
to demonstrate greater egalitarianism (Arts & Gelissen, 2001), empathy (Davis,
1983), and disdain (Druschel & Sherman, 1999). Gilligan (1982) argued that the
morality of girls and women did not follow Kohlberg's one true path but developed along *two* paths: an ethic of justice and also an ethic of care that could not be
derived from the former. Thus, greater critic and inquiry on the psychological
impact of terrorism would allow us to find and describe difference in personality
formation toward participating in terrorist act that was not possible before.

Lastly, given that this sample consisted of mostly African Americans differences in foundational morality, comprehensive justice and perception of terrorism may vary from the extent of research conducted. Since psychocultural and
social political forces have impacted the current state and conditions of African
Americans, these results must be carefully examined. While some may think

that one can move beyond politics, the internalization of sociopolitical forces may undoubtedly affect this group's ideation of equal justice and collective experience of terrorist acts by the very government designed to protect them. This begs the question, what are the differences in moral foundation, comprehensive justice, and perception of terrorism by race in the United States?

Limitations

This limitation in this research cannot answer this question. The sample chosen for this research was that of a convenient sample, mostly consisting of a younger African American population that may not stay up on current trends in the news. In addition, this sample may have limited participation in politics and carry out acts of justice. Haidt (2007) expressed that "While research may demonstrate slight differences between Eastern and Western cultures the small effect sizes for all the East-West differences suggest that variation within cultures (e.g., by gender or political ideology) will exceed the East-West variations given so much attention in cross-cultural research." In fact, the marginalization of this political group has been traumatic and continues to be challenged by multiple forces, such that only when one becomes conscious of their political, cultural, and gender-specific identify will they begin to critically examine their morals and beliefs about justice and terrorism.

Shweder et al. (1997) projected that throughout the world, we live by tripart of ethics: protection of autonomous individuals, preservation of social order and organization, and divinity or supreme guidance. Future research should examine these constructs in relation to cultural values and other psychosocial variables that may impact the degree to which we truly evaluate psychological impact of terrorism. Turiel's (1983) definition of moral province refers to "prescriptive judgments of justice, rights, and welfare pertaining to how people ought to relate to each other." In the end, Kohlberg (1969), Gilligan (1982), and Turiel (1983) all view that morality is concerned with interpersonal relationships, safe from harm, and deference to other persons. More importantly, what are the psychological predictors of one's participation in terroristic acts, while the impact of terror exist in others from varied cultural backgrounds and their perceived threat to terrorism poses, a desire to understand terrorism rationales, and faith in the government to protect its citizens from further attacks.

> While those who identified, when asked, to describe in detail the nature and development of their own religious and moral beliefs, conservatives and liberals engaged in dramatically different forms of moral discourse. Whereas conservatives spoke in moving terms about respecting authority and order, showing deep loyalty to family and country and working hard to keep the self pure and good, liberals invested just as much emotion in describing their commitments to relieve the suffering of others and their concerns for fairness, justice, and equality. (McAdams et al., 2008, p. 987)

Future Implications

There are several implications emanating from this research. First, the examination of how African Americans view terrorism is paramount. When we examine the Maafa experience, systematic destruction of a people, we will undoubtedly recognize the psychological effects on their psyche, even within evolutionary psychology. In fact, seminal works of Akbar (1991) and Azibo (1990) have begun to recognize and acknowledge specific psychological disorders as a result of the Maafa experience. Second, the examination of moral foundation and political affiliation for African Americans remain non-existent in research. While it remains unclear and oftentimes conflicted when examining moral values for this population, the thrust and paradigm continue to remain the same—the use of white racial framing perspective (Williams & Wilson, 2016). Black psychology's investigation of the theories presented in this study (the IET, SJT, and MFT) warrants a sense of humanity to the population studied in this research. Lastly, while this research attempted to conduct such research, further layer of cultural examination should be conducted—specifically, how do cultural values, African narratives, and African episteme shape, harness, and guide people of African descent in relation to moral foundation, comprehensive justice, and fear of terrorism.

References

Ajzen, I. (1985). From intentions to action: A theory of planned behavior. In J. Huhl & J. Beckman (Eds.), *Will; performance; control (psychology); motivation (psychology)* (pp. 11–39). New York, NY: Springer-Verlag.

Akbar, N. (1991). Mental disorder among African Americans. In Jones, Reginald L. (Ed.), *Black psychology* (pp. 339–352). Berkeley, CA: Cobb & Henry Publishers, 794.

Arts, W., & Gelissen, J. (2001). Welfare States, Solidarity and Justice Principles: Does the Type Really Matter? *Acta Sociologica, 44*, pp. 283. Retrieved March 2017, from https://doi.org/10.1080/00016990152696385.

Azibo, D. A. (1990). Advances in Black/African personality theory. *Imhotep: An Afrocentric Review, 2*(1), 22–47.

Brown, D. (1991). *Human universals*. San Francisco, CA: McGraw-Hill.

Davis, M. H. (1983). Measuring Individual Differences in Empathy: Evidence for a Multidimensional Approach. *Journal of Personality and Social Psychology, 44*, 113–126. Retrieved March 2017, from http://dx.doi.org/10.1037/0022-3514.44.1.113.

Department of Defense Dictionary of Military and Associated Terms. (2010). Joint Publication 1-02 (As Amended Through 15 February 2016).

Druschel, B. A., & Sherman, M. F. (1999). Disgust sensitivity as a function of the Big Five and gender. *Personality and Individual Differences, 26*, 739–748.

Gilligan, C. (1982). *In a different voice: Psychological theory and women's development*. Cambridge, MA: Harvard University Press.

Goodwin, R., Willson, M., & Gaines, S. (2005). Terror threat perception and its consequences in contemporary Britain. *British Journal of Psychology*, 1–19. Retrieved December 18, 2015, from http://www.brunel.ac.uk/~hsstrbg/BJP%20terror%20proofs.pdf.

Graham, J., Haidt, J., & Nosek, B. (2009). Liberals and conservatives use different sets of moral foundations. *Journal of Personality and Social Psychology, 96,* 1029–1046.

Graham, J., Haidt, J., Koleva, S., Motyl, M., Iyer, R., Wojcik, S. P., & Ditto, P. H. (2012). Moral foundations theory: The pragmatic validity of moral pluralism. *Advances in Experimental Social Psychology.* Retrieved March 13, 2016, from correction submitted https://www.sciencedirect.com/science/article/pii/B9780124072367000024?via%3Dihub.

Graham, J., Nosek, B. A., Haidt, J., Koleva, S., Iyer, R., & Ditto, P. H. (2011). Mapping the moral domain. *Journal of Personality and Social Psychology, 101*(2), 366–385. doi:10.1037/a0021847

Greenberg, J., Solomon, S., & Pyszczynski, T. (1997). Terror management theory of self-esteem and social behavior: Empirical assessments and conceptual refinements. In M. P. Zanna (Ed.), *Advances in experimental social psychology* (Vol. 29, pp. 61–139). New York, NY: Academic Press.

Grunig, J. E. (Ed.) (1992). *Excellence in public relations and communication management.* Hillsdale, NJ: Lawrence Erlbaum.

Haidt, J. (2007). The new synthesis in moral psychology. *Science, 316*(5827), 998–1002. doi:10.1126/science.1137651.

Haidt, J. (2012). *The righteous mind: Why good people are divided by politics and religion.* New York, NY: Pantheon. RighteousMind.com.

Haidt, J., & Graham, J. (2007). When morality opposes justice: Conservatives have moral intuitions that liberals may not recognize. *Social Justice Research, 20*(1), 98–116.

Huddy, L., Feldman, S., Taber, C., & Lahav, G. (2005). Threat, anxiety, and support of antiterrorism policies American. *Journal of Political Science, 49*(3), 593–608.

Hudson, R. A. (1999). *Who becomes a terrorist and why-The 1999 government report on profiling terrorists.* Guilford, CT: The Lyons Press.

Inbar, Y., Pizarro, D., Iyer, R., & Haidt, J. (2012). Disgust sensitivity, political conservatism, and voting. *Social Psychological and Personality Science, 3,* 537–544. doi:10.1177/1948550611429024

Janoff-Bulman, R., & Carnes, N. C. (2013). Surveying the moral landscape: Moral motives and group-based moralities. *Personality and Social Psychology Review, 17,* 219–236.

Jarudi, I. N. (2009). Everyday morality and the status quo: Conservative concerns about moral purity, moral evaluations of everyday objects, and moral objections to performance enhancement. Doctoral dissertation, Yale University.

Jost, J. T., Banaji, M. R., & Nosek, B. A. (2004). A decade of system justification theory: Accumulated evidence of conscious and unconscious bolstering of the status quo. *Political Psychology, 25*(6), 881–919.

Jost, J. T., & Banaji, M. R. (1994). The role of stereotyping in system-justification and the production of false consciousness. *British Journal of Social Psychology, 33,* 1–27.

Kalb, J. (2014). The moral divide between progressives and traditionalists. *Crisis Magazine.* Retrieved August 21, 2014, from http://www.crisismagazine.com/2014/moral-divide-progressives-traditionalists

Kohlberg, L. (1969). Stage and sequence: The cognitive development approach to socialization. In D. A. Goslin (Ed.), *Handbook of socialization theory* (pp. 347–480). Chicago, IL: Rand McNally.

Kohlberg, L., Levine, C., & Hewer, A. (1983). Moral stages: A current formulation and a response to critics. *Contributions to Human Development, 10,* 174.

Kowoll, S. L. (2012). Theorist meets terrorist: A reviewing examination of the impact of threat and efficacy beliefs on fear of terrorism. Retrieved from http://essay. utwente.nl/61607/1/Kowol l%2C_S.L._-_s0192260_%28verslag%29.pdf

Lee, J. E. C., & Lemyre, L. (2009). A social-cognitive perspective of terrorism risk perception and individual response in Canada. *Risk Analysis: An international Journal, 29*(9), 1265–1280.

Lerner, J. S., Gonzalez, R. M., Small, D. A., & Fischhoff, B. (2003). Effects of fear and anger on perceived risks of terrorism: A national field experiment, *Psychological Science, 14*(2), 144–150.

Luttig, M. (2013). The structure of inequality and Americans' attitudes toward redistribution. *Public Opinion Quarterly, 77*(3), 811–821.

Mackie, D. M., Smith, E. R., & Ray, D. G. (2008). Intergroup emotions and intergroup relations. *Social and Personality Psychology Compass, 2*(5), 1866–1880.

Major, A. M., & Atwood, L. E. (2004). Assessing the usefulness of the U.S. Department of homeland security's terrorism advisory system. *International Journal of Mass Emergencies and Disasters, 22*(2), 77–101.

Mapping Police Violence. (2016). Retrieved March 13, 2016, from http://mappingpoliceviolence.org/unarmed/

Marshall, G. J. (2007). Short communication half-century seasonal relationships between the Southern annular mode and antarctic temperatures. *International Journal of Climatology, 27*, 373–383.

McAdams, D. P., Albaugh, M., Farber, E., Daniels, J., Logan, R. L., & Olson, B. (2008). Family metaphors and moral intuitions: How conservatives and liberals narrate their lives. *Journal of Personality and Social Psychology, 95*(4), 978–990.

Miller, E., & Jensen, M. (2015). American Deaths in Terrorist Attacks.The National Consortium for the Study of Terrorism and Responses to Terrorism (START). Retrieved from https://www.start.umd.edu/pubs/START_AmericanTerrorismDeaths_FactSheet_Oct2015.pdf

Nellis, A. (2009). Gender differences in fear of terrorism. *Journal of Contemporary Criminal Justice 25*, 322–340.

Overberg, P., Upton, J., & Hoyer, M. (2013). Behind the bloodshed: The untold story of America's mass killings. *USA Today*, December 3, 2013. Retrieved March 13, 2015, from http://www.gannett-cdn.com/GDContent/mass-killings/index.html#title

Piaget, J. (1965). *Etudes sociologiques*. Geneva, Switzerland: Librairie Droz. (Note: my page indication refers to the Italian translation by Barbetta, 1989.)

Rai, T. S., & Fiske, A. P. (2010). Psychological studies are ODD (observation and description deprived). *Brain and Behavioral Sciences, 33*, 106–107.

Richman, J. A., Cloninger, L., & Rospenda, K. M. (2008). Macrolevel stressors, terrorism, and mental health outcomes: Broadening the stress paradigm. *American Journal Public Health, 98*(Suppl 1), S113–S119.

Rogers, R. W. (1975). A protection motivation theory of fear appeals and attitude change. *Journal of Psychology, 91*, 93–114.

Schwartz, S. H., & Bilsky, W. (1990). Toward a theory of the universal content and structure of values: Extensions and cross-cultural replications. *Journal of Personality and Social Psychology, 58*(5), 878–891. doi:10.1037/0022-3514.58.5.878

Seger, C. R., Smith, E. R., & Mackie, D. M. (2009). Subtle activation of a social categorization triggers group-level emotions. *Journal of Experimental Social Psychology, 45*, 460–467.

Shweder, R. A., Much, N. C., Mahapatra, M., & Park, L. (1997). The "big three" of morality (autonomy, community, and divinity), and the "big three" explanations of suffering. In A. Brandt & P. Rozin (Eds.), *Morality and health* (pp. 119–169). New York, NY: Routledge.

Shweder, R. A. (1990). In defense of moral realism: Reply to Gabennesch. *Child Development*, 6(61), 2060–2067.

Sinclair, S., & LoCicero, A. (2006). Development and psychometric testing of the perceptions of terrorism questionnaire short-form (ptq-sf). *The New School Psychology Bulletin*, 4(1), 8–43.

Tajfel, H., & Turner, J. C. (1986). The social identity theory of intergroup behavior. *Psychology of Intergroup Relations*, 5, 7–24.

Tamborini, R., Eden, A., Bowman, N. D., Grizzard, M., & Lachlan, K. A. (2012). The influence of morality subcultures on the acceptance and appeal of violence. *Journal of Communication*, 62(1), 136–157. doi:10.1111/j.1460-2466.2011.01620.x

Trump, K. S., & White, A. (2015). *Does inequality activate the system justification motivation?* Presented at the 2015 Aage Sorensen Memorial Conference. Retrieved March 17, 2016, from http://scholar.harvard.edu/files/arwhite/files/trump_white_inequalitysjt_ draftmay2015.pdf?

Turiel, E. (1983). The development of social knowledge: Morality and convention. Cambridge, UK: Cambridge University Press. Translated to Spanish and published by Editorial Debate, Madrid, Spain, 1984.

White, J. (2011). *Terrorism and homeland security* (7th ed.). Belmont, CA: Wadsworth.

Wilcox, P., May, D. C., & Roberts, S. D. (2006). Student weapon possession and the "fear of victimization hypothesis;" Unraveling the temporal order. *Justice Quarterly*, 23, 502–529.

Williams, V., & Wilson, D. (2016). White racial framing and its impact on African-American male mental health (in 2nd Volume of the African American Male series) *Counseling African American Males: Effective Therapeutic Interventions and Approaches*. (Ed. William Ross) Charlotte, NC: Information Age Publishing.

Wilson, D., & Williams, V. (2013). Ubuntu: A model of positive mental health for African Americans. *Psychology Journal*, 10(2), 80–100. Retrieved from www.psychologicalpublishing.com

Witte, K. (1992). Putting the fear back into fear appeals: The extended parallel process model. *Communication Monographs*, 59, 329–349. doi:10.1080/03637759209376276

9

AFRICANA PHILOSOPHY

A Preliminary Study of the Nature of Spirit and Soul

DaVonte Lyons

In the Africana world, the fundamental mode and basis of social and cultural reality are centered on a philosophy of spirit and soul. Traditional African societies identify spirit-soul as the organizing force and essence of phenomenal reality, which give meaning and dynamism to existence. Nonetheless, there are cosmological, ontological, epistemological, and axiological ideas that permeate throughout African tradition, illustrating concepts of beingness, space and time, morality, and ethics. All these ideas are motivated and sustained by a fundamental understanding of essence grounded in the notion of the oneness of being. Basically, the resolve of this paper is to analyze and fuse the various philosophical conceptions of the nature of spirit and soul, as they relate to monotheism, human beingness, and immortality.

Africana Philosophy

According to the Kemites, before the emergence of the known universe, there was the primordial Nun. The "Pyramid Text" states that Nun existed "before sky came into being, before earth came into being, before that which was to be established came into being, before fear inspired by the Eye of Horus came into being" (Obenga, 2004). Thus, Nun is essentially the absolute infinity, depicted as an ethereal fluid, indeterminate matter, containing unlimited possibilities. Even more, Nun was said to have existed before the creator; in effect, the prefiguration of creation, by the creator, would take place within Nun. Specifically, the "Papyrus Bremner Rhind" states that there I [Ptah/Ra] created the modes of being with the energy in me. There I created in Nun, while still drowsy, while I had yet to find ground on which to stand upright. But then in my heart was filled with energy the design of creation appeared before me, and I accomplished everything I wanted to do, being alone. Conceiving designs in my heart, I created a different mode of existence and multitudinous ways of being were born of the Existent. (Obenga, 2004)

Correspondingly, Ptah (Amon-Ra), realizing self, was the first to rise out of Nun and initiate the process of creation. Ptah, as stated in the "Papyrus Bremner Rhind," "conceived of creation in his heart then proceeded to create the multitudes of existence." In Kemetic tradition, the heart (ib) is considered to be the base of intellectual comprehension and/or soul (ba) (Obenga, 2004). Additionally, the ba signifies "essence" or "vital energy," and it is noted that "everything that lives, and all creations shares the essence of Ptah"; therefore, Ptah is both the creative mind and "essence" of all being (Obenga, 2004). Moreover, Ptah, the developing consciousness within Nun, would achieve the process of creation by merging with Atum, in effect becoming "creative utterance" (Obenga, 2004). Furthermore, having its origins in Nun, the universe is described as a conscious entity, Ptah (soul), that is versed with the spiritual energy of Atum (Obenga, 2004).

Similar to the Kemites, the Akan people, located on the Ivory coastal region of Ghana, West Africa, also have three creative principles, Onyame, Onyankopon, and Odomakoma. Onyame represents the "fundamental nature" of the universe and its "natural order"; Onyankopon is known as the "experiencing and knowing principle"; and Odomakoma is the "universe of the idea" (Danquah, 1968). Concurrent to Kemetic philosophy, the Akan also considered the universe to be a living entity, which they describe as the "All Thing," (Odomakoma) (Danquah, 1968). Specifically, the "All Thing" is considered to be an "Adee," an expanding and/or living idea in the mind of Odomakoma, who is seen as the "Great Architect" and/or "universal spirit of the entire Thing" (Danquah, 1968). Equally important, the "All Thing," within itself, is considered to be "a becoming," where creation is indefinite (incomplete) but possesses "every possibility of ever and always becoming perfect" (Danquah, 1968). Subsequently, the essence of the "All Thing" is the Honhom, "pure ethereality" and the "ideal perfection," which is achieved through the "perfect identification" between the "universes of experience," Sunsum (spirit), and the "universe of the Ideal," Okara (soul)—Onyankopon and Odomakoma (Danquah, 1968).

The Dogon conception of the universe is yet another example of cultural continuity in Africa. According to the Dogon, before the emergence of the known universe, there was Amma, depicted as a "cosmic egg," containing the po, the amma bummo; "266 signs of Amma," the "word"; and all other materials that will inhabit the universe (Griaule & Dieterlen, 1986). Accordingly, in the process of creation, Amma, as the nyama (soul), synonymous with the "spiral," "whirlwind," and "word," positioned himself at the center of the Po to give it an "internal movement (life)," in addition to placing all the material that would make up the universe within the po (Griaule & Dieterlen, 1986). Consequentially, the po represented the "image of the origin of matter," in addition to being; the "smallest of things" and the bummo signified the initial idea (Griaule & Dieterlen, 1986). Moreover, Amma, as the "word," which is the articulation of his/her initial thoughts (bummo), caused the po to "vibrate" and eventually "burst," releasing all the material that will make up the universe (Griaule & Dieterlen, 1986). In effect, the Nommo, similar to Atum and Onyame, will act as the "creative word," the force that "protects, directs, and controls" all universal phenomenon (Griaule & Dieterlen, 1986; Karenga, 2010).

In relation to traditional African thought, contemporary Aeronautics and mathematics professor, Gabriel A. Oyibo, in the 1990s, introduced a theory known as the "God Almighty Grand Unified Theorem (GAGUT)" or the "Theory of Everything," which challenged prior theories and introduced a wide variety of new ideas that have, since then, gone unchallenged and been virtually ignored by modern scientist. According to Dr. Oyibo, the four known universal force fields, gravitational, electromagnetic, strong, and weak, can be configured into GAGUT, to provide a unified force field solution to Albert Einstein and Isaac Newton gravitational force fields. Additionally, Oyibo states that GAGUT can provide explanations for the String theory and other general Hyper-space theories (Oyibo Preface). There are three main formulas associated with GAGUT, the unified field, space time variable, and the union of the first two, the Grand Unified Theory (Oyibo, 2004):

1. $\left(G_{j_0}\right)_t + \left(G_{j_1}\right)_x + \left(G_{j_2}\right)_y + \left(G_{j_3}\right)_z = 0$

2. $\eta_n = g_{n0}t^{n+!} + g_{n1}x^{n+1} + g_{n2}y^{n+1} + g_{n3}z^{n+1} + \ldots$

3. $G_{ij,j} = 0$

In equation 3, "$Gij, j = 0$," "Gij" represents the unified force field (unification of all known forces), the comma is an indication of change, and "0" represents the absolute infinity (unchanging value). The second equation represents the "characteristic trajectories" of the perpetual motions of the universe, where "nn" represents the "space time variable," "$n0$" represents "the motion of waves," and "$n1$" is the trajectories of the wave particles and their geometrical characteristics (forms) caused by force concentrations. Specifically, the orbiting of planets around the sun and the orbiting of electrons around the nucleus of an atom, under the direction of gravitational and electromagnetic forces, are ellipses, one of three "conic sections" (Oyibo, 2004). From Oyibo's analysis, motion is considered to be a fundamental character of the universal reality and force is its causation. Moreover, since force is the cause of motion, he asserts that the universe is essentially a "force field," from which the concentration of waves by the universal force field produces matter (particles) (Oyibo, 2004). With GAGUT, Oyibo concludes that the universal life force (God), as related to cosmic order, could "exist in the form of waves," which he believes is spirit and/or soul (Oyibo, 2004). With that being the case, Oyibo's analysis of the universe originating as a Great Wave (spirit) seems to be consistent with traditional African conceptions.

Accordingly, the creative "word," of Amma-Nommo, Ptah-Atum, Odomakoma-Onyame, which represented "authoritative utterance of exceptional insight (Husia)," is an energy wave or "sound wave"—spirit (Karenga & Carruthers, 1986; Oyibo, 2004). Phrased another way, the "word of the thinking mind" constitutes the origins of the universe, where the word (sound wave) is the concentration and/or expression of the mind (soul force) (Carruthers, 1995). Even more interesting, some of the above deities are symbolized as the sun. Specifically, Atum and Ptah, setting sun and midday sun, exemplify the sun's rays, essentially energy waves (Carruthers, 1995). Comparatively, the "$n0$," in Oyibo's space time variable, maintains that energy waves are implicit to sound waves, sun waves, electromagnetic waves, and other energy waves or particles (Oyibo, 2004). Thus, if the universe is an entity, mind, according to the African view, and all universal interactions are the result of forces (gravitational, electromagnetic, etc.), this would imply the entity (mind) to be a unified "force field" (Oyibo, 2004). Moreover, if matter (particles) is simply "high force field intensity" and it has its origins in energy waves, then that would denote that matter and waves (spirit) are interchangeable; as a result, matter is the coagulation of energy waves (spirit) (Oyibo, 2004). African philosophy provides further examples to explain the above argument.

Specifically, the Dogon state that, "when Amma broke the egg of the world and came out, a whirlwind arose. The po, which is the smallest, was made invisible, at the center; the wind is Amma himself. It is the po which Amma let come first" (Griaule & Dieterlen, 1986). As noted in previous paragraphs, the "whirlwind" is Amma as nyama (soul force) and the po is essentially spirit (wave). Therefore, the Dogon are implying that spirit preceded soul; the Kemites have a similar narrative. According to the "Text of Prt Em Hru," "the souls come forth to do the will of their Ka's and the soul of Ausar Ani cometh forth to do the will of his Ka" (Nelson, 2011; Budge, 1965). Once again, it is the spirit (ka) that moves ahead of the soul (ba). In the Akan notion, "Onyankopon is the Sunsum (spirt) and Odomakoma is the Okara (soul)." Odomakoma, separated from Onyankopon, is "only soul and not an experiencing being, an individuality or personality"; moreover, it is noted that "it is the sunsum that experiences, and its end is okara, the ideal to be lived or experienced" (Danquah, 1968).

Consequentially, force (soul) causes spirit to emerge into existence first, so that it may have a medium for experience; in other words, the spirit is the experiencing vessel for the soul.

Ntu-Rohoumbo

The previous explanations of cosmic reality give us a foundation to explore the deeper implication of spirit and soul as they relate to human beingness. However, for the purpose of this study, it is imperative that the fundamental concepts presented above are unified into a coherent set of terms; the Zulu tradition has provided an outline. The Zulu believe that everything that exists in the universe is a "constituent" of UQOBO, "living consciousness" (Nobles, 2006). According to the Zulu, UQOBO is an "infinite cluster of forces," where "life, law, and energy," constitute some of its essential qualities (Asante, 1996). Correspondingly, personal and collective development is depended on an individual's involvement and responses to the "appearing law, Umthetho weMvelo, the demands of one's nature, Isimu, and perpetual evolution, Ukuma Njalu" (Nobles, 2006). Furthermore, since all things are essentially a phenomenon of UQOBO, "Uluthu," human beings are a "self-defining value" of phenomena, whose destiny is rooted in "perpetual evolution," in response to the translation of Umthetho weMvelo (law) (Nobles, 2006). Concurrent to the "self-defining value," the Zulu consider the "self-evolving value" of life to be Ntu (Asante, 1996).

In relation to the Zulu conception, the Kemites, Akan, Dogon, and Oyibo's GAGUT illustrates several parallels that provide the basis for the creation of a cohesive set of terms that will allow us to continue or explore spirit and soul. To begin, Nun, indeterminate matter, is essentially potential energy—impending possibility. Correspondingly, the Akan concept, Honhom, "pure ethereality," is presented as the essence of the universe, rooted in the integration of the Great Triad, Onyame, Onyankopon, and Odomakoma (Danquah, 1968). Even more, Honhom is the "informing ideal" in which the universe, "All Thing," is "to become" (Danquah, 1968). Both the Honhom and Nun are uncreated and inactive, until the emergence of the Creative Force. Ptah, Odomakoma, and Amma are all depicted as the Universal Mind and/or life force (soul). Moreover, Atum, po, Onyame, Onyankopon (sunsum), and Nommo together form the "creative word," the force that "protects, directs, and controls" all universal phenomenon; collectively, they can also be identified as "spiritual-physical fluidity" (Griaule & Dieterlen, 1986; Jahn, 1961; Karenga, 2010). Consequently, universal ("All Thing") desire, mind, and word are the Husia, "authoritative utterance of exceptional insight"; thus, Dr. Oyibo's GAGUT is an amalgamation of the Creative Principle, existing as a unified force field. In effect, the combined principles will be equated to the Zulu concept UQOBO, "living consciousness," with Ntu being UQOBO's "self-evolving" aspect (Asante, 1996).

To complement Ntu, the author will borrow another term from the Bantu language. From the Swahili language, I have combined the terms roho, "spirt," and umbo, "shape or form," to create Rohoumbo, to mean spirt form (Hinnebusch & Mirza, 1998). Particularly, Rohoumbo is meant to represent the "universe of experience," in which Ntu becomes individualized (Danquah, 1968). Moreover, Rohoumbo is the concentrations and/or motions of spirit (energy waves), similar to Oyibo's terms "$n0$" and "$n1$," which fluctuate in form (i.e., solid, liquid, gas, and plasma) due to the force(s) of UQOBO. Comparatively, the Zulu believe that what is perceived and experienced in universal reality is form, as an "unchaining value" of UQOBO. In relation, the Zulu see the "cosmic order [as] an indefinite total of forms," which "metamorphoses into a phenomenon"; this is what is implied by Rohoumbo (Asante, 1996). Accordingly, Ntu and Rohoumbo are counterparts of UQOBO, that is, to say, they are "diunital" (uniting opposites) qualities of the same principle (Myers, 1988). Specifically, Ntu is UQOBO as the animating spirit and/or invigorator, and Rohoumbo is the vessel (form), derived from UQOBO's essence, which provides Ntu with conscious experience. Furthermore, Rohoumbo is the substance that is shared by all cosmic entities, while Ntu constitutes the individual essence that becomes personal experience (uniqueness).

Ntu-Rohoumbo is a phenomenon that emerges from the desire, thought, word, and action of UQOBO, as Husia, "authoritative utterance of exceptional insight" (Karenga & Carruthers, 1986). This is imperative in understating the African conception of human beingness as it relates to sprit and soul, which we will refer to as Rohoumbo and Ntu. Specifically, as stated in previous paragraphs, the "Word" is the transmission of energy waves, as well as the expression of the thoughts. Thus, the concentration of wave energy not only creates forms but also encases energy within them, such as the relationship of the sun to organic life. Thus, Ptah, "as a form of Atum," symbolized as the setting sun, "transmitted his power to all the gods and their ka's, in truth through his heart [mind], this tongue [utterance] through which Horus came into existence, and Djehuty came into existence as Ptah" (Obenga, 2004). In effect, as Dr. Wade Nobles implies with "Sakhu," the body, as the container of God's energy, becomes an "illumination," which, in turn, gives off its own energy; this is the relationship between Ntu and Rohoumbo (Nobles, 2006).

Equally important to the notion of energy transfer is the idea of universal mind and/or consciousness. Specifically, if the universe is ultimately an entity, "living consciousness," and phenomenon is the result of "Divine Speech," then the universe within itself is a "Divine script," containing the symbols, signs, and laws that constitute natural order (Nobles, 2006). Consequently, as the "self-evolving" aspect of UQOBO, Ntu is a conscious force and/or energy that can be transmitted. Moreover, the energy concentrations within the bodies of living beings, the atoms responsible for chemical bonds and compounds, and the cells that facilitate organelle functioning are all conscious organisms that transfer information (energy). In fact, as Dr. Nobles has analyzed in his work, the heart cells are producers of "strong electromagnetic singles that radiates" approximately "twelve to fifteen feet beyond [the body]." As a result, not only are the living systems in the body exchanging conscious energy, but also energy is projected outside of the body to other "energy-vibrating" beings (Nobles, 2006). By and large, consciousness is socially linked and is therefore stimulated by transpersonal phenomenon, as we will see in later paragraphs.

All things considered, existing before universal reality was Nun, indeterminate matter. Residing within Nun was UQOBO, "living consciousness," who existed but had the desire to become and thorough the power of Husia, "authoritative utterance of exceptional insight," emerged as the universe ("All Thing"), which is UQOBO as multitudinous-self (Karenga & Carruthers, 1986). Equally important, UQOBO is Maat and the essence and "informing idea" of which UQOBO is "to become," is Honhom, "pure ethereality" (Danquah, 1968). Maat, "truth, righteousness, justice, order, balance, harmony, and reciprocity" is the "appearing law" that regulates, commands, and guides cosmic equilibrium (Asante, 2014; Nobles, 2006). Correspondingly, using its essence (Honhom) as substance, UQOBO, originally a singularity (whole), expanded and/or separated self, conceptually, in order to know (experience) self—engendering infinite expansion. As a result, from "pure ethereality," Rohoumbo (sprit form) emerged as the vessel for UQOBO experiencing Ntu (self-evolving soul), thus becoming the central axis of universal phenomena.

Ontology of Ntu-Rohoumbo

By the power of Husia, "authoritative utterance of exceptional insight (Husia)," the four categories of beingness emerged: Muntu, Kintu, Hantu, and Kuntu. The highest level, Muntu, represents human beingness; Kintu represents "things (animals and nature)"; Hantu represents "space and time"; and kuntu represents "modality force" (Jahn, 1961). All of the above categories exemplify the union of Ntu-Rohoumbo, as the "self-evolving (Ntu)" matures through the experience of phenomenon (Rohoumbo)—Rohoumbo is the determinative Mun, Kin, Han, and Kun, and Ntu is the stem (Jahn, 1961) (Asante, 1996). Correspondingly, Muntu is a unique agent of Ntu; specifically, as a "self-defining value," Muntu possesses the capacity to rise to higher levels of conscious awareness and beingness (Nobles, 2006). Dr. Nobles has provided us with an explanation of Muntu's distinctiveness grounded in the Kemetic conception; he writes:

> the human being as well as human reality were all governed by divine law and the basic divine law was simply to be and in being, one was the creative cause which made humans divine. This divine law was, in turn, translated into an enduring moral mandate which stated that to be was

permanently guaranteed by the human instinct to become and in becoming, humans revealed their belongingness to God (liness); i.e., capacity to
be creative cause. (Nobles, 2006)

Nobles further emphasizes that "being" is related to a "mortal element (visible)"
and an "immortal element (invisible)." This is implied in Rohoumbo and Ntu
(Nobles, 2006). With attention to the above, Muntu represents multiple divisions of psychic awareness (individualized Ntu). For instance, in the Kemetic
tradition, there are seven aspects of Ntu: the Ka, "spirit or principle body"; Ba,
"soul or breath of life"; Khaba, "veil"; Akhu, "intelligence/mental perception";
Seb, "self-creative power of being"; Putah, "mental maturity"; and Atmu,
"eternal soul" (Nobles, 2006). Additionally, the Yoruba believe that there are
four aspects of Ntu: Emi, "the breath"; Iponri, "one's personal destiny"; Ojiji,
"a person's shadow"; and Ori, "one's head" (Asante, 2007). In effect, the body
(i.e., organs, blood, etc.) belongs to the "mortal elements," while the energy/
force categories (i.e., Ka, Ba, Emi, Iponri, etc.) belong to the "immortal elements" (Nobles, 2006).

Central to the African concept of soul (Ntu) is the idea that human beings
(Muntu) are divinely endowed with an inner sense of right and wrong, conscience. Central to this idea is the human heart. For instance, the Yoruba believe
that Olodumare engendered man with an "Ifa aya (oracle of the heart)," an
inherited conscience that will be judged upon the conclusion of physical existence; in Yoruba tradition, the Okan, "heart-soul," is the "seat of man's energy
and emotion" (Asante, 2007). Comparatively, in the Kemetic view, in addition
to the heart (ib) being the "seat of emotion and reason," it is believed to be a
"guide and witness" of moral conduct that will be judged by the creator upon
physical death (Karenga, 2004). In relation to the above, it is also believed that
God granted human beings "free will," the capacity to choose between right
and wrong. As an illustration, the Kemetic narrative the "Four Good Deeds of
Ra" states, "I [Ra] made every man like his fellow. I did not command that
they do evil, it was their hearts that violated what I had said" (Karenga, 2004).
Essentially, in African tradition, the heart is the developing center of moral
and conscious growth; as one matures in consciousness, they must also grow
conscientiously (Nelson, 2011). In other words, the heart is an implication of
character, a quality of conduct in relationship to awareness and response—that
response being words, actions, etc. Concurrently, the heart is essentially a symbol for Ntu, the "self-evolving" essence, which is never disconnected from its
substance of experience, Rohoumbo (spirit-form). This leads us to the African
conception of self.

Particularly, in traditional African thought, the notion of self is rooted in
the ontological idea of the "oneness of being," which places value on social
"interdependence" (Nobles, 2006). Dr. Marimba Ani's illustration of the Zulu
concept Umuntu, "human beingness," best elucidates this point. Specifically,

Ani uses the phrase, "Umuntu Ngu Muntu Nga Bantu," meaning "a person is a person because there are people" (Nobles, 2006). Contrary to this understanding is the notion of sight and insight; sight is a sense perception that enables a person to see beyond themselves, and insight is more of an intuitive capacity that can only be realized through outer experience. Thus, involvement with other people and phenomenon allows a person to become cognizant of purpose, potential, direction, moral values, etc. Evan more, through transpersonal relationships, an individual acquires identity by name, culture, history, and tradition. A fundamental characteristic of human beingness is speech. As has been noted, the word is a transfer of energy, the relative force; it is the word that causes one to become conscious of self; as a result, that consciousness expresses itself in speech. In fact, as Dr. Jacob Carruthers has assorted in his work, "Mdw Ntr," it is by the transfer of speech that we know; therefore, knowledge and speech coincide. According to Dr. Carruthers, "knowing is the result of divine, universal and integrational conversation among God the creator, the cosmos, nature and the creatures of the earth, especially human beings" (Carruthers, 1995). In effect, as Muntu, we are able to define reality and other people through the transfer of ideas. This exchange of verbal energy not only becomes the cause that leads to all action but also provides the building blocks of knowledge.

"Collective Immortality"

Intimately related to social organization is the notion of space-time and historical memory. As noted by Dr. Ani, the African concept of time is "multidimensional" and is grounded in the concentric nature of the African communal experience (Ani, 1994) Specifically, the African community is metaphysical and is composed of the living, physically deceased (ancestors), and the unborn, who coexist in one divine space, encompassing "past, present, and future," establishing "sacred time" (Ani, 1994). Equally important, place and name are essential to social-historical development; that is to say, through geographical-ecology, people create, confirm, reflect, and reaffirm their existence (Nobles, 2006). With that in mind, the divisions of Ntu (soul) are essentially referring to spiritual-physical ties that human beings have with other life forms and phenomenon. Specifically, a person is connected to other people through genealogy, marriage, procreation, deeds, and essence (Rohoumbo) (Mbiti, 1969). Correspondingly, in the Akan divisions of Ntu; the mogya, "blood"; and the abusua, "clan" signify the material ties, while the okra, "soul," and sunsum, "spirit," represent the invisible links (Asante, 2007). As noted before, the Akan believe that when a person finds the "perfect identification" between the "universe of experience," Sunsum (Rohoumbo), and the "universe of the Ideal," Okara (Ntu), they will be able to transcend Hantu (space-time) and become one with the source, Honhom (Danquah, 1968).

Thus, the African notion of immortality is grounded in the discovery of the relationship between Rohoumbo (material) and Ntu (immaterial), in conjunction with collective memory. John Mbiti introduced two concepts relating to collective memory, "personal immortality" and "collective immortality." The former deals with genealogical and/or family ties, and the latter represents the community and wider society (Mbiti, 1969). The above concepts are implying that a person continues to live after physical death through the memory of other people, in the context of deeds and/or character (i.e., works, marriage, conduct, procreation, etc.) (Mbiti, 1969). As previously mentioned, the heart, a symbol for the developing character (Ntu), is continuously being guided and critiqued by other people, constituents of UQOBO. With that in mind, in African tradition, character is expressed as one of the highest values of human beingness. It is rooted in the harmonizing of consciousness and conscience, reason and emotion. Even more, character is developed through an awareness of the relationship between Ntu and Rohoumbo; therefore, on physical death, a person is ultimately remembered by their character. Thus, immortality is linked to collective memory (i.e., rituals, stories, reiteration of ideas, etc.) (Mbiti, 1969). In the event that the physically deceased does not leave a part of their selves in the material world, in the form of children, deeds, ideas, etc., they will be forgotten; although they may continue to exist spiritually, they will be dead to the community and therefore disconnected from the physical world. Furthermore, the African conception of immortality has physical and spiritual implications. On a physical level, immortality is relative to the collective memory, and on a spiritual level, Rohoumbo (energy in form) can never be destroyed or created but reorganized. Thus, an alteration of Ntu involves its harmonizing with Rohoumbo—constituting character and the Kemetic notion, "know thyself."

"Know Thyself"

The maxim, "everything is everything," spoken by the Asante people of Ghana, West Africa, asserts that the bird, river, tree, sky, human, emotion, will, etc., are all of the same essence (UQOBO) and are, therefore, indivisible. Thus, within UQOBO, self-knowledge and human beingness are one. However, critical insight of the nature of cosmic indivisibility requires a consistent social-ecological interchange, within place, space, and time, that is guided by the "appearing Law," Maat (Asante, 1990). In effect, culture is a mechanism that establishes cohesiveness in thought and behavior, facilitating collective experience. Particularly, there are four basic components of culture: history, motif, ethos, and mythology. History represents a coherent chronicling of human events; motifs are signs, symbols, and icons that communicate aesthetic expression; ethos represents a people's emotional (spiritual) character as it relates to "shared group reactions and responses"; and mythology is a

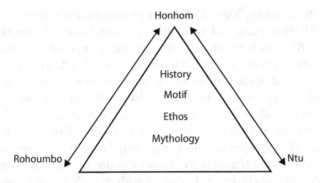

FIGURE 9.1 Developing cultural-spiritual clarity and order

system of reasoning and historical documentation that deals with metaphysical truths concerning a person's place in space-time (Ani, 1997; Asante, 1990). The following diagram seeks to aid in the union and identification of Ntu and Rohoumbo as they relate to culture (Figure 9.1).

Within the pyramid, each cultural aspect must be stable in order to identify and unify Ntu and Rohoumbo. Moreover, through the harmonizing of Ntu and Rohoumbo, a person is able to gain insight, be knowledgeable of personal and extended self, and ascend to Honhom (equilibrium); as a result, each member becomes a link to the collective development and perpetuity of the culture.

Accordingly, the ethos is associated with reflective memory and obligation, within the context of cultural exchange and inheritance. That is to say, every generation is accountable for the maintenance, management, and transference of cultural legacy to the next generation (Conyers, 2001). Moreover, motifs reaffirm collective identity and, through myths, are synthesized to aid in conscious cohesion and the translation of personal and collective experience (Ani, 1997). As noted previously, history, in a traditional African conception, operates concentrically, to merge past, present, and future into one divine space. Correspondingly, the Akan concept, Sankofa, ritualizes the above aspects in a way that redefines, reaffirms, and reinvigorates culture. Specifically, Sankofa, which means "to go back and fetch what you forgot," merges history and consciousness (Akoto, 1992). As a result, Sankofa is an expression of agency and/or centrism—the interrogation, critique, and use of one's history to authenticate their place in space and time (Asante, 1990). Equally important, Sankofa deals with metaphysical existence, the union between physical and spiritual reality. Furthermore, Sankofa, as a reflective search of harmony, is affirmed by Maat, the divine idea and process that facilitates cosmic order.

By and large, the fundamental nature of human beings, as explained in African philosophy, is to "create order out of chaos," that is, to develop an awareness of one's own self-beingness and, in effect, become "creative cause"

(Asante, 1996; Nobles, 2006). In Kemetic philosophy, Ptah represents the pathway for Khepera (process of becoming), perpetual descend from the source, UQOBO; Khepera is essentially chaos waiting to be ordered. Concurrently, order and chaos are essentially one force experienced as different qualities; it is only in our identification of one or the other that we become aware of both. For instance, a person may experience chaos and seek to establish order; in contrast, an individual may create disarray in the midst of order. Either way, when both principles are realized, conceptually, they form a whole, reestablishing equilibrium—this represents the eternal cycle. Consequently, Sankofa can be seen as an illustration of the Kemetic notion of order and arrangement. Specifically, Sankofa is depicted as a bird with its body facing forward and its head turned backward, signifying the need to use the lessons of one's past to guide their present and future. Thus, the body of the bird, chaos, indicates perpetual movement away from the source, while the head represents chaos looking back on itself to reestablish order. Thus, Sankofa, united with Maat, is a ritual that facilitates cultural harmony and restoration. Furthermore, Ntu-Rohoumbo, in a cultural sense, deals with Sankofa, as an affirmation of history, motif, ethos, and mythology, within the consistent pursuit to establish/reestablish Maat, "truth, righteousness, justice, order, balance, harmony, and reciprocity" (Conyers, 2001; Asante, 2014).

The diagram below is an illustration of the aforementioned points. In the figure, Ntu-Rohoumbo is the core of Sankofa, which indicates that harmony, order, unity, and an awareness of the relationship between Ntu and Rohoumbo depend on the spiritual character, ethos, of a person being in alignment with Maat. In sum, self-knowledge, collective memory, obligation, and character are not only essential to the idea of immortality but also correspond to cultural perpetuity and continuity (Figure 9.2).

FIGURE 9.2 Recentering and illuminating African character

References

Akoto, K. A. (1992). *Nationbuilding Theory and Practice in Afrikan Centered Education.* Washington, DC: Pan Afrikan World Institute.

Ani, M. (1994). *Yurugu: An Afrikan-Centered Critique of European Cultural Thought and Behavior.* Washington: Nkonimfo Publications.

Ani, M. (1997). *Let the Circle Be Unbroken: The Implications of African Spirituality in the Diaspora.* New York: Nkonimfo Publications.

Asante, M. K. (1990). *Kemet, Afrocentricity and Knowledge.* Trenton, NJ: African World Press.

Asante, M. K. (2003). *Afrocentricity: The Theory of Social Change.* Chicago, IL: African American Images.

Asante, M. K. (2007). *Spear Masters: An Introduction to African Religion.* Lanham, MD: University Press of America.

Asante, M. K. (2014). *Facing South to Africa: Towards an Afrocentric Critical Orientation.* Lanham: Lexington Books.

Asante, M. K. (2015). *African Pyramids of Knowledge: Kemet Afrocentricity and Africology.* Brooklyn: Universal Write Publications LLC.

Asante, M. K. & Abarry, A. (1996). *African Intellectual Heritage.* Philadelphia: Temple University Press.

Budge, E. A. W. (1965). *The Book of the Dead: The Papyrus of Ani in the British Museum.* New York: Dover Publications.

Carruthers, J. (1995). *Mdw Ntr Divine Speech: A Historiographical Reflection of African Deep Thought from the Time of Pharaohs to the Present.* London: Karnak House.

Conyers, J. L. (2001). *African American Jazz and Rap Social and Philosophical Examinations of Black Expressive Behavior.* Jefferson, NC: McFarland & Company.

Danquah, J. B. (1968). *The Akan Doctrine of God: A Fragment of Gold Coast Ethics and Religion.* London: Frank Cass and Company.

Diop, C. A. (1991). *Civilization or Barbarism: An Authentic Anthropology.* Brooklyn: Lawrence Hill Books.

Finch III, C. S. (2007). *The Star of Deep Beginnings: The Genesis of African Science and Technology.* Georgia: Khenti.

Griaule, M. & Dieterlen, G. (1986). *The Pale Fox.* Paris: Afrikan World Books.

Hinnebusch, T. & Mirza, S. (1998). *Swahili: A Foundation for Speaking, Reading and Writing.* Lanham, MD: University Press America.

Jahn, J. (1961). *Muntu: African Culture and the Western World.* New York: Groves Press.

James, G. G. M. (1954). *Stolen Legacy.* New York: Eworld.

Karenga, M. (2004). *Maat The Moral Ideal in Ancient Egypt: A Study of Classical African Ethics.* New York: Routledge.

Karenga, M. (2010). *Introduction to Black Studies.* Los Angeles: University of Sankore Press.

Karenga, M. & Carruthers, J. (1986). *Kemet and the African Worldview Research Rescue and Restoration.* Los Angeles: University of Sankore Press.

Mbiti, J. (1969). *African Religions and Philosophy.* New Hampshire: Heinemann Educational Botswana.

Myers, L. J. (1988). *Understanding an Afrocentric World View: Introduction to an Optimal Psychology.* Dubuque, IA: Kendall/Hunt Publishing Company.

Nelson, T. (2011). *KaAbBa: The Great Pyramid Is the Tree of Life.* Mattapan: Library of Congress Cataloging in Publication.

Nobles, W. (1986). *African Psychology: Toward Its Reclamation, Reascension, and Revitalization*. Oakland: A Black Family Institute Publication.

Nobles, W. (2006). *Seeking the Sakhu Foundational Writings for An African Psychology*. Chicago: Third World Press.

Obenga, T. (1992). *Ancient Egypt and Black Africa: A Students Handbook for the Study of Ancient Egypt in Philosophy, Linguistics and Gender Relations*. London: Karnak House.

Obenga, T. (2004). *African Philosophy: The Pharaonic Period 2780–330 BC*. Paris: Per Ankh.

Opoku, K. A. (1978). *West African Traditional Religion*. Accra: FEP International Private Limited.

Oyibo, G. (2004). *Grand Unified Theorem: Discovery of the Theory of Everything and the Fundamental Building Block of Quantum Theory*. New York: Nova Science Publisher.

Sertima, I. V. (1989). *Egypt Revisited*. Piscataway, NJ: Transaction Publishing.

Sertima, I. V. (1994). *Egypt Child of Africa*. London: Transaction Publishers.

Zubay, G. (2000). *Origins of Life on the Earth and in the Cosmos*. New York: Academic Press.

10

BLACK IDENTITY AND WHITE CULTURE

Jacqueline Gerard

Lauded as the artistic voice for black women, *Lemonade* (Beyonce, 2016) examines the identity and self-image of black women today, in the past, and in the future. After its release in April of 2016, many critics applauded its portrayal of the female self-image and its connection to black culture as well as black beauty. *Lemonade*'s critical success reflects the female's wish to control her self-image through obtaining her own identity, especially for black American women. *Lemonade*'s popular/entertainment success stemmed partly from the reference of "Becky with the good hair," the woman who supposedly hurt Beyonce and Jay Z's relationship, the woman whose ethnicity suggests a white ethnicity and not a black ethnicity. A social phenomenon, *Lemonade* encompasses the black feminine identity saturated in a culture concerned with ethnicity and scandal. It mirrors what black women must examine, own, and empower in a predominantly white culture today. In an attempt to control their self-image and social identity through their culture and their beauty, black women find that their self-image changes and their social identity is affected and affects the goals of group when enveloped in a white environment.

A black woman's self-image, directly related to identity, body image, and self-esteem, is molded from her environment. "Shaped by individual and collective experiences" between "famil[ies], neighborhood[s], school[s], communit[ies], and culture[s]," self-image reflects self-worth and value, which feed into self-esteem and how a woman views her body and her identity (Hesse-Biber, Livingstone, Ramirez, Barko, & Johnson, 2010). With a healthy self-image, women can create a positive social identity, allowing women "to make some positive contribution" to society (Thomas, Hacker, & Hoxha, 2011). Leah Miller,[1] a black woman and graduate of Harvard University, believes that black women see their self-image in relation to others. Because of "colonization and slavery and other general patriarchies throughout history, black women have been socialized to see their worth in relation to the men and children in their life" and their surroundings. She believes that this self-image forces them to "fight" and "prove" their own self-love to others. In order to "fight" and "prove" their self-love, many black women rely on their heritage and community to find their identity.

When surrounded with a proud, black community, black women tend to have higher self-esteem, which creates a positive self-image and social identity. In an all-black, female community, women tend to compare themselves to one another as well as find their social identity. They embrace Afrocentric values, "spirituality, communalism, harmony, movement, verve, spontaneity, expressive individualism, oral tradition, social time, and perspective"; this leads to a sense of pride for their heritage (Thomas et al., 2011). Inclined to be black nationalists, these women who hold Afrocentric values "believe they should be in control of their own social, economic, and political institutions" and not the mainstream culture, which is not their culture (Eaton, Livingston, & McAdoo, 2010). The ability to control their social, economic, and political institutions grants agency, and agency leads to not only a positive self-image but a social identity as well. Even women who grew up in an all-white community with no connection to their heritage or a black, nationalist group can begin to "understand blackness through the lens of black peoples' words and the way that black people thought about blackness" when placed in an all-black community (Miller, 2016). In their all-white community, women can believe "there's something wrong with [them]" because of others' reactions to the women's "blackness" when the black women "didn't do anything" (Miller, 2016). Within the black community, they no longer feel abnormal and realize that these poor reactions to their "blackness" stems from ignorance and racism "sown into the logic and fabric of [The United States]" (Miller, 2016). A positive community that looks at and experiences what an individual looks like and experiences can inspire confidence in that individual.

As stated above, a black community can inspire confidence in that individual, creating a positive self-image and social identity; however, what occurs when an individual surrounds herself in an all-white community? For some, such as for Leah Miller, an all-white community in childhood can create ignorance and the questioning of values and feelings, but what happens when a woman is aware of her white surroundings and has already embraced her black heritage? Can she still lose her self-image, her social identity, and her self-worth, or does it change depending on the environment? Research indicates that primarily a black woman's self-image can change and mutate into one microcosm of the self-image: body image. Within school and the media, a woman's body is the instinctual factor that affects a woman's self-image.

Black women who attend primarily white colleges can become dissatisfied with their bodies, even when rooted in their black heritage. A myth exists that black women are not affected by white Western body image ideals because their own culture does not adhere to the same standards (Hesse-Biber et al., 2010). While this may be true for some individuals, many black women who attend primarily white colleges can still be affected by the surrounding norms, adapting to the norm of the campus. Eating disorders and body dissatisfaction run rampant on many predominantly white college campuses, and those black women who tend to have "more fluid and flexible" "self contingencies" can easily develop an eating disorder and want a white woman's "body shape" (Hesse-Biber et al., 2010). Even with roots in their own heritage, although most likely not strong, black women can absorb white Western standards and then hold themselves accountable to those standards, believing that these standards are the correct standards. This sentiment rings truer, especially when "predominately black colleges report fewer eating disorders symptoms" (Hesse-Biber et al., 2010). Clearly, black women's idea of self-image changes when surrounded by those who do not identify with their race.

If a black woman wants to avoid a social climate of body dissatisfaction, she still cannot escape because she constantly is inundated with media, a media that the white Western world has constructed. Most of Hollywood, which is responsible for most of the films and television series, is orchestrated by white Western culture. White "voices, values, and beliefs echo in [the] brains" of black women because Hollywood is primarily white (Hooks, 1995). White Hollywood has caused the need for television channels such as BET and films that directly market to the black community, so that black voices, values, and beliefs can echo in the minds of blacks; however, even with a distinct effort to separate from White Hollywood, "the prevailing values in society, values created and sustained by white supremacist capitalist patriarchy," still overflow into black film and television (Hooks, 1995). For example, Gangsta rap, a genre distinctly created to rebel against white Western culture, appeals to white Western men. Why? The violence and hatred found in the genre stem first from the violence and hatred perpetrated during the American slave trade (Hooks, 1995). This is further emphasized with the size of black women in hip-hop music videos. Black women in hip-hop music videos tend to be slimmer when the video's subject features materialism and slimmer in general (Dixon, Zhang, & Conrad, 2009). Why? Although the hip-hop music videos are made with a black audience in mind, those who are funding, producing, and watching these videos are white. Why are women slimmer, especially in videos featuring materialism? Capitalism, a cause for materialism, stems from the white Western world. It would only be fitting for the video, which values white Western monetary values, to value the same ideal body image as the white Western culture. And now that the bodies in the music video are abnormally slimmer, a black woman can easily feel self-conscious about her own body image, even while avoiding an all-white community (Hooks, 1995). The white Western values infiltrate the black community even when trying to separate.

In both school and media, women fell prey to the beauty myth, the belief that they had to encompass the same body image and values as their white peers; however, what is her social identity in a white environment? Is her social identity negatively affected? Can she achieve her individual goals as well as the goals of the group? Research indicates that a black woman struggles with a positive social identity in a prominently white environment but can still contribute to achieving the group's goals within the work environment and social settings.

When studying a group of black female police officers, the women were able to keep their individuality and their femininity, but they struggled with social identity among their co-workers. Despite feelings of confidence, the women admitted that they tried to "fit in" and be "truly accepted," but most of their time in the force, they never quite achieved acceptance (Burns, 1997). They believed in the idea that their co-workers were their "brothers and sisters in blue," but their co-workers didn't always feel the same, which made the black female officers feel "powerless" (Burns, 1997). Lacking these relationships, the women saw how their work negatively influenced their outside relationships because they were less trusting of others. Many of these women had to maintain friendships within their black communities as well as become more active in the black community in order to keep their self-image and work toward a social identity (p. 105). While their self-image was intact in these contrasting work environments, their social identity was not.

Similar to the police officers, Leah Miller attends a predominantly white church in a white neighborhood. Leah chose the church because of its teachings and doctrines, and she chose the neighborhood because it is located in the same neighborhood as the church. Most of her friends are from her friends and many of her social activities are with church friends and are church events. In her interview, Leah stated that she loves her church and loves her friends but that her time there has "been really difficult." Before her current church, she lived in a different area of the United States and attended a church that was very diverse in age, race, and class. Her church now primarily consists of white women between the ages of 22 and 32. Leah believes her previous church was so diverse because it intentionally wanted to be diverse but did not force the diversity; in contrast, her current church does not intentionally seek diversity. She believes that a church that states that "they love all of God's children" and even "desire diversity" does not try to "serve cross-cultural groups." As an individual, Leah does not struggle to make friends, but she believes it hurts the goals of the church. The church wants to share their love for the Lord they worship to all they encounter, especially locally, but she believes this is more difficult when the church thinks similarly and looks similarly. Her social identity may not be harmed, but the social identity and the goals of the church are nullified.

When immersed in an all-white community, black females have the struggle to know their self-image, keep their self-image, and create a social identity that does not hurt them or the groups they encounter. In a world that seems more divided by ethnicity and yet is forced to share the same space, it is important for black females to have their self-image and social identity. Whether or not *Lemonade* is an artistic visual album, a social phenomenon, the best album of the year, a media ploy, a wannabe artistic expression, or any other title that has been allotted to it, it has become a symbol for black women to know their heritage and to know the self in order to create a social identity. Positive self-image and social identity are necessary for black women to have a voice, agency, and location. And only when all have a voice, agency, and location will the racial and social divides begin to erode.

Note

1 Leah Miller's name has been changed at her request.

References

Beyonce. (2016). Lemonade. *TIDAL*. N.p., April 24, 2016. Web. August 10, 2016.

Burns, L. J. (1997). *Self-perceptions: Effects of being black, female and a police officer*. Ann Arbor, MI: The Union Institute.

Dixon, T. L., Zhang, Y., & Conrad, K. (2009). Self-esteem, misogyny and Afrocentricity: An examination of the relationship between rap music consumption and African American perceptions. *Group Processes & Intergroup Relations, 12*(3), 345–360.

Eaton, S. C., Livingston, J. N., & McAdoo, H. P. (2010). Cultivating consciousness among Black women: Black nationalism and self-esteem revisited. *Journal of Black Studies, 40*(5), 812–822.

Hesse-Biber, S., Livingstone, S., Ramirez, D., Barko, E. B., & Johnson, A. L. (2010). Racial identity and body image among black female college students attending predominately white colleges. *Sex Roles, 63*(9), 697–711.

Hooks, B. (1995). *Killing rage: Ending racism*. New York: H. Holt.

Miller, L. (2016). Personal interview. August 10.

Thomas, A., Hacker, J., & Hoxha, D. (2011). Gendered racial identity of black young women. *Sex Roles, 64*(7–8), 530–542.

11

CRITICAL ANALYSIS OF RECLAIMING THE BLACK PSYCHE THROUGH RESEARCH METHODS IN AFRICANA STUDIES

Tanisha Stanford

Within the black community, there seems to be a lack of a common consciousness regarding the status of black people globally and why it is a necessity for all people of Africana descent to unite. Sadly, many people of African descent see no point in trying to get on one accord for the progression of the people, because of the hate that they possess toward one another and sometimes themselves. In other words, Africana people are not putting Africana thought and values at the center of their world, hearts, and minds. Furthermore, this proves problematic in the type of research done for, on, and by some people of color. Much of the research done on people of color isn't really done for the progression of the people and thus is not done with methods and instruments that reflect issues and needs of the black community. All of this to emphasize the essentiality of exploring research methods through Afrocentricity in order to properly assess black mental health and reclaim or awaken the black psyche.

First, one must understand the term Afrocentricity and explore its ideas along with the benefits that persist once its methods are put into place in the daily lives of black people. According to Asante (2003), Afrocentricity is a way of thinking; it's theoretical; it's a kind of behavior that one must possess. Basically, it has to be first in every aspect of life; the way one acts; the way one thinks; the way one moves and interact in the social world. More specifically in terms of research, Afrocentricity can be defined as assuring that African interest and prosperity are a central concern or measurement in analysis (Asante, 2003, p. 2). Afrocentricity is a concept that has the magnitude to eliminate any negativity imposed on people of color through European colonization. Simply put, it not only takes into context of the struggles and triumph are experiencing and have been experiencing in recent centuries—it also takes into account, the values, origins, and traditions of Africana people globally.

Most importantly, Afrocentricity grants a sense of agency to Africana people. Agency is really important to any person, because it gives them a sense of cultural history (Asante, 2003, p. 3). As an African within the diaspora, this is more important than most other people because, due to colonization, many of them believe that they originate from slavery or wherever they reside at the time. Moreover, this creates an internal conflict in a person when they try to integrate into a culture that they consider their own and they are not accepted. Even more than acceptance, Afrocentricity provides a clear lens for people of African descent to properly perceive institutions, people, and just the world in general. Through Afrocentricity, there would be no more confusion and no more self and national hate among Africana people.

However, Afrocentricity is a complex concept and takes a certain kind of mentality for it to be properly lived and enforced throughout life. Likewise, there is relevance in the retention, reclamation, uplift of Africana spirituality and ethos. Awakening the black psyche and utilizing Afrocentricity essentially form a cycle because one uses Afrocentricity to awaken the black psyche, yet, by awakening the black psyche, one is interested and capable of understanding the true purpose of Afrocentricity. One could start in either direction, but for the purpose of this essay and reclaiming the black psyche, Afrocentricity would be the second step. In this day and age, there are so many Africana people lost in the world because their sense of thought and culture has been forcefully stripped away from them. Thus, the first step would be that realization, and once one has realized their reality, the black psyche is tapped but not necessarily awake. Likewise, one could be aware of their reality and not act upon it because they really are not in control. Therefore, one must want to control their own mind; it must be an infatuation for one to claim their mind and what it believes.

In claiming one's mind, it is a necessity to recreate one's whole mentality and being because the person only knows the customs and traditions of the colonial culture. "The person's images, symbols lifestyles, and manners are contradictory and thereby destructive to personal and collective growth and development" (Asante, 2003, p. 3) According to Daudi Ajani ya Azibo (2015), there have been a number of scholars, activists, and social scientist, from Dr. King, to John Henrik Clark and even Michael Bradly, who have urged Africana people to create a new man that forsakes any social structures and even religions that do not genuinely portray African values and cultures. In essence, people of African descent must decolonize their minds, in order to liberate their entire being. Once a person can liberate themselves, it is their divine duty to pass on the knowledge and feeling of mental and spiritual liberation, whether it is to peers or family, and assure that they too continue the cycle of spreading the gospel of black unity and liberation.

Moreover, it is imperative that black people educate their children before society can do so, considering it would be much more effortless to incorporate

Afrocentric ideas into the lives of children, and create habits young, instead of trying to disarrange their minds once they are adults and personally see and feel the discrimination.

> Afrocizing involves Black adults recognizing that the early and critical development years must be used to socialize Black children to become significant links in our collective liberation struggle. Parents' noble responsibility is to communicate to African youth that they must have a cardinal interest in the dignity, prosperity, survival and sovereignty of African people. (Azibo, 2015)

Essentially, this means obliterating one's whole mental being, everything that they were taught to worship and even the family structure; their whole rhythm through life and how they relay information as a unit would have to follow a completely different tune. Consequently, this particular rhythm is one that is familiar to most Africana people but often goes unnoticed. Innately, most people of African descent possess African habits, mentalities, and customs (Azibo, 2015), but because they are not recognized by the colonial culture, they are forced to repress things that feel natural to them. "Just as the puppy is endowed with the propensity to develop a 'dog's mind' (rather than a 'sheep's mind'), so is the African endowed with the propensity to develop psychological Africanity…" (Azibo, 2015). However, black people are forced to think as Europeans, and this creates a sense of mental distress in most, if not all, unconscious Africana people. Even those who are aware and conscious have trouble adjusting to certain aspects of the ideas of mental and spiritual liberation as well as the power of uniting African people on the continent and within the diaspora. Furthermore, this mental distress can potentially be the cause of many of the mental health problems and disorders that persist within black communities globally.

Anxiety disorders are a group of psychological disorders that have been highly understudied among black people yet are very prevalent within the black community. Due to the ambiguity surrounding anxiety disorders within the black community, many studies previously done suggested that black people experience more anxiety than white people, but they primarily focused on lower socioeconomic status, and thus, the findings were void (Walker & Hunter, 2009). A nationally recognized organization known for studying mental health did a study and found that "African Americans have lower rates of anxiety disturbances relative to European Americans, although anxiety disorders in African Americans have a more chronic course… researchers have suggested that the chronicity of disease is due to sparse coping resources" (Walker & Hunter, 2009).

Further, there are certain encounters with anxiety disorders that are distinct to black people. Consequently, these particular distinctions are more than likely a result of colonization and attempting to integrate into a culture that isn't accepting of them and repressing natural habits and ideas because they are not familiar to the colonizing culture. According to Walker and Hunter (2009), "African Americans may demonstrate a unique experience of anxiety that is yet to be articulated in diagnostic texts." This is yet one more reason to conduct investigative research and writing related to concern of the black community.

Another prevailing psychological disorder within black community is depression. In many instances, black people will not seek professional help for depression or receive inadequate treatment because many believe that sadness is the only symptom of depression, but it is much more than the occasional feeling of sorrow. Of course, if anybody has to repress feelings and customs that come naturally to them, there would definitely be an imbalance in emotion because one would feel sad or confused and wouldn't understand why. Not realizing reasoning behind their emotional imbalance could potentially discredit their feelings when they are being assessed by a mental health professional. "Much of the depression literature relevant to African Americans has been characterized by conflicting reports that yield an unclear picture of the prevalence, risk, and severity of symptoms associated with depression in African Americans" (Walker & Hunter, 2009). Further research from Walker and Hunter (2009) suggests that though people of color were no more likely than other ethnicities to be diagnosed with clinical depression, they experienced more associated symptoms of psychology. Basically, as an ethnicity, black people are more likely to have depressive symptoms but not enough to be diagnosed with clinical depression. Sadly, those possessing symptoms without a diagnosis are more likely to develop permanent psychological distress.

Due to the lack adequate treatment for anxiety and depressive disorders for black people, there seems to be an increase in suicidal tendencies within the black community. Naturally, there is a common misconception that people of African descent do not engage in suicidal behavior, but contrary to popular belief, suicide is the sixteenth leading cause of death for African Americans. Further, the attitude that black people do not commit suicide may be due in part to the fact that many African American suicides are categorized as a homicide or an accident or they are not reported at all (Walker & Hunter, 2009).

More importantly, another reason that the Africana people's suicide rates go unnoticed is due to the idea that many of the self-harm done by black people are common community habits and do not immediately kill the victim, thus the term "slow" suicide, coined by Early and Akers. Moreover, this is the most common, yet misinterpreted form of suicide within the black community (Walker & Hunter, 2009). Even more, this is problematic for the community because there is no awareness of this kind of suicide. Consequently, speculation provides no context to describe and evaluate, how chronic drug use and alcohol are forms of substance abuse, which the outcome assessment can lead to suicide. Ironically, many of these types of behaviors are considered dysfunctional coping strategies for distress, whereas they impose a life-long threat on the lives of many people (Walker & Hunter, 2009). With no awareness of such things, there could be no proper preventions methods to be promoted in the community.

> Contemporary studies are needed to operationalize self-destructive behavior across the life span in African American communities. Inclusion of self-destructive behavior in its many forms (e.g., alcohol and drug abuse, victim-precipitated homicide) in response to interpersonal, socio-political, and psychological difficulty should be considered in conceptualizations of suicide. (Walker & Hunter, 2009)

Society has created mental instability in black people due to disparity and by forcing assimilation, but oddly, many feel that it is this same society's job to fix and heal these mental problems. That is completely arbitrary and contradictory of why certain institutions were put into place; thus, it is absolutely absurd to believe that the systems meant to destroy Africana people would all of a sudden be willing to admit their wrongs and fix the problems they have created. Further, this only makes it more apparent of why there must be methodology and sciences that are African-centered and are in place for the progression and uniting of all Africana people. Uniquely, African-centered psychology as well as other indigenous psychologies do exist and are very much affective for the people they are intended for, but, of course, they are not mainstream and are not utilized as much.

By creating or utilizing social sciences and humanities instruments of evaluation, there is the formulation of interpretative analysis which describes and evaluates Africana culture from an Afrocentric perspective. It is detrimental that Afrocentric scholars pursue research and Africana studies from an Afrocentric perspective. Further, it is imperative that these scholars take advantage of methods such as interpretive analysis and the benefits it grants toward the advancement of people of color. More importantly, methods such as Afrocentric perspective and interpretive analysis must be implied in any theory, publishing, and assessment that pertain to reclaiming or awakening the black psyche.

Surely, one must be able to comprehend terms such as Afrocentric perspective and interpretive analysis, the benefits of them, and how the two go hand in hand when conducting research concerning social change and the systems in place hindering Africana people. Both methods are important in helping set a tone, as well as give significance to Africana people and their perspective of the world as they know it and experience it.

According to Erickson, interpretive analysis is defined as studying the acts and meanings of certain events provided by a particular subject. It is important to note that acts are distinguished from behaviors because acts are meant to only be understood from the particular subjects' point of view (Smith, 2006). In many instances, black people's experiences are not understood from their point of view, which explains the incentive feelings that other ethnicities possess toward people of color. Further, some Africana people are not even aware that there is a way of interpreting things that is significant to them and their experiences. Interpretive analysis is something that shapes and formats research because it provides constructs for the research to be filtered through. Moreover, interpretive analysis gives way to acceptance of the personal relationship between the researcher and what is being researched. This is important because many do not understand that people perceive things differently based on their environment and experiences. Thus, a black man explaining or publishing from his very own point of view is much more beneficial to the progression of black people and awakening their minds than that of a European.

Interpretive analysis could potentially be seen as a key component to an Afrocentric perspective, simply because it helps to personalize what is being researched to the person possessing an Afrocentric perspective. According to Asante (2003), an Afrocentric perspective is one that places people of the African diaspora at the primary focus point of analysis or research. Once a person of African descent realizes the importance of placing African ideas at the center of their research, they have awakened their mind; it places them in a place to help others reach that same liberation. An Afrocentric perspective is important to researching because it gives Africana people a sense of agency. Moreover, the rationale behind an Afrocentric perspective is for one or all of the diaspora to be proactive in its history and culture. In conclusion, the purpose of Afrocentric perspective would be to help create a national consciousness across the whole diaspora.

Once one understands the type of methods needed to create sciences and assessments that are beneficial for the betterment of black people and reclaiming the black psyche, one understands why Western-based psychologies are not effective in securing the mental well-being of Africana people. Further, Africana people will understand the importance of creating more assessments and social science concepts specifically for their own kind. Fortunately, there are many great examples to build off of. One great example is African-centered psychology because it follows many of the essential concepts within Afrocentricity. According to Utsety, Belvet, and Fischer (2009), "African-centered Psychology has its origins in ancient Kemet (often misnomered Egypt) and is grounded in the worldview and philosophical systems of African culture." The most essential components of an African-centered psychology should include self-definition, spirit, nature, metaphysical interconnectedness, and communal disorder (Utsety et al., 2009). Most, if not all, of the studies that evaluate personality and behavior are not of these standards and thus would not be able to properly analyze Africana people. However, if there were policies in place that required mental health professionals to apply an African-centered psychological viewpoint when diagnosing and treating black people, there would be far fewer Africana people being labeled ill-adjusted by the mental health field. Likewise, once Africana people understand that they are not ill-adjusted to society and that they are simply being discriminated against, it will light a fire in the black psyche so enlightening that it will force them to focus on awakening the minds of their brothers and sisters.

However, there has to be more than a concept; there must be ways of practicing and assessing the black psyche effectively. Specifically, there has to be some form of empirical examination of behavior and personality that is centered from an Afrocentric perspective of reality. Utsety et al. (2009) feel that this structure must meet certain criteria that include "(1) the study's conceptual framework is grounded in an African-centered theoretical method; (2) the study's constructs are readily identifiable African centered; and (3) the study is clearly empirical, employing either quantitative or qualitative research methods." Joseph Baldwin created a measurement that embodies the criteria mentioned above and is probably the most widely known and used method of measuring the personality of black people. His development is called the ASC, which stands for African Self-Consciousness Scale. Therefore, this scale is used to "assess the respondent's attitudes, beliefs, values, and interest regarding his or her awareness and knowledge of the history, culture, and philosophical position of African Americans" (Utsety et al., 2009). Moreover, there must be policies that require that scales such as ASC and others like it be utilized for psychological and emotional well-being in black people.

People of African descent are by far some of the most self-destructive people because they fight the most indigenous parts of themselves. Furthermore, until Africana people cease their internal mental battle, it is impossible to awaken their true consciousness, making it even more impossible for all African people, on the continent and the diaspora, to reach a single consciousness. "Amilcar Cabral of Guinea-Bissau says the cessation of self-destruction by ADPs is motivated through one route only—a journey back to renewing myths of our pre-colonial origins" (Azibo, 2015). Hence, the importance of knowing and understanding their origins in Africa and how returning to their customs cultivates their collective memory and ethos. Finally, when this realization of liberation and certainness in their origin exists, the black psyche is alive and thriving and ready to spread itself among the masses.

References

Asante, M. K. (2003). *Afrocentricity: The theory of social change*. Chicago, IL: African American Images.

Azibo, D. A. (2015). Can psychology help spur the re-birth of African civilization? Notes on the African personality (Psychological Africanity) Construct: Normalcy, Development and Abnormality. *The Journal of Pan African Studies, 8*(1), 146–186.

Smith, M. L. (2016). Publishing qualitative research. In J. L. Conyers (Ed.), *Qualitative methods in Africana studies* (pp. 34–36). New York, NY: University Press of America.

Utsety, S. O., Belvet, B., & Fischer, N. (2009). Assessing African-centered (africentric) psychological constructs. In H. A. Neville, B. M. Tynes, & S. O. Utsey (Eds.), *Handbook of African American psychology* (pp. 75–87). Thousand Oaks, CA: Sage.

Walker, R. L., & Hunter, L. (2009). From anxiety and depression to suicide and self-harm. In H. A. Neville, B. M. Tynes, & S. O. Utsey (Eds.), *Handbook of African American psychology* (pp. 401–415). Thousand Oaks, CA: Sage.

12

TAKING ACTION ON HOPE

An Analysis on Culture-Based Education in the School Districts of New Orleans

Lanetta Dickens

The public and charter schools in New Orleans have seen some progress and downfall. Although the graduation rate had a steady increase between 2013 and 2016, the dropout rate is still effectively high at 23.1%. Since the disaster of Hurricane Katrina in 2005, an average of 65 students moved back to the New Orleans' school districts per year between 2007 and 2011. Most of the survivors have relocated to different cities due to the damages within New Orleans. Families wanted a better life and sought better opportunities for their children. Throughout the 11 years since Hurricane Katrina, public schools have not reached to the standard level of academic excellence for all of their students. In 2008, Louisiana had made a drastic decision regarding school reform. The state dismissed their school board and welcomed charter operators to conduct and build new schools in their districts, especially in New Orleans. Since the Knowledge is Power Program (KIPP) charter school program's goal is to have 100% of all freshmen to graduate by their senior year; unfortunately, that is far from reality. Due to problems of their environment, peer pressure, and health disparities, some high school students still have trouble with their schoolwork. Despite the KIPP program's goal to succeed all students, only 73% of high school students in the city of New Orleans graduate in a 4-year period. In order to shift the graduation and dropout rate, educators, administrators, and parents need to be culturally relatable and more attentive to high school students.

Being more culturally relatable to students simply means practicing a culture-based education. According to Dr. Molefi Asante (1980), "culture is the totalization of the historical, artistic, economic, and spiritual aspects of a people's lifestyle" (Afrocentricity, 134). In other words, a culture-based education is a form of instruction where students learn and process the curriculum through their way of being. Since the 1600s, educators have tried to practice Americanism, which is an act of assimilation meant to help "children learn to think, believe, and behave according to the white Anglo-Saxon Protestant ways while divesting non-WASP children of cultural practices that differed from the mainstream" (Pai & Adler, 1990).

In order for a student to become successful in the "white-dominated" society, he or she must be accommodating to Western practices in education. In unpropitious terms, Westernized thought in education marginalizes students of color. They are unable to relate to European or American culture because their experiences do not necessarily reflect the lifestyle. The phenomenon of the Americanization of educating non-white students has continued well into the twenty-first century. Despite the middle- and upper-middle-class families moving their children out of the public schools and into the private institutions, white American values are still being taught in the classroom.

Students of color often feel uncomfortable in white-dominated spaces. In an excerpt by Michael Omolewa (2010) from his encyclopedic entry on education, he states that:

> Such a child's basic introduction to Western values had been incomplete, and when he left school he belonged neither to the traditional African way of life nor to the Western world. Thus, cultural alienation and destabilization of traditional values, life, and cultural identity resulted from Western education. (p. 333)

A student may have difficulty in implementing the European ideology of writing, reading, and speaking with their current life experiences. A young African American boy will most likely distance himself from the classroom if he does not understand or cannot relate to the lesson being taught in class. Learning about William Shakespeare without some reference to a students' lifestyle or way of living can disconnect the student from the learning process. Instead, educators can associate the conflict between the Capulets and the Montagues in *Romeo and Juliet* with the conflicts of ideas in the political parties. The example may be overly simplified but provides a good counteraction with the students' comprehension skills and the lesson.

Students of color, especially African American students, should have a reason to deny their identity, in the case that there is a perceived idea that their culture or identity has no value. For centuries, African, Native, Latino/a, and Asian Americans were taught that their values were inferior to European Americans. In fact, "many suggest that the legacy of inequity continues, as some public and private school curriculums are biased and likely to include Eurocentric values, cultures, and ways of knowing," which "marginalizes some students of color whose ways of knowing, language, and dress are informed by popular culture" (Carter, 2011). While it is plausible to say that some students of color can easily adapt to the structural European curriculum, others have difficulty processing the information, which can leave them behind.

If a student of color loses their sense of identity in a constricted learning environment, their self-esteem is reduced. A young person has the desire to learn more about themselves in the classroom through an effective teacher. Students who doubt their capabilities of achieving in school are predestined to settle in a low socioeconomic status, where their dreams may be altered due to their lack of confidence. A prominent example is narrated in the book *Hope Against Hope: Three Schools, One City, and the Struggle to Educate America's Children* (Carr, 2013). A young 14-year-old girl in the book is unsure of her ambitions and goals because of her questionable future. The author, Sarah Carr, illustrates the student's fear: "No one in her immediate family had attended college, and despite her good grades in middle school, she remained deeply insecure about her 'book smarts'" (2013, p. 9). Insecurity builds in a child's mental health if it is not treated properly through accurate instruction and guidance from the people who help train their development.

Culture-based education denies the thought of insecurity and self-esteem by cultivating a way of learning that benefits all students but directly to African Americans. A good scenario can be illustrated through the following: a 16-year-old student causes disruption in the classroom because he is not sure how to complete the assignment that was given to him 10 minutes ago in class. The instructor becomes frustrated, because he or she is not sure how to handle the situation. According to Pai and Adler (1990), "teachers should be mindful of giving clear-cut explanations of what is to be done and how the work can be accomplished by providing specific instructions" (p. 230). The assignment was not instructed through a familiar interpretation and may be outside of his experience. The student loses confidence in his studies and therefore misbehaves in an open environment. However, if the assignment was instructed through a point of view that he may understand, whether it is related to pop culture, a familiar acquaintance that he remembers, or a past experience, then the 16-year-old student is no longer in a bewildered place. Thus, he focuses on his work and is no longer interrupting the classroom.

Oftentimes, most young students who live in the New Orleans district have a large disparity of income in their families' households. African American students are also underemployed in the city of New Orleans. After graduation, high school graduates suffer at a 19.5% unemployment rate within the district that they live in (Davis, Kimball, & Gould, 2015). Through a culture-based education, students learn more about themselves, seek value in themselves, and do better for themselves. For example, parents who have not received a "proper" education are inspired by their children to pursue their dreams that they did not have the chance to follow due to a lack of resources. Or, parents encourage their adolescent children to make the right choices in life, so they won't follow similar paths.

Along the idea of obtaining economic stability through income, students who learn through a culture-based curriculum has a greater advantage of improving their current lifestyle. Processing the history and experiences of the ancestors will give students a proper evaluation of their current situation, involving their environment, their peers, and their identity. Changing your environment can happen through the eyes of the oppressed. Learning about the racial and discriminatory history that leads to the result of a student's environment will awaken their consciousness (Asante, 1980, p. 62). Culturally speaking, their environment affects their families, other students, and can sometimes misinterpret their economic status.

Consequently, students may feel overwhelmed or pressured into success through a large amount of schoolwork, balancing their time with friends and family and participating in extracurricular activities. In order for students to suppress the tension, family relatives can enact in culture-based education through family narratives. Relating a child's experience to one's own journey indicates reassurance and hope within the student. The student, preferable African Americans, are better equipped of what life will bring and not feel defeated by having to complete so many duties and tasks. The weight is lowered, and the student becomes more relaxed.

Teaching an African American student or any student of color the values of family, commitment, and love for one another is a good strategy that is directly positioned in culture-based learning. Charter programs such as KIPP try to implement these aspects in their curriculum. Their main approach for all students is to prepare them for college and to lead fulfilling lives through good choices (kipp.org). Although their goal is to enhance collegiate success, not every student will want to go to college.

There is an uncertainty as to whether or not charter schools such as KIPP provide intellectual equality between regular students and overachievers. Gifted and talented students are not necessarily overachievers, but a general definition of the status is needed for this critique. Regular students in public and charter schools in the city of New Orleans continue to struggle with their schoolwork and the new procedures in their school programs. Dr. John Hope Franklin (2007) was familiar with the common distinction between public and private schools: "Not only is there no equality of opportunity in education, there is also no quality of resources among school districts" (p. 27). Would students in a charter school need additional disciplinary training to succeed? Public schools do not have strict guidelines in curriculum, but public and charter schools must follow procedures that are aligned with government funding. Also, the private schools in New Orleans do not participate in harsh punishment that could be detrimental to the students. However, the cost of high tuition for a lenient curriculum is taken into consideration. Why should public and charter schools learn different materials that are based on money?

Enhancing a student's sense of success is legitimate if they have an internal knowledge of self. The knowledge of self "is based on reality...if you use logic outside of yourself, you know that it is artificial...only the logic, symbolic relationships, derived from your center can create the necessary power for reconstruction" (Asante, 1980, p. 113). A student can achieve their goals by knowing who they are as individuals in society and learning to love themselves first. Then, when a student has a sense of who they are, they can succeed in whatever career they choose. Not all occupations require a degree, maybe some form or document that credits a skill or trade. Encouraging all students to go to college and teaching them self-worth and self-value are two different approaches. However, one is more effective than the other as far as the student's need for prosperity and growth.

African American male students are more likely to be misdiagnosed with medication relative to special education and/or learning disabilities than European Americans (Codrington & Fairchild, 2012). Young African American boys also represented 20 percent of the total population in school who are classified as mentally retarded (National Education Association, 2011). Statistical information concerning African American boys is very crucial because they are often viewed as inferior and incapable of learning. Instead of African American adolescents being diagnosed, educators and parents should find alternative strategies to engage students into learning. One of the strong suggestions is to instill an Afrocentric worldview into the minds of young African Americans.

Afrocentricity, or the Afrocentric thought, is a concept in which the ideas, perspectives, and interests are centered on African people. Dr. Asante claims that "Afrocentricity is a philosophical perspective associated with the discovery, location, and actualizing of African agency within the context of history and culture" (Asante, 1980, p. 3). With the rate of low graduates and higher dropout rates than the national average, the city of New Orleans can gather collective data on the impact of cultural-based education. Educators need to study systemic research in order to address the problems that connect to society's overall concern about education for all students (Walker, 2016). One of the methodologies that could be studied is a method that is studied under a certain cultural phenomenon that young students are noticing. Educators and administrators could acculturate the phenomenon into the lesson plan. A common aspect to popular culture that is discussed in the education field for further analysis is hip hop. In the past, the musical genre was a type of sound that was generated in urban cities. Presently, hip hop is a cultural trend and is formed in a certain pedagogy, so that students could comprehend the activity to their experience. Hip hop is a universal way of knowing, which is similar to the Afrocentric worldview. Hip hop was created by people of African descent; therefore, the culture itself is centered in the perspective of the creators of the culture.

Educators must encourage reliability with their students. During the early millennium, many candidates from the *Teach for America* program migrated to urban areas with a heavy population of underprivileged children. *Teach for America's* missionary model is to help make the country a better place by teaching poor children how to read and do math (Carr, 2013). New graduates from predominant elite or middle-class institutions are traveling to large cities where the people and demographics are different. For example, a young privileged graduate who settles in New Orleans to gain a teaching experience may feel overwhelmed with the economic and educational disparities that are occurring in the community. Students in the classroom are unimpressed with the teachers' lack of knowledge about their world and are doubtful of their teaching skills.

Active listening is a great strategy to cultivate a culture-based environment. Repeating yourself multiple times to the whole class does not stimulate active listening. Since there is an accepted statistic that African American children are more verbal and oral in class than other ethnic groups, implementing listening techniques to the students would be interesting. One of the positive characteristics of a culturally effective learner is to be a participant, speaker, and listener. There is a difference between regular listening and active listening. Regular listening requires careful attention in response to instruction. Active listening involves full concentration and reciprocating the instruction that is heard through an activity or assignment. Although not all African American are verbal learners, active listening should be required for students of different learning styles. Culture-based education uses this technique to bring full engagement in the classroom.

Whether it is hard to believe this thought, adolescents have the desire to be positively relatable to their peers, relatives, and educational leaders. Teachers and students who have experienced different ways of life can have a closer, professional connection through culture-based education. In *Hope Against Hope* (Carr, 2013), an educator named Aiden had a rough start with the students in the Science and Math Academy in New Orleans. However, he did his research and began launching a comfortable conversation with his students about their interests. What he did was extraordinary. Aidan used their experience as a learning mechanism for himself as a new teacher and for his students in the classroom.

A cultural-based education overall embodies the significance of connection and identity with students who have different experiences. The technique not only gravitates a sense of freedom within the classroom, it also "...positively impacts [a student's] socio-economic well-being" (Kana'iaupuni, Ledward, & Jensen, 2010). Students who especially suffer from living in low-income neighborhoods, are marginalized, and/or are misidentified as mentally unstable to learn can factor the way other students learn through an acculturated education.

Ensuring a qualified, cultured education requires solutions to the present problem of curriculum and instruction in institutions, especially in New Orleans. One solution is to apply Afrocentric values, history, and ways of knowing in predominate African American schools. Another factor is to place more value in culture-based education in administrative board meetings, so that authoritative leaders will recognize the importance of culture. Educators especially need to teach students how to think and become culturally connected with each other instead of by Eurocentric norms. If a school administration is reluctant in initiating a culture-based program, leaders can organize an alternative culture-base program on the weekends or after school for deeper study. All students of color should have access to an education that matters to them.

References

Asante, M. K. (1980). *Afrocentricity: The theory of social change.* Chicago, IL: African American Images.

Carr, S. (2013). *Hope against hope: Three schools, one city, and the struggle to educate America's children.* New York, NY: Bloomsbury Press.

Carter, S. (2011). Education: Public and private. In J. C. Smith (Ed.), *Encyclopedia of African American popular culture* (pp. 446–449). Santa Barbara, CA: Greenwood.

Codrington, J., & Fairchild, H. (2012). Special education and the mis-education of African American children: A call to action. *The Association of Black Psychologists.* February 13. Accessed August 11, 2016. http://www.abpsi.org/pdf/specialedpositionpaper021312.pdf.

Davis, A., Kimball, W., & Gould, E. (2015). The class of 2015: Despite an improving economy, young grads still face an uphill climb. *Economic Policy Institute,* May 27. Accessed August 11, 2016. http://www.epi.org/publication/the-class-of-2015/#epi-toc-4.

Franklin, J. H. (2007). "The national responsibility" for equality of educational opportunity. *The last word: The best commentary and controversy in American education* (pp. 23–29). San Francisco, CA: Jossey-Bass.

Kanaʻiaupuni, S., Ledward, B., & Jensen, U. (2010). Culture-based education and its relationship to student outcomes. *Culture-Based Education.* Kamehameha Schools Research & Evaluation Division, 1. Accessed July 29, 2016. http://www.ksbe.edu/_assets/spi/pdfs/CBE_relationship_to_student_outcomes.pdf.

National Education Association. (2011). Race against time: educating black boys. Focus on Blacks. February. Accessed August 11, 2016. http://www.nea.org/assets/docs/educatingblackboys11rev.pdf.

Omolewa, M. (2010). Education. In F. A. Irele & B. Jeyifo (Eds.), *The Oxford encyclopedia of African thought* (Vol. 1, p. 333). New York, NY: Oxford University Press.

Pai, Y., & Adler, S. A. (1990). *Cultural foundations of education.* Upper Saddle River, NJ: Merrill Prentice Hall.

Walker, H. (2016). Methods of research. *Qualitative methods in Africana studies: An interdisciplinary approach to examining Africana phenomena* (pp. 3–30). New York, NY: University Press of America Print.

13

RACE TALK AT THE INTERSECTIONS OF GENDER AND CLASS

Examining White Men's *Intersectional* Talk

Brittany C. Slatton

Introduction

According to discourse analysts, language is more than just words. "People use language 'to do things' [and] to achieve certain ends" (Augoustinos, Tuffin, & Sale, 1999, p. 91). Over the last several decades, scholars across the disciplines have utilized myriad theoretical and methodological approaches to examine the ways in which whites use their discourse or race talk to accomplish certain racial ends (Augoustinos & Every, 2007). Research shows that whites employ race talk as a form of "'storytelling' in which a master narrative ('White talk') depicts historical and cultural themes of racial progress, of a fair and just society, of equal access and opportunity, of meritocracy, and of colorblindness" (Sue, 2013, p. 665; Bell, 2002, 2003; Bolgatz, 2005; Pollock, 2004; Bonilla-Silva, 2010). According to Augoustinos and Every (2007), whites employ five common rhetorical strategies to justify, persuade, blame, and defend their racial positions—to people of color, members of their own social group, and to themselves—in ways that make them appear non-prejudicial (Goodman, 2014; Billig, 1987, 1988). The first strategy is the "denial of prejudice," whereby respondents claim that they are not racist before or after making a statement that many would perceive as indeed racist (Goodman, 2014; Augoustinos & Every, 2007; Van Dijk, 1992). The second common strategy is "grounding one's views as reflecting the external world." The third strategy is when speakers present a "positive self and negative other presentation." Hence, whites might present themselves as favorable and tolerant while discrediting other racial groups. The fourth strategy is when individuals engage discursive deracialization, whereby they remove "race from debates that could (at least potentially) be viewed as about race." The fifth common strategy is when whites make "liberal arguments for illiberal ends" (Goodman, 2014, p. 149; Augoustinos & Every, 2007, p. 125). Eduardo Bonilla-Silva (2010) also argues that whites rely on the discourses of colorblindness to talk about blacks (and other racial groups) in racist ways, without appearing racist. He identified four discursive frames: (1) abstract liberalism (decontextualized political and economic liberalism that allows whites to oppose policies that redress inequality while appearing moralistic), (2) naturalization (rationalizes racial separation and inequality as a natural human process, as opposed to a racially motivated one), (3) cultural racism (biologization of "cultural practices" and the rationalization of such practices as the root of racial inequality), and (4) minimization of racism (racism no longer or rarely contributes to the societal experiences of people of color) (Bonilla-Silva and Dietrich, 2011; Bonilla-Silva, 2010).

Ultimately, scholars find that through race talk, whites accomplish racism, "sustain and legitimate social inequalities" (Wetherell, 2003) and resist programs and policies that can attend to social inequality (Hastie & Remington, 2014). While race talk/discourse scholars have provided great insight into the ways in which whites (as well as other racial groups) talk about race— including defending, justifying and legitimating racism—few research studies have examined race talk at the intersection of other categories of difference, such as gender and class (Slatton, 2014; Embrick & Henricks, 2015).

If language does something—as many scholars argue—we must address all the ways in which language is used to accomplish certain ends. The current study seeks to address this issue by presenting data on the ways in which white men use intersectional patterns of talk and rhetorical arguments to construct themselves and black women in the context of romantic relationship.

I argue that talk or discourse should be examined from an intersectional framework. I begin by introducing the theoretical concept of intersectionality, addressing its machinations, criticisms, and scholarly responses to those critiques. I then apply the multidimensional framework of intersectionality to my discursive analysis of white men's *talk* on relationships with black women. My analysis gives attention to the ways in which respondents implicitly and/or explicitly draw on a hierarchical intersectional context to construct themselves, black women, and other social actors. Lastly, I discuss the major findings and the value of an intersectional approach to discursive studies.

Race, Gender, and Class as Intersectional Categories

Kimberle Crenshaw (1989) developed the concept of intersectionality to critique analyses of race and gender from a single-axis framework. A single-axis framework treats categories of race and gender as "mutually exclusive" and distorts their multi-dimensionality (Crenshaw, 1989). By placing black women at the center of analysis, Crenshaw showed how the experiences of black women were often erased, marginalized, and excluded. She found that the courts assumed that black women's sex discrimination experiences were the same as white women and their race discrimination experiences were the same as black men. Hence, the courts refused to acknowledge black women's "combined race and sex discrimination" claims and deemed it unnecessary to recognize black women as a "distinct social group" (Crenshaw, 1989; Carbado, 2013). Courts viewed black women as too "different" to represent gender or race—when the "class of plaintiffs" included white women or included black men, respectively (Carbado, 2013).

Crenshaw (1989) also addressed the ways in which feminist theory and antiracist politics, at times, excluded or marginalized black women by ignoring experiences that result from the interaction between race and gender. By focusing on "women's experiences" or "the black experience," some feminist theorists and antiracists essentialized the gender and race experiences of white women and black men. Simply adding black women into existing single-axis gender or race frameworks does not solve the problem, because the interactional dynamic of race, gender, class, and other categories is not attended to. As Crenshaw (1989, p. 166) notes:

> If any real efforts are to be made to free Black people of the constraints and conditions that characterize racial subordination, then theories and strategies purporting to reflect that Black community's needs must include an analysis of sexism and patriarchy. Similarly, feminism must include an analysis of race if it hopes to express the aspirations of non-white women. Neither black liberationist politics nor feminist theory can ignore the intersectional experiences of those whom the movements claim as their respective constituents.

The intersectional approach is not without criticisms. This approach is often critiqued as only being about race or gender or black women and for focusing primarily on subordinate groups and oppression, as opposed to groups with privilege. These critiques are not wholly accurate (Carbado, 2013). First, other scholars have successfully used the theory of intersectionality to examine more than race and gender. Some scholars have examined the intersection or interactions among class, citizenship, immigration, disability, and sexual orientation among other categories of difference. Second, Crenshaw and other scholars employed black women as a representational element of the intersectional framework to show how certain groups become invisible or excluded when intersections are not considered. According to Carbado (2013), this inaccurate critique potentially arises from scholars conflating intersectionality with double jeopardy theory. The theory of double jeopardy assumes that "the greater the number of marginal categories to which one belongs, the greater the number of disadvantages one will experience" (Carbado, 2013; Purdie-Vaughns & Eibach, 2008). Black women are a major part of this theory, because it is assumed that "they experience the double jeopardy of racism and sexism" (Carbado, 2013). Intersectionality, however, is not a derivative of double jeopardy theory. It does not assume that in every situation, poor black women or black lesbians, for example, will be more disadvantaged than other groups who occupy only one or two "marginal categories" (Carbado, 2013). Intersectionality is not concerned with adding up oppression to decipher who is the most oppressed group in society but instead seeks "to specify the distinctive forms of oppression experienced by those with intersecting subordinate identities" (Purdie-Vaughns & Eibach, 2008).

Lastly, scholars have shown how the intersectional approach is useful for analyzing the ways in which race, gender, class, and other social categories interact with each other in ways that create both oppression and privileges (Carbado, 2013; Ferber, 2012; Collins, 2000). Carbado's research employed intersectionality to address the categories at "the top of the social hierarchies," such as masculinity, whiteness, and maleness. For example, Carbado (2013) articulated a colorblind intersectionality and a gender-blind intersectionality to show how whiteness and gender "help to produce and is part of a cognizable social category but is invisible or unarticulated as an intersectional subject position." Carbado (2013) finds that when colorblind and gender-blind intersectionality go "unnamed and uninterrogated," privileged categories are further normalized as the "baseline" by which everyone else is "intersectionally differentiated."

Research Context

Since the achievement of *de jure equality*, contemporary polls and surveys show marked differences in white attitudes toward blacks—specifically in terms of social interactions and marriage. A recent poll finds that 84% of white Americans approve of interracial marriage between whites and blacks, as opposed to 17% in 1968 (Jones, 2011). And a 2005 Gallup poll finds that whites are quite receptive to white men dating black women (Jones, 2005).

These progressive attitudes are seemingly in vast contrast to a time period when whites defined black women as unsuitable and illegitimate partners for white men. As early as the fifteenth century, influential white men—who were travelers, scientists, doctors and politicians—used their prestigious platforms to write and talk about African women in ways that constructed them as strong, masculine, brutish, unmarked with the curse of Eve (childbirth pain), akin to the orangutan and other animals, and as possessing insatiable animalistic sexual appetites—evidenced by "disfigured" and "primitive" sexual body parts (Long, 1774; Gilman, 1985; Sharpley-Whiting, 1999; Morgan, 2002). The writings and pseudo-scientific findings of these influential men provided "evidence" that black women were biologically inferior to Europeans and thus at the bottom of the intersectional hierarchy. They also justified black women's enslavement and sexual objectification and denigration at the hands of white men. According to reports, during U.S. slavery, close to 60% of enslaved black women between the ages of 18 and 30 were raped by white men (West, 2006). White men (and women), however, asserted that "black women could not be raped, that they were seductresses" with a "lascivious nature" (Slatton, 2014). This argument was supported by legal institutions, as black women were considered property and had no legal recourse in the courts.

During legal segregation, whites continued to institutionally uphold beliefs in the biological inferiority of blacks and oppose interracial social interactions—particularly open relationships and marriage. White men continued to construct black women as sexual objects with animalistic sexual tendencies, who were nothing more than convenient bodies to quench their sexual desires. This construction was upheld legally—the laws continued to provide little recourse for black women who were raped by white men—and socially. In his 1914 book *Race Orthodoxy in the South and Other Aspects of the Negro Question*, Thomas Pierce Bailey detailed the attributes of black women in the post antebellum era:

> And the memory of antebellum concubinage and a tradition of animal satisfaction due to the average negro woman's highly developed animalism are factors still in operation. Not a few "respectable" white men have been heard to express physiological preference for negro women. If therefore animal appetite may become more powerful than race pride, it is not surprising that race hatred is superinduced upon those who offend against race purity; for abnormal sexuality easily develops brutality... Thus the element of kindliness that often belongs to concubinage yields to a mere animal convenience that may be consistent with race enmity on the part of the white offender...Thus does the negro woman become more and more a cheap convenience of the occasional sort, and the purity of the white race is protected at the expense of the white man's appreciation of the negro woman's personality. (Bailey, 1914, p. 43)

Although, contemporary society has certainly seen changes since the open discourse expressed by Thomas Pierce Bailey, current research on white men's dating and marriage behaviors with respect to black women finds that, in general, white men are not as racially progressive as contemporary polls might suggest. According to the U.S. Census Bureau (2010), whites have the lowest interracial marriage rate of all racial groups (Lin & Lundquist, 2013). And when whites marry across racial-ethnic lines, they are most likely to marry Latinos, Native Americans, and Asian Americans and least likely to marry blacks (Qian & Lichter, 2007). Intermarriage between white men and black women is one of the least likely interracial couplings and represented only 147,000 of the 504,000 black-white non-Hispanic marriages of 2010 (U.S. Census, 2010).

Studies also find that parity in education does not lead to a significant increase in black women's intermarriage rate with white men (Qian & Lichter, 2007; Iceland, Weinberg, & Steinmetz, 2002).

An analysis of internet dating profiles found that white men are open to interracial dating, just not with black women (Robnett & Feliciano, 2011; Feliciano, Robnett, & Komaie, 2009; Lin & Lundquist, 2013; Phua & Kaufman, 2005). One particular study found that when white men specified a racial preference, 93% excluded black women as a dating option (Robnett & Feliciano, 2011; Feliciano et al., 2009). Another recent study on online dating behavior found that white men were most likely to contact white women, followed by Hispanic and Asian women, and equally likely to "respond to messages from Asian, Hispanic, and white women" (Lin & Lundquist, 2013). However, white men avoided contacting black women and rarely responded to messages from black women. Black women, on the other hand, responded equally to messages from all racial groups. Higher education levels among black female online daters did not improve their likelihood of receiving responses from white men online. In fact, college-educated black women were excluded more than any other education group (Lin & Lundquist, 2013).

The contemporary data presents contradictory findings between white attitudes—expressed on polls—and actual behaviors. The present study approaches this area of inquiry from a discourse analytic framework. I examine the ways in which contemporary white men *talk* about black women in the context of romantic relationships, as opposed to identifying attitudes on Likert scale surveys. Through the analysis of white men's talk, I can ascertain how white men construct relationships with black women, the "variability" in what they say, and the function or end their talk serves (Augoustinos et al., 1999).

Method

One-hundred and thirty-four white men completed in-depth online self-administered questionnaires for this study. The respondents answered open-ended questions on their dating behaviors with black women and their thoughts on black women as relationship partners.[1] The participants accessed the questionnaire online, completed it anonymously and in the privacy of their own homes.[2] The sample is not representative, and the participants self-selected for the study. However, the sample reflects a broad selection of white males in all four regions, of varying ages, education, and income levels. See Table 13.1 for demographic information.

The data was collected in 2009 using a backstage methodological approach. This approach derives from Goffman's dramaturgical model of social interaction, which contends that people are social actors who engage in varying human performances depending on the social setting and the audience. Goffman defined two main social settings: the front region (known as the frontstage)

TABLE 13.1 Demographic information, $n = 134$

Region	Age range, yrs	Education	Dating relationships w/black women
44%—South	29%—18–29	42%—some college	54%—never dated
20%—Northeast	21%—30–39	30%—bachelors degree	45%—dated
24%—Mid-West	28%—40–49		34%—short term
12%—West	23%—50 and up		30%—sexual relationships
			14%—long term
			0%—long-term marriage
			20%—other[a]

a Friendships or combination of short-term, sexual, and long-term relationships.

and the back region (known as the backstage). In the frontstage, social actors are tasked with putting on the appropriate performance befitting of normative expectations of society. Whereas in the backstage, social actors can relax, joke, and "step out of character," because they generally do not have to concern themselves with the expected norms of society (Goffman, 1959).

Using Goffman's metaphor of human performances, backstage researchers argue that whites engage in different racial performances depending on the setting (Embrick & Henricks, 2015; Slatton, 2014; Picca & Feagin, 2007; Meyers, 2005; Hughey, 2001; Myers & Williams, 2001). In the frontstage—representative of racially diverse settings—whites are influenced by social desirability bias and hence may be more likely to perform societal expectations of colorblindness. In the post-civil rights era, society has normatively adopted color-blind/oppression-blind and even post-racial ideology—at least in theory. It is socially unacceptable for whites to appear openly racist or sexist in society, and individuals labeled as racist or sexist often face the consequences of sanctions and public shame (Embrick & Henricks, 2015; Anderson & Lepore, 2013; National Research Council, 2004). Hence, whites in the frontstage engage in what Goffman (1959) refers to as impression management, whereby social actors "attempt to guide audiences' reactions to achieve a positive self image in their eyes" (Embrick & Henricks, 2015).

The backstage is representative of private, exclusive white spaces. While in the backstage, whites can "express views that counter social norms," "are socially unacceptable," and hence contradict their frontage performances (Embrick & Henricks, 2015). Backstage researchers find that whites are quite likely to talk in openly racist ways in the backstage and often "do not define such performances as problematical" (Picca & Feagin, 2007). I contend that the talk of whites in the backstage is not just racial but also intersects with other categories of difference, such as gender and class. I used the approach of in-depth self-administered questionnaires because it is an accessible approach that is particularly useful for researchers of color attempting to capture whites in the backstage. Research shows that whites are less likely to provide open statements on race (Hatchette & Schuman, 1975) and other "sensitive" topics when the researcher is a person of color. Hence, it was advantageous for me to employ the in-depth questionnaire, as opposed to other approaches.

The overall findings of the questionnaire reveal that respondents overwhelmingly defined black women as less desirable relationship partners, and some respondents asserted explicit old-fashioned expressions of intellectual and biological inferiority among black women. See Slatton (2014) for more details on the overall results of the questionnaire. In the current study, I rely on the questionnaire data to discuss how white male respondents used common patterns of intersectional talk to construct themselves, black women, and other social actors in the context of romantic relationships and the rhetorical tools they employed to justify their arguments. My primarily goal is to illustrate—in broad strokes—the intersectional context of respondents' statements, as opposed to a more comprehensive overview of data.

Analysis and Discussion: White Men's Intersectional Talk

All social actors embody intersectional identities, in terms of race, gender, class, sexuality, and so forth. Hence, I use the multidimensional framework of intersectionality, as opposed to a single-axis race framework to examine the discourse of white male respondents in this study. I rely on Crenshaw (1989) and Carbado's (2013) articulation of intersectionality to assess how respondents draw on a hierarchical intersectional context to construct themselves, black women, and other social actors and the ends that such a context provides. I also give attention to the types of rhetorical arguments respondents employed to justify their claims and social standing and deflect criticism (Billig, 1988).

My analysis of the data finds that white men implicitly and explicitly drew on a hierarchical intersectional context—and other rhetorical tools—to explain, defend, and justify the construction of themselves and other social actors favorably and black women unfavorably in the context of romantic relationships. A major finding is that white men treated black women's race as "always already particularizing her" gender, femininity, and beauty and treated whiteness as an implicit or normative category for the expression of gender, femininity, and beauty (Carbado, 2013). The following quotes by Walter, Dan, James, and Ross illustrate[3]:

> [I] think their vagina is just not right looking, the black lips and the pink inside is just a total turn off (Slatton, 2014).
>
> *Walter*

I tend to read African features as somewhat masculine. The "blacker" the person, the less femininity I tend to see (Slatton, 2014).

Dan

Do not find attractive—facial features, hair, skin. Occasionally a black woman whose black features are less prominent will be attractive, but rarely. Most of the black women I find attractive... are of mixed ethnicity and appear more white than black (Slatton, 2014).

James

Sexual attraction for me is a combination of physical and personal attributes. If I find a "black" woman attractive, it is because their hair type and facial features are more representative of the [C]aucasian race. If that aspect is attractive, then their speech and intelligence level would have to be more representative of that found more prevalent in other races (such as [C]aucasian or [A]sian—i.e.: anthropological mongoloids) (Slatton, 2014).

Ross

In the first two quotes, Walter and Dan racialize the physical features of black women—in terms of hair, skin color, facial features, and genitalia—as either less "black" or more "black." In order to define a person's degree of blackness as less or more beautiful, there must be a comparison or baseline. Whiteness is that unarticulated baseline. The discourse of Walter and Dan reflects Carbado's (2013) articulation of colorblind intersectionality because, in their extracts, "whiteness is doing racially constitutive work…but is unarticulated and racially invisible as an intersectional subject position." To elaborate, whiteness is the default racial category by which gender, beauty, and femininity are expressed (Carbado, 2013); black women have no representational capital, because their race already adulterates their gender, femininity, and beauty. As the quote by Walter illustrates, even a black woman's genitalia have no representational capital because it is part of a gendered body that is raced.

James and Ross explicitly name white women as the standard or normative category by which beauty and other characteristics, such as intelligence and speech, are expressed. For them, black women are not beautiful unless they look like white women. Hence, whiteness is not always an invisible, unarticulated backdrop for gender and beauty; some whites clearly express whiteness as the category by which other characteristics are expressed and by which others are evaluated.

The data also shows that white men at times considered other racial/ethnic groups of women as closer to meeting the default beauty, femininity, or intelligence quotient. Latina women and Asian American women were differentiated along the intersectional hierarchy by white men; however, white men evaluated these groups as being much closer to meeting the intersectional baseline. For example, Davis asserted that the only attractive black women are those mixed with other racial groups:

> There are some black women who are attractive. And they aren't full black. The only black women I find attractive are a mix of black and [E]uropean, black and [L]atino, or black and [A]sian. They end up with the tan complexion, and hair that doesn't look frizzled or like a [B]rillo pad (Slatton, 2014).
>
> *Davis*

White men also drew on an intersectional context to construct culture, class, and personal attributes as well. Positive culture, attitudes, and ways of living one's life were attributed explicitly and implicitly to whites, while "black" culture was negatively evaluated from the normative baseline of whiteness. Below, Greg, Mark, Gibson, Roger, and Andre illustrate[4]:

> Some black women that I have met are absolutely wonderful .... I know I've been blessed to come away from those meetings with incredible and unique friends. Still, even in the small town and rural settings that I am used to, I see a large number of black women, young and old, simply unable and unwilling to form relationships with men that last more than a few months to a few years.... I don't know the root of it, but I do see it as a major contributor to a continuing "state welfare" lifestyle where they believe they are entitled to a monthly paycheck, and all the trimmings, so long as they keep churning out children... actual fathers are unnecessary. This needs to stop. I think at the heart of the matter, black women (as a whole, and in the media) need to stop seeing themselves as an oppressed minority, and look forward to building a future, one step at a time like everybody else, rather than expecting it to be done for them. I wish them luck, it's not easy, but it's doable (Slatton, 2014).
>
> *Greg*

> Black women are like black people, which are different tha[n] white people. This is not a racist comment (doesn't that sound defensive?) we are just different socially, morally, physically... etc. This does not mean one is better than the other, just different. I think most of us are attracted to those who share similar values, thus I am attracted to white women. Black women generally have different morals, values and social etiquette than white women, and I don't find the differences exemplified by black women attractive (Slatton, 2014).
>
> *Mark*

No, they usually have body shapes that I don't like (usually their butts are too big), and don't value education as much as white and Asian women. I have known a few black women who were raised around whites, and they don't have these traits (Slatton, 2014).

Gibson

I like the ones who live in the suburbs. Who are respectful of other people and who can keep their voices at an average level. Who dress like normal people. Who can speak proper [E]nglish. Who doesn't swear every other word. Who doesn't shake their necks when they talk. Black women can be beautiful as long as they act like a normal human being. I like their hair, when they straighten it (Slatton, 2014).

Roger

Some women really take care of themselves and get educated and like nice things but [I] feel that the most of the black race are too lazy to start at the bottom and work their way up as [I] had to do. [I]n all my schooling and diplomas [I] went to school with very few black men or women for they seem to like not being educated and living on the poor or welfare over and over with 5 kids and 4 dads (Slatton, 2014).

Andre

In the above extracts, whiteness or whiteness and gender operate(s) as an invisible or recognized but uninterrogated default for ideal culture, class, values, and etiquette. In Roger's extract, whiteness is unarticulated in the following descriptors: "suburbs," "normal people," "proper English," "normal human being," straight hair, and necks that don't shake. Although, Roger does not explicitly identify whiteness or white female as the normative standard by which he is differentiating black women; his implicitness has the same impact and fulfills the same ends—the reproduction of privileged and oppressed statuses along intersectional lines—as Gibson, Mark, and Andre's explicit statements. Whiteness or white woman is the clear baseline by which Gibson, Mark, and Andre evaluate black women. They construct black women as having bad "morals, values, and social etiquette," denigrating education, relishing poverty, and a welfare lifestyle and hence unsuccessful in meeting the normative cultural standard. Because whiteness or whiteness and gender play a role as producer and product of constructions of culture and class, black women on the whole are thus too intersectionally different to provide a general representation of ideal culture and class. Instead, they are intersectionally differentiated from the normative (white) baseline and assessed on how close or far away they are from the norm. Black women who live in white neighborhoods (suburbs) and express themselves in ways constructed as *less* black and female (neck doesn't shake when she talks, for example) are closer. But it does not matter how many black women meet the normative standard, because black women collectively do not have the representational "currency" to express culture, class, etiquette, and so forth.

Rhetorical Arguments

Rhetorical arguments and other discursive tools were employed by the respondents to save face, protect themselves against criticism, and justify their arguments to themselves and the readers of their comments (Billig, 1988). For example, immediately after defining black women as different from white people, Mark stated that "this is not a racist comment." The denial of racism is one of the most common discursive tools employed by contemporary whites (Goodman, 2014; Van Dijk, 1992). This is a disclaimer statement that allows whites to "attend" to a "positive self-presentation...but also allow what otherwise would be 'unsayable' to be said" (Augoustinos & Every, 2007). Mark followed up his disclaimer with "doesn't this sound defensive?" He recognized the discursive move of prefacing his comments with an "I'm not a racist" claim. Other disclaimer statements included those expressed by Greg and Roger. The opening sentence of Greg's comment "[s]ome black women I have met are absolutely wonderful" is an "advance justification" designed to deflect criticism away from his series of follow-up sentences that negatively construct black women as poor relationship partners, welfare users, and victims (Billig, 1988, p. 98). Roger started his statement by differentiating a deviant black woman from the normative baseline for woman—white women. His closing sentence, "Black women can be beautiful as long as they act like a normal human being," acts to justify himself as a decent person and someone who cannot be prejudicial against black women if he thinks they have the potential to be beautiful—only if—of course—they can meet the normative cultural standard. The discursive frame of minimization was also employed. According to Greg, seeing themselves as an oppressed minority is what hold's black women back. This statement implies that oppression is no longer an issue for black women, and hence, he minimizes its impact on black women's lives.

Conclusion

An analysis of white men's talk from a multi-dimensional framework of intersectionality illustrates the ways in which whiteness and gender produce and are part of social concepts/categories such as beauty, culture, education, femininity, and masculinity, yet are invisible, unarticulated, recognized but uninterrogated, and/or normative as an "intersectional subject position" (Carbado, 2013). Respondents both legitimated and sustained intersectional privileges and oppression by naturalizing whiteness and/or gender—implicitly and explicitly—as the baseline for femininity, beauty, class, and culture. Black women were "intersectionally differentiated" from this normative baseline and overwhelmingly defined as falling short of the standard. Black women do not have representational capital for beauty, femininity, gender, and culture, because respondents treat whiteness and/or whiteness and gender as the default for such categories. Rhetorical arguments—such as disclaimers, advance justifications, and minimizations—along with other discursive tools allowed white men to deflect criticism from themselves and justify the intersectional hierarchy.

The research findings illustrate that language accomplishes more than just racial ends. And if discursive scholars are to capture all those ends, talk must be analyzed multidimensionally at the intersections.

Notes

1   The quotes of the respondents in this essay are word-for-word from the written responses to the questionnaires. Ellipses, capitalizations, all-caps words, and statements in parenthesis are the way the respondents wrote the response.
2   According to a Census Bureau report on computer and internet use in the United States, White men have the greatest access to a computer and to the internet (Davie et al., 2005), thus the online questionnaire used in this study did not create a barrier to reaching potential study participants. The author advertised the questionnaire in all 50 states on a popular advertisement website that reaches over 40 million people each month.
3   Walter, James, and Ross are responding to questions on what they find physically and sexually attractive or unattractive about black women.
4   Greg's comments are in response to a question that asked him to share his thoughts on black women. Gibson's comment is in response to "whether he believes he can find his ideal woman among black women."

References

Anderson, L., & Lepore, E. (2013). Slurring words. *Nous*, 47(1), 25–48.

Augoustinos, M., & Every, D. (2007). The language of "race" and prejudice: A discourse of denial, reason, and liberal-practical politics. *Journal of Language and Social Psychology*, 26(2), 123–141.

Augoustinos, M., Tuffin, K., & Sale, L. (1999). Race talk. *Australian Journal of Psychology*, 51(2), 90–97.

Bailey, T. P. (1914). *Race orthodoxy in the South: And other aspects of the Negro Question.* New York, NY: The Neale Publishing Company.

Bell, L. A. (2002). Sincere fictions: The pedagogical challenges of preparing white teachers for multicultural classrooms. *Equity and Excellence in Education, 35*, 236–244.

Bell, L. A. (2003). Telling tales: What stories can teach us about racism. *Race, Ethnicity, and Education, 6*, 3–28.

Billig, M. (1987). *Arguing and thinking: A rhetorical approach to social psychology.* Cambridge, UK: Cambridge University Press.

Billig, M. (1988). The notion of "prejudice": Some rhetorical and ideological aspects. *Text, 8*(1–2), 91–110.

Bolgatz, J. (2005). *Talking race in the classroom*. New York, NY: Teachers College Press.

Bonilla-Silva, E. (2010). *Racism without racists: Color-blind racism and the persistence of racial inequality in the United States* (3rd ed.). Lanham, MD: Rowman and Littlefield.

Bonilla-Silva, E., & Dietrich. D. (2011). The sweet enchantment of color-blind racism in Obamerica. *The Annals of the American Academy of Political and Social Science Policy, 634*, 190–206.

Carbado, D. (2013). Colorblind intersectionality. *Signs: Journal of Women in Culture and Society, 38*(4), 811–845. [1–42]. Retrieved June 10, 2016. http://papers.ssrn.com/sol3/papers.cfm?abstract_id=2291680.

Collins, P. H. (2000). *Black feminist thought: Knowledge, consciousness, and the politics of empowerment* (2nd ed.). New York, NY: Routledge.

Crenshaw, K. (1989). Demarginalizing the intersection of race and sex: A black feminist critique of antidiscrimination doctrine, feminist theory, and antiracist politics. *University of Chicago Legal Form, 1*(8), 139–167.

Day, J. C., Janus, A., & Davis, J. (2005). "Computer and Internet Use in the United States: 2003." US Census Bureau.

Embrick, D. G., & Henricks, K. (2015). Two-faced-isms: Racism at work and how race discourse shapes classtalk and gendertalk. *Language Sciences, 52*, 165–175.

Feliciano, C., Robnett, B., & Komaie, G. (2009). Gendered racial exclusion among white internet daters. *Social Science Research, 38*(1), 39–54.

Ferber, A. L. (2012). The culture of privilege: Color-blindness, postfeminism, and Christonormativity. *Journal of Social Issues, 68*(1), 63–77.

Gilman, S. L. (1985). *Difference and pathology: Stereotypes of sexuality, race, and madness*. Ithaca, NY: Cornell University.

Goffman, E. (1959). *The presentation of self in everyday life*. Garden City, NY: Doubleday.

Goodman, S. (2014). Developing an understanding of race talk. *Social and Personality Psychology Compass, 8*(4), 147–155.

Hastie, B., & Remmington, D. (2014). "200 years of white affirmative action": White privilege discourse in discussion of racial inequality. *Discourse & Society, 25*(2), 186–204.

Hatchette, S., & Schuman, H. (1975). White respondents and race-of-interviewer effects. *Public Opinion Quarterly, 39*, 523–528.

Hughey, M. W. (2001). Backstage discourse and the reproduction of white masculinities. *The Sociological Quarterly, 52*(1), 132–153.

Iceland, J., Weinberg, D. H., & Steinmetz, E. (2002). *Racial and ethnic residential segregation in the United States 1980–2002*. Washington, DC: U.S. Government Printing Office.

Jones, J. M. (2005). Most Americans approve of interracial dating. *Gallup*. October 7. Retrieved June 1, 2016, from http://www.gallup.com/poll/19033/most-americans-approve-interracial-dating.aspx.

Jones, J. M. (2011). Record high 86% approve of black-white marriages. *Gallup*. September 12. Retrieved June 1, 2016, http://www.gallup.com/poll/149390/record-high-approve-black-white-marriages.aspx.

Lin, K.-H., & Lundquist, J. (2013). Mate selection in cyberspace: The intersection of race, gender, and education. *American Journal of Sociology, 119*(1), 183–215.

Long, E. (1774). *The history of Jamaica, or, general survey of the ancient and modern state of that island: With reflections on its situation, settlements, inhabitants, climate, products, commerce, laws, and government.* London: T. Lowndes.

Meyers, K. A. (2005). *Racetalk: Racism hiding in plainsight.* Lanham, MD: Rowman & Littlefield.

Morgan, J. L. (2002). "Some could suckle over their shoulder": Male travelers, female bodies, and the gendering of racial ideology, 1500–1770. In K. Wallace-Sanders (Ed.), *Skin deep, spirit strong: The black female body in American culture* (pp. 37–65). Ann Arbor, MI: The University of Michigan Press.

Myers, K. A., & Williamson, P. (2001). Race talk: The perpetuation of racism through private discourse. *Race and Society, 4*(1), 3–26.

National Research Council. (2004). *Measuring racial discrimination.* Panel on Methods for Assessing Discrimination, Committee on National Statistics, Division of Behavior and Social Sciences and Education, R. M. Blank, M. Dabady, & C. F. Citro (Eds.), Washington, DC: The National Academies Press.

Phua, V. C., & Kaufman, G. (2005). The crossroads of race and sexuality: Date selection among men in internet "personal" ads. *Journal of Family Issues, 24*, 981–994.

Picca, L. H., & Feagin, J. R. (2007). *Two-faced racism: Whites in the backstage and frontstage.* New York, NY: Routledge.

Pollock, M. (2004). *Colormute: Race talk dilemmas in an American high school.* Princeton, NJ: Princeton University Press.

Purdie-Vaughns, V., & Eibach, R. P. (2008). Intersectional invisibility: The distinctive advantages and disadvantages of multiple subordinate-group identities. *Sex Roles, 59*(5–6), 377–391.

Qian, Z., & Lichter, D. T. (2007). Social boundaries and marital assimilation: Interpreting trends in racial and ethnic intermarriage. *American Sociological Review, 72*, 68–94.

Robnett, B., & Feliciano, C. (2011). Patterns of racial-ethnic exclusion by internet daters. *Social Forces, 89*(3), 807–828.

Sharpley-Whiting, T. D. (1999). *Sexualized savages, primal fears, and primitive narratives in French.* Durham, NC: Duke University Press.

Slatton, B. (2014). *Mythologizing black women: Unveiling white men's deep frame on race and gender.* New York, NY: Routledge.

Sue, D. W. (2013). Race talk: The psychology of racial dialogues. *American Psychologist, 68*(8), 663–672.

U.S. Census Bureau. (2010). *Table 60. Married couples by race and Hispanic origin of spouses.* Washington, DC: U.S. Government Printing Office.

Van Dijk, T. A. (1992). Discourse and the denial of racism. *Discourse & Society, 3*, 87–118.

West, C. M. (2006). Sexual violence in the lives of African American women: Risk, response, and resilience. *National Online Resource Center on Violence against Women,* 1–11.

Wetherell, M. (2003). Racism and the analysis of cultural resources in interviews. In H. van den Berg, M. Wetherell, & H. Houtkoop-Steenstra (Eds.), *Analyzing race talk: Multidisciplinary approaches to the interview* (pp. 11–30). Cambridge, UK: Cambridge University Press.

14

THE THIRTEENTH AMENDMENT

James L. Conyers, Jr.

Introduction

History is defined as the record of human events, shaped in the image and interests of the narrator or reporter (Karenga 2010, p. 66). Subsequently, the Thirteenth Amendment and the African American agency are a compelling and adjusted topic of discussion. Phrased another way, African Americans are the descendants of involuntary migrants who were forced to migrate outside the continent of Africa. Maulana Karenga points out about the impact of the political legislation of the Thirteenth Amendment, writing the ensuing: "Congress passed three cornerstone Amendments directed toward integration of Blacks in the social fabric on the basis of equality, i.e., the Thirteenth, Fourteen, and Fifteenth Amendments" (Karenga 2010, p. 131). Using institutional and systemic punitive forms of subordination and restraint, Blacks were placed in a position of captivity for a period of almost five centuries.

Paradoxically, these institutional barriers have impacted the current state of privilege and racism, ranked in the United States. Figure 14.1 outlines the breakdowns and breakthroughs of enslavement and the holocaust of the systemic extermination of Africana phenomena. The three layers of analysis are enslavement, manumission, and Jim Crow segregation. Collectively, all three of these institutional barriers restrained and subordinated the sovereignty of Africana people and culture.

Likewise, the contemporary climate of race relations in America has provided context for the reflection, reclamation, and reflexivity of the Civil War. Extracting a selected quote, I pause for the succeeding commentary, offering the preceding: "It's hard to tell time by revolutionary clocks. Everything, including time, changes in a revolutionary time, and the clocks inherited from the old

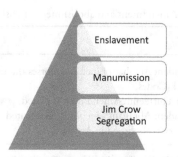

FIGURE 14.1 Breakdowns and breakthroughs of enslavement

regime are usually too slow or too fast. A real revolution introduces a new time and a new space and a new relation to both time and space" (Bennett 1972, p. 11).

Addressed in the thesis of this essay, the passage of the Thirteenth Amendment pursued the declaration of the Emancipation Proclamation of 1863. Both documents addressed the bondage and systemic subordination of African Americans. Melvin Drimmer mentions:

> The Thirteenth Amendments, prohibiting slavery, was adopted in 1865, immediately after the war. The southern states responded by enacting the Black Codes, which restricted the rights of the newly freed Negroes and effectively made them serfs. Some of these laws, for example, forbade Negroes to own land outside towns or do any work but farming without a special license. (Drimmer 1969, p. 425)

Additionally, Michael Conniff and Thomas Davis continue to write about this visage in Americana history, saying:

> Emancipation did much the same. Rather than being a private act, emancipation was public act: The government declared that some class of slaves, whether small or large, was free...Thus, in northern states such as New York, New Jersey, and Pennsylvania, it was not state action but the Thirteenth Amendment to the U.S. Constitution that in 1865 abolished the legal basis of slavery. (Conniff and Davis 1994, p. 144)

Table 14.1 provides a brief chronology of the Thirteenth Amendment and other political affairs, which shaped the social ecology for the abolishment of enslavement.

For organization purposes, this essay will examine four areas regarding the Thirteenth Amendment: (1) Civil War, (2) Emancipation Proclamation, (3) justification for succession, (4) methodology, and (5) the overall impact of the Thirteenth Amendment passage before the close of the Civil War. Accordingly,

TABLE 14.1 Thirteenth Amendment and abolishment of enslavement

Date	Event
January 1, 1863	President Abraham Lincoln endorses the Emancipation Proclamation.
January 1, 1865	Black Codes.
January 31, 1865	The Thirteenth Amendment is passed.
April 15, 1865	President Abraham Lincoln is assassinated.
December 6, 1865	Slavery is abolished in America.

Source: Timetoast timeline, TJSTERK. "13th Amendment Timeline." Timetoast, https://www.timetoast.com/timelines/13th-amendment-timeline.

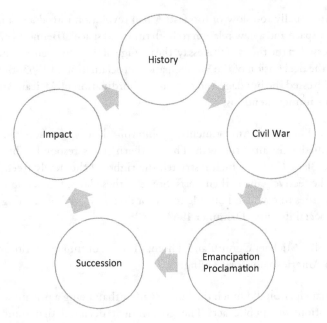

FIGURE 14.2 Research framework

I will be using secondary analysis to collect data, which will be composed of books, articles, and primary sources. Figure 14.2 outlines the framework of this research paper.

Civil War

The basis for the Civil War, resting on the Southern Confederacy of States who attempts to succeed as a sovereign nation within itself. Removed from the Union of the United States, President Abraham Lincoln attempted to draw the differences between the concept of rebel and sovereign nation. In this way, he identified that the states were still connected to the Union, however, the personnel who lived in these states were committing treason, in the way of advancing the separation of the state and the continuation of the enslavement of African Americans.

Lerone Bennett provides a description of the landscape of the Civil War, by writing the following:

> In the two decades preceding the Civil War, a great many slave holders expressed hopes that slaves would stop writing books. Scores of slaves escaped and told; and the abolitionists audience increased. Slave narratives became a new form of literature, An English clergyman, Ephraim Peabody, observed that 'America had the mournful honor of addition a new department to the literature of civilization—the autobiography of escaped slaves. (137, Before the Mayflower)

Earl Lewis advances this idea by writing the following, with concern to African American historiography:

> Ironically, the study of slavery enslaved African-American historiography, at least in the pages of the *AHR*. Through 1945, scholars writing for the journal conflated slavery and blacks, viewing African Americans through the prism of the Peculiar Institution. Most of these early articles painted a picture of slavery heatedly disavowed later, but it was a portrait that the generation of scholars who lived through the Civil War or came of age during Reconstruction found quite appealing.[8] To a certain degree, the story of slavery was not just about the bygone days of a "once upon a time" era; rather, slavery occupied a prominent place in the nation's memory because it framed the building of the Jim Crow era and situated the continuing contestation of power and race. (Lewis 1995, p. 767)

Emancipation Proclamation

Precisely, our focus is on the year of 1865. Historically, two years earlier, America experienced the signage of the Emancipation Proclamation, which is, ironically, a document that purports to provide liberation for African Americans. Ronald Walters addresses the institutional impact of racism and enslavement by correlating the following analysis:

> Indeed, one of the striking things about the character of the modern discourse about the reason for the persistence of overt and covert racism and the way in which it affects various aspects of American life is that it appears de-linked from the past history of the United States as a slave society. Although slavery is an institution that dominated American

race relations for 250 years and persisted in various forms and intensity for another one hundred years after it was declared illegal, it is rarely discussed by social scientists as the foundation for modern racial dynamics such as the socioeconomic conditions for African Americans and the racial attitudes of white Americans. Nevertheless, the realm and reach of its proximity to modern problems should still inform the work of scholars today. However, the unarticulated impact of slavery has fostered in whites and many African Americans alike the notion that in the 21st century, African Americans themselves are totally responsible for having created and maintained the situation in which they find themselves. (Walters 2012)

Yet, the United States was under the guild of the Civil War, whereas the Southern Confederacy of States succeeded from the Union and recognized themselves as a sovereign nation. Specifically, this was a war time act of expediency, which did not allow or prohibit the liberation of African Americans who were living in the South, under the authority of the rebels. Bethany Johnson provides some discourse threaded to this discussion relative to the Thirteenth Amendment and slavery, reviewing Foner notes in the following:

> These characteristics, however, stemmed in part from the recognition by African-American intellectuals that what slavery *meant* to their contemporaries in the early twentieth century was at least as important, if not more, than what slavery *was* in the past.[7] Moreover, as Eric Foner has stressed, African Americans possessed special authority over the meaning of slavery. While white Americans could profitably forget or "sugarcoat" slavery, for blacks "slavery was a historical experience, which would remain central to their conception of themselves and their place in history". (Johnson 2000, p. 32)

Justification of Succession

There are a number of reasons justified for the purpose of the development of the Southern Confederacy of States, which address sovereignty. Yet, the creation of subordinate group status lends discussion to involuntary, voluntary, annexation, and colonialism (Schaefer 1993). Nonetheless, there is a need to mention as a sidebar note the issues of annexation and colonialism of the Native American community. The Dakota nation of indigenous people is also referred to as part of the Native American population of the United States. However, in the year 1500, there were a reported number of 10 million Native Americans in the United States. Regrettably, by the year of 1900, there were less than two-hundred and fifty-thousand Native Americans in the United States. Much of this is relegated to the holocaust committed against the Native Americans. Holocaust can be defined as the systemic genocide or extermination of a selected group of people.

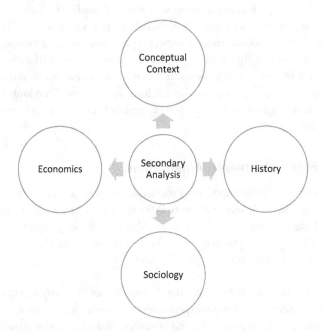

FIGURE 14.3 Collection of data and context

Methodology

The method of collection of data for this research assignment is secondary analysis, with the use of some primary sources, with a conceptual formation and organizational design. Equally important, secondary analysis refers to use of books and article already in print. Additionally, I will use scholarly articles through databases online and in print. Books will comprise studies that have examined the passage of the Thirteenth Amendment. Worldview is relevant in my interpretation of the literature of discussion. Likewise, I am using a conceptual approach to collection of materials for this research assignment. This refers to using a matrix that assigns a social science analysis for the development of this essay. Figure 14.3 offers the framework for the collection of data and contextual boundaries of locating the topic of discussion in place, space, and time.

As noted previously, the Thirteenth Amendment passed before the end of the Civil War. What did this mean for the Southern Confederacy? Under the presidential administration of Abraham Lincoln, the Republican Party advanced the idea of restoring peace to the nation. Johnson builds on this discussion by writing about the position and ethos of Frederick Douglass, saying:

> What Douglass realized, and what later historians have argued, was that the meaning of emancipation was not fixed, despite its historical reality. "Emancipation was a central dynamic of southern history," LaWanda Cox

has written, "forcing a reconstruction of southern society of which Reconstruction after the Civil War was but an episode."[3] To participate in this restructuring of society, the former slaves assigned meaning to freedom through building independent institutions like churches and schools by structuring economic relationships that preserved aspects of their autonomy in a generally exploitative system. Freedom, therefore, was as much a cultural concept as a legal or literal reality. (Johnson 2000, pp. 30, 31)

Impact of the Thirteenth Amendment

Nonetheless, the Emancipation Proclamation was a war time measure. The heart of the disclosure was, were African Americans property or humans with civil rights. Here, the point directed were Blacks property or was the Southern Confederacy a sovereign nation. Lewis inserts his analysis concerning the body of literature on this topic, documenting:

> During the years 1886–1990, the *Political Science Quarterly* and the *American Political Science Review* published twenty-seven articles each about African Americans. Comparatively, the *American Historical Review* printed a total of fifty-one substantive articles about blacks: twenty-nine essays on slavery, thirteen on African Americans, and nine on race relations-between 1895 and 1994. Just as important, sixteen of the twenty-nine articles on slavery had appeared in the *AHR* by 1945. (Lewis 1995, p. 768)

There stood the possibility that if the war ended first, the rebels would walk back the idea to retain slavery and create disruption.

Compelling with discussion about the Thirteenth Amendment are two queries: (1) the abolition of enslavement, and (2) the ending of the Civil War. It is paradoxical that there was intersection between these two points. Whereas the abolition of enslavement impacted the sovereignty of the Rebels in the Southern states. Political, economic, and sociological aspects of enforcement of racism were prioritized. Nonetheless, the ending of the war allowed the union to retain political and economic expediency. Presenting these two points in a structural manner dismisses the impact and subordination of Black cultural history and thought. Another aspect of passage of the Thirteenth Amendment lied in the thought of President Abraham Lincoln going into his second term of office.

Here lies the thought of the Civil War occupying three quarters of the Lincoln administration. He was challenged with the opposition of having the Rebels, living in the Southern states, and acknowledging themselves as the Southern Confederacy of States, possibly attempting to ratifying the Thirteenth Amendment, if brought back to the union, without the passage of this amendment to the constitution. Contrary to the contemporary political landscape, it was the Republican Party that opposed the continuity of enslavement of African Americans. On the other hand, it was the Democratic Party, with representatives from free Midwestern and Middle colony states, who supported the enslavement of Blacks. Ratification of the amendment was a concern.

Enslavement is oftentimes described and evaluated from a structural lens. On the other hand, a cultural analysis describes this era in the context of African American history as a holocaust, rather than trade. Simply put, a holocaust is defined as systematic genocide of a selected group of people.

The status of African Americans in 1619, when arriving in Jamestown, Virginia, was transitional between: indentured servants, enslaved persons, and lifelong property. Reflecting, this period is during the early settlements in the United States and the formation of the first colonies along the eastern colonies. Whereas the London Virginia Company was established by the English as a colony in the year of 1619. Yet, the concept of indentured servitude was misleading, whereas the thought, African Americans were servants, but could work as laborers and eventually earn their freedom as citizens with human rights.

This idea was short lived, in the view of the American colonialists who sought the idea of enforcing the Eurocentric hegemonic perspective and imposing Blacks in a systematic status of enslavement. In this way, the colonial forces could justify their actions concerning the subordination of African people, by implementing their thoughts, philosophies, and ideas into law and public policy. Expectations imposed on enslaved Africans were for them to be free laborers, with having no overhead for labor or product to the early colonial pioneers. Phrased another way, it meant all profit, while subjugating Black life. The practical aspect of the enslavement of Africans rested on their knowledge and familiarity of residing in an agrarian societies (Bennett 1969, p. 48).

Ironically, some historians have referred to the system of enslavement as being benign and civilizing, economically profitable, and a system of barter and trade. Irrespective, the system was institutional holocaust. Phrased differently, a holocaust means the systematic genocide and termination of a selected group of people. In the case of the British, using the term trade removes the fact that we are referring to humans being trafficked. From a common sense perspective, the idea is rendered and justified; one was not violating the rights of humans but rather providing culture and humanism to chattel property. African people were the commodity to be exterminated (Conyers 2016, p. 91). Likewise, the system of enslavement was intentional, whereas Black people, in 2017, are still affected and impacted from the traumatization of the system of bondage imposed on African people. Interesting, some historians, in light of using the justification of racism to rationalize the support and enabling of enslavement, used the terminology of a peculiar institution.

This peculiar institution was the basis of the creation and consequence of the subordinate status of African people for over five centuries. With attention on the Eastern seaboard communities of North Carolina and South Carolina, the crops of tobacco, cotton, and rice were commodities that the colonial forces used to establish their wealth and power status in the United States. Consequently, the result of free African labor has an impact on the current economic and political status of African Americans (Bennett, 1972). Likewise, in Haiti, this nation state of Africans experienced the exploitation of both the French and the British. Overall, the movement and transit of African people were traded for merchandise.

The query centers a discussion on God, race, and slavery. My approach to the discussion takes the position of defining terms and outlining the basis of the difference between religion, theology, and spirituality of African people. First, religion can be defined as "thought, belief, and practice concerned with the transcendent and ultimate questions of life" (Karenga 2010, p. 55). Equally important, some general characteristics and general themes in African religions were "belief in one supreme God" (p. 55). Nonetheless, the basis for why enslaved Africans converted to Christianity was to reinforce, justify, and maintain dominance (p. 55). Still, the historical role of the Black church presented itself to be a spiritual sanctuary. Moreover, the point of relevance was that religion was imposed and enforced on African people. With a Eurocentric hegemonic translation of the King James Version of the Bible, the British community interpreted analysis of the sacred text and sanctioned God to be visually perceived in the image and interest of Europeans. Likewise, the mortality of this folklore extended itself that Europeans on earth resembled and were the living images of God, using the high case "G." At the heart of this discussion, Europeans labeled African traditional religions as polytheist, referring to Blacks as being heathen like. Without the human element of Black people having a traditional culture located in Africans, Europeans dismissed the fact that they did not speak the indigenous languages or understand the sacred and secular aspects of Africana culture and history. Ironically, using God and race, the British justified their racist acts of enslaving and subordinating African people.

Conclusion

In conclusion, what has been learned, discovered, and evaluated from examining the Thirteenth Amendment to the U.S. constitution? First, the institution of enslavement still has lasting effects on the Africana world community in contemporary times, meaning that Black people experienced a holocaust, which can be referred to as the systemic genocide of a selected group of people.

Enslavement of African Americans has been a paradoxical issue of engagement. Yet, while discussing the Thirteenth Amendment, the concept of abolishing enslavement was considered a tool to weaken the Southern Confederacy of the states in America. Nonetheless, in contemporary times, we are still impacted and restricted by the demarcation lines of racism regionalization. Equally important, America has not and continues to evoke a state of denial for correctness, concerning the systemic patterns that intentionally subordinated the human status of African Americans. Such denial has archived the institutional leveraging of privilege in this country for Euro-Americans. On the other hand, Blacks are given a referendum of self-help, which is the remedy for upwardly mobility. Likewise, the deficit, destitution, and deconstruction of Black America have been almost totally ignored, with reference to education, economics, and historical memory. Lastly, the Thirteenth Amendment was a critical document of political legislation, which was the precedent for the establishing grounds for the passage of the Fourteenth and Fifteenth Amendments to the U.S. Constitutional Law. Perhaps studies in contemporary research will describe and evaluate the Thirteenth Amendment, the abolishment of enslavement, and the intentional subordination of Africana phenomena from a cultural context and Afrocentric perspective.

References

Bennett Jr., L. *Before the Mayflower: A History of Black America*. Chicago: Johnson Publishing Incorporated, 1969.

Bennett Jr., L. *The Challenge of Blackness*. Chicago: Johnson Publishing Company, Incorporated, 1972.

Drimmer, M. (Ed.). *Black History: A Reappraisal*. New York City: Doubleday & Company, Incorporated, 1969.

Conniff, M. L. and Davis, T. J. (Eds.). *Africans in the Americas: A History of the Black Diaspora*. New York: St. Martin's Press, 1994.

Conyers Jr., J. L. (Ed.). *Africana Faith: A Religious History of the African American Crusade in Islam*. Lanham, MD: Hamilton Books, 2016.

Johnson, B. Freedom and slavery in the voices of the negro: Historical memory and African American identity, 1904–1907. *The Georgia Historical Quarterly*, 84, 1 (2000), 29–71.

Karenga, M. *Introduction to Black Studies*. Los Angeles, CA: University of Sankore Press, 2010.

Lewis, E. To turn as on a pivot: Writing African Americans into a history of overlapping diaspora. *The American Historical Review*, 100, 3 (1995), 765–787.

Schaefer, R. T. *Racial and Ethnic Groups*. New York: HarperCollins College Publishers, 1993, pp. 18–23.

Timetoast timeline, TJSTERK. "13th Amendment Timeline." Timetoast. Accessed November 27, 2017. https://www.timetoast.com/timelines/13th-amendment-timeline.

Walters, R. W. African Americans and movements for reparations: Past, present, and future. *The Journal of African American History*, 97, 1–2, (2012), pp. 111–112.

INDEX

Note: Page numbers in italics and bold refer to figures and tables, respectively.